Clutter

A Poetic Experiment of Language, Consciousness, and Time.

Published by **Ramiform Press**

ISBN: 979-8-9944111-0-0

Printed in the United States of America

Dedication

To Patricia, whose faith makes things happen.

Table of Contents

Introduction to Clutter: Structure and Purpose

---•---

A Monument of Time

The job of the poet is to write and recite, that of the listener is to read and listen. But meaning is something that each person derives from the experience of the moment, the actual impact of the words as they unfold in time.

These poems have multiple "themes" and perhaps multiplicity itself is the thread that unites them. You know that in the next few minutes or hours information and experience will bombard you from diverse sources from all over the planet. How do you survive all that without fragmenting? How do you keep all that from burying you in anonymity?

By writing, by reciting, by reading, by listening ...

Listen:

If Mount Rushmore, The Great Wall of China, or the Pyramids at Gaza are monuments of space, *Clutter* is a monument of Time. And like the Fresh Kills landfill site on Staten Island, which is the largest object on the East Coast of the United States and can be seen from space, *Clutter* is a monument of cast offs, subjective impressions gathered together in identically formed units, each composed from the happenstance of the day in which it was formed.

Numbers and Dates

Clutter is composed of four phases of 108 poems each. The number 108 has been revered in a variety of contexts and in many cultures, so much so that it is assumed to have divine or esoteric qualities, which enables it to serve as a portal, or contemplative entity, with the power to open into other domains of consciousness. Is this true? Maybe or maybe not, but I think that as one pursues these chains of significance, the number itself leads us to consider, accept or reject, layers of meaning which expand one's knowledge, and maybe even one's awareness. At any rate, this number was used in *Clutter*, as a scientist might use a microscope or a telescope, to reveal possible connections between what might otherwise appear to be disparate things or events. I used the sequence 4 times so that the poem might cover, not just the days of the year in the individual poems, but also embody the 4 seasons of the year, as the work encompasses both smaller and larger units of Time.

Another feature of *Cutter* as a monument of Time is that, although it is a sequence of 432 calendar dates, beginning with 13 October, 2015 and ending 17 December, 2016, it is not merely a sequence. The larger poem has a mid-point. This is a kind of barycenter between the poems of 15 May, 2016 and 16 May, of the same year.

At this invisible point, how the poems are enumerated changes: the poem following poem 216 is not identified as number 217, but by the inverse of 216, namely 612.

The poems that follow are all numbered as the inverse of the strictly numerical initial 216 poems. There is a backward precession of the poems, as poems 216/612 are related thematically, as are poems 215/512, 214/412, and so forth, to the last poems of *Clutter*, which being single digit numbers in the first sequence, have no inversions. The last thematically matched poems share the single digit numbers counting down from 9 to 1.

I am not trying to be cute or obtuse here, what I am trying to do is establish the symbolic or metaphoric qualities of numbers, in addition to their numeric values. By using numbers in this way, I am able to link poems that are not sequential.

The Time monument now has another shape, a pyramid, whose apex contains poems both closely related in themes and also in Time, and whose base contains poems, although closely related in theme, have become more and more distantly related in Time. Clutter can be read sequentially, or in what might be called a parallel fashion, and hopefully in both ways.

Rhyme Scheme

Clutter's units are all 21-line poems each written in real time in four phases of 108 poems, for a total of 432 poems written one each day for 432 days.

Each-poem follows the same pattern: a 9-line stanza, a 3-line stanza, and another 9-line stanza. The lines are counted syllabically, not metrically. Each line having no less than 14 syllables and no more than 15. In practice, one should read it as one would read prose, and although not metrical, since English speech almost exclusively falls into duple or triple rhythms, the poems should still be musical enough, and with a music that is naturally characteristic of normal English speech.

The rhyme schemes are as follows: In the first and third 9-line stanzas:

Line 1 rhymes with line 9.
Line 2 rhymes with line 8.
Line 3 rhymes with line 7.
Line 4 rhymes with line 6.
Line 5, the middle line, rhymes with the middle lines of all three stanzas.

The 3-line stanza dividing the two 9-line stanzas, follows this pattern:

Lines 1 and 3 rhyme.
Line 2 — the middle line — rhymes with the middle lines in the other 2 stanzas.

Since English is a rhyme-poor language, rhymes can either be vowel rhymes or consonant rhymes. There are no eye-rhymes, and the sounds follow my Mid-Western American pronunciations. The intent was to create a subtler kind of music which works unobtrusively without becoming monotonous or singsong. Readers should read the words out loud, or at least with a strong inward vocalization. Like sheet music, which must be played by an instrument or sung with the performer's own interpretation, these visual words on the page or on a screen must be recited by a human voice to be musical.

A Visual Schematic

The schematic on the next page gives a visual representation of the poetic units of *Clutter*, the 0's representing the syllables, with the end letters A, B, C, D, E indicating the rhymes. All this may be a bit hard to decipher with the explanations above, but it is easy enough to see in the schematic, and even easier to hear in recitation.

The feature that stands out is that the rhymes "collapse" toward the mid-lines of the stanzas, becoming closer in time to one another until they reach the pivot-point of the center. The sound sequences then take on a shape, or we could say, that Time takes on a shape, which allows us to have some insight into Time, which a sequential unfolding of sounds never reveals.

RHYME SCHEME SCHEMATIC FOR "CLUTTER'

```
                  1   2   3   4   5   6   7   8   9
                  o   o   o   o   o   o   o   o   o
                  o   o   o   o   o   o   o   o   o
                  o   o   o   o   o   o   o   o   o
First             o   o   o   o   o   o   o   o   o
Nine-Line         o   o   o   o   o   o   o   o   o
Stanza            o   o   o   o   o   o   o   o   o
                  o   o   o   o   o   o   o   o   o
                  o   o   o   o   o   o   o   o   o
                  o   o   o   o   o   o   o   o   o
                  o   o   o   o   o   o   o   o   o
                  o   o   o   o   o   o   o   o   o
                  o   o   o   o   o   o   o   o   o
                  o   o   C   D   o   o   o   o   o
                  A   B               E   D   C   B   A
```

```
                          1   2   3
                          o   o   o
                          o   o   o
                          o   o   o
                          o   o   o                 All lines of the poem
                          o   o   o                 syllabically measured —
Three-Line                o   o   o                 each line 14 or 15 syllables
Central Pivot             o   o   o
                          o   o   o
                          o   o   o
                          o   o   o
                          o   o   o
                          o   o   o
                          o   o   o
                          A   E   A
```

```
                  1   2   3   4   5   6   7   8   9
                  o   o   o   o   o   o   o   o   o
                  o   o   o   o   o   o   o   o   o
Second            o   o   o   o   o   o   o   o   o
Nine-Line         o   o   o   o   o   o   o   o   o
Stanza            o   o   o   o   o   o   o   o   o
                  o   o   o   o   o   o   o   o   o
                  o   o   o   o   o   o   o   o   o
                  o   o   o   o   o   o   o   o   o
                  o   o   o   o   o   o   o   o   o
                  o   o   o   o   o   o   o   o   o
                  o   o   o   o   o   o   o   o   o
                  o   o   o   o   o   o   o   o   o
                  o   o   o   o   o   o   o   o   o
                  o   o   o   o   E   o   o   B   o
                  A   B   C   D           D   C       A
```

The above rather abstractly considered and described procedures are expressed so that *Clutter* as a whole can embody a kind of linguistic instrument in which the junk pile of sensations, arbitrary habits, the weather, the events of everyday life, the collision of the so-called subjective and the so-called objective can be seen, heard, and experienced from a number of temporal angles.

My Obsession

In other words, I've tried to explore what I've come to call my "obsession", namely, the conflation — language/consciousness/time. I have invented other procedures in other works that give insight into this phenomenon. From all these, over many years, I've come to imagine the experience of each present moment as the nadir of a funnel, where memory and foreshadowing spiral down to create the Now.

I suspect that poetry is a legitimate way to examine and express this mystery — one that is at least as fruitful as the methods pursued by philosophers, theologians, cosmologists, physicists — et al. With the arrogance of a poet, I've gone a bit further, saying poetry is perhaps the most suitable of these approaches because of its flexibility. It appeals to both intellect and emotion. It has the ability to not only express its propositions, but also to embody the phenomenon. Poetry has the power to simultaneously assume a metaposition to itself and thereby explore both its own simplicities and its own intricacies. Thus poetry continues in the linguistic realm what organic evolution does in the physical realm. Namely, poetry extends the domain of Time itself, and proliferates Time's already proliferating manifestations.

Three examples from Clutter:

A Nostalgia for Agitated Breath
Clutter 212
Written 20 May, 2016

In this once-definitive and now outdated book on
Imagery and healing, I read: "Our understanding of how
The brain functions has come from the study of damaged brains."
For seven years, I studied, with my own anguished limbic
Brain, my father's brain, as its fabric's tissues, like stretched dough,
thinned,
And then tore into lesions with no remembrance, the wreck
That remained still warm with limbic affection. Now an insane
Calmness provokes me. He died three weeks ago. So? Why now
This relief? Because all that piecemeal pain is completely gone.

The substrate is destroyed, the necrosis in the tissue
Has no host, and what remains is numbness. And yet when the wind
Shakes the trees, tearing new apertures for the sun to drop through …

I am reminded of how inextricably he remained
A part of Nature — not ever really being tamed. The boy in
The crude log hut with the hard dirt floor kept growing like the sod
Of the cabin's roof, a part of the living meadow, reaching
Sunward, not quite content to be part of a house, and blend
Its wildness with domesticity. Perhaps he is growing
Still, though his brain is burned to ashes, and his son throws these odd
Words into the wind. Like wind, I thrash about as if — in
The throes of limbic violence — I might rouse a cherished pain.

Passion
Clutter 702
Written 25 May, 2016

When I returned to the Black Hills after my father's passing,
I had to confront the question of the forest. Years of
Drought and the infestation of a certain beetle had turned
The pinegreen into dead-needle-russet, and fire had burned
Whole mountainsides to black. The miniature heaven that my
Mind maintained as nostalgia was killed by a vision that churned
In the gut, not the brain, a vision that I try to turn
Away from, but cannot. I have invested so much love
In the dying or the dead — my little heaven is burning.

Perhaps it has always been burning — this strange nostalgia for
Perishable fathers and forests. Perhaps these little mind
Forays are only ersatz models for something stranger.

I see it — Him — as a shadow behind this fire, a shadow
That *lights* this fire — a presence as featureless as a father's
Or a forest's ashes — this terrible arsonist, who
Has no face, no form, yet twists all faces to his own image.
He is the God of the sober poet, the masculine cry
That wakens the feminine muse, the words that hotly rampage
Through the gut to light the larger heaven of the heart. And you,
Who read this in your cool pine-shade, entranced by the fine weather,
You drowse, and cannot feel his breathing stirring the shadows.

Food For Thought
Clutter 012
Written 22 May, 2016

The ability to visualize is so crucial
To that ritual of rebirth known as "getting ready
For it." Billions of Human beings devouring billions of
Non-human beings, insect over insect — that is the vision.
Naturally it leads to a feeling of anonymity.
When this isolating sickness comes over me, I can
See my granddad in the woods burying a flour sack, his rough
Hands scraping a hole for his stillborn son. Now I am ready.
I know the grammatology of the past — its taste, its smell.

I obtain my potency from that anonymous relic's
Bones. The insects have stripped them so thoroughly that only
The memory remains — a taste, a smell, which can cure the sick.

The disposition to illness, or the rite by which demons
Conjure illness, has a name. It is called: "The Un-Ready,"
The premature or aborted stillborn, exposed too early
To the vision. One insect is as hungry as the next,
And as anonymous. If I imagine a baby
Buried in a flour sack, anonymously, why should that vex
The readers of this text or the ears that hear this poetry's
Stridulations? Fame cannot stick to the unborn baby's
Bones, nor words move humans consumed by inhuman demons.

PHASE ONE

Waste Management
Clutter 1
Written 13 October, 2015

————————— • —————————

The afternoon is crushingly oppressive, not just with heat,
But with the junk of discarded feelings — accumulating.
This breeds methane, and mashes everything to toxic gruel.
The sky, ironically, is crystal blue, and this makes us
Think that above such dumps are tens of thousands of gulls —
So many scavenging thoughts of fear and hate.
They add chaotic flight to underground pressure, the booming
Of propane cannons, scaring aloft white choirs of maddened shrieks.

The medial pre-frontal cortex teems with incessant fret,
As the relentless machinery of habit denies us
Closure. Past jealousies intrude unbidden. We re-act.

Old men and old women speak of old loves with a mixture
Of relief and regret. And still, still, heat's crushing weight remains.
And no one is immune, since even the young — heartbroken —
Grow instantly old, as the genius of sorrow grows dense
Or flies about, seeming to be two things, combined in us
As dumped and scavenged words, words starved for salvaged sense.
But love is the gift of nonsense. That is its grace. Love blends
The wondrous madness of frantic flight with buried pain.
Love is a cannon-shot that knows no closure.

Riddle

Clutter 2

Written 14 October, 2015

Sadly, every epoch creates its wandering searchers,
Men, women, who roam the roads as mendicants,
Or knights or knaves errant, uprooted for lack
Of a visceral understanding of that terrible,
Wonderful word. The computational approaches
Of neuroscientists attempt to expunge all
Our poetic descriptions, claiming to act
On behalf of cognitive progress, but the rant
Goes on in bedrooms and in song — its curse its cure.

(We are blind Platonic cave fish, compelled to seek it,
And those who find it, luminous in their darkness,
Become its spirit, yet cannot define it.)

Once there were symbols for it, all subject, like the thing,
To intense perversion. Like the swastika sun sign
Found carved in mammoth tusks, or tattooed on bikers' skin,
Or worshipped in Hindu processions, or flying over death camps,
It can show divergences centered at a cross
Point, or show that cross point blown apart by chance.
It is the trusting touch of hand to hand, the virtuous sin
Of sex in lustful primates, the crush of hope, whose wine
Incites all war, or that which forges bonds in wedding rings.

Zenith and Nadir
Clutter 3
Written 15 October, 2015

———— • ————

"High" — a condition not dissimilar
To actual flying, wherein the afflicted travel
Through the troposphere at the very edge of space.
I look into your eyes. There is no Earth below me,
Just these amorphous webs of white, immaculate
As light from infant stars. There is no bar above me,
And Time, no longer a line, becomes a lake, a lake
Of lustrous blue that glows like cobalt, a cobalt that swells
Into absolute, vitreous calm — which pulses splendor.

In that state of dejection known as "normal," the undead
Hear hyperbole in these words. For them "high" is a state
Of drunken numbness, a blurriness inside the blurry head.

The webs of white have splayed into a haze, a vaporous
Bluing and blurring of the Earth, which spreads below me,
Showing wrinkled veins, creasing the mountains, merging
In sinuous rivers, and checker-boarding into purple
Fields, which prove the harvest is at last complete.
Your eyes grow weary and your soft lids fall.
I feel the intimate warmth of your slow breathing.
"Slow" — a lowness not dissimilar from "high," a state where we —
The earthbound, the afflicted — sink into depths of stars.

Musing Invocation
Clutter 4
Written 16 October, 2015

———————— • ————————

Sunset in a new old place, where yellow pythons
And tawny lions still startle the mediocrity
Of small town evangelical America. Here
Loves that you most love and still most pine for can still
Be threatened by these old Biblical beasts, and you
Still impotent to rescue. Time passing kills
Time past, and the words, *scriptio continua,* still pour
Like water over pebbles. Oh Intimate Lady
Of Infinite Compassion, speak from your waves of emotion ...

And hear me in this instant of gladness. I am here
Where I most want to be. Bright Lady make me new —
As the prodigal father who does so love his daughter.

And so when I close my eyes, I see, stretched across
A deep and comforting darkness, an array
Of exquisite lights. They look like cities at night
Seen from exquisite heights, only these lights are like jewels.
They are like jewels with voices, voices involute
With innocence, as when a mother reads to still
Her drowsy child. And so I can speak and say "I
"Am happy. Happy." Then I can say "The threat has gone away.
"I am with family. I have found what I had lost."

Itinerant Raconteur
Clutter 5
Written 17 October, 2015

—————— • ——————

Except for love, there is no reason to leave the vibrant
Coastal cities and return to those squalid
Inland towns, and most who do return, have nothing to say
That is not the spare redundancy of their hopelessly
Repeated myth: "The past is the true, pure self."
And yet, woven through the chin lace of the demented, we
Do occasionally hear glimmerings that the decay
Of the past is not complete, and that amidst the squalid
Relics, those too feeble to hobble, still might dance.

For you who are busy in your cities at the cusp,
These observations will seem the blandest drivel.
But I say, through chin lace spittle: "Something unites us."

There are bronze statues in the past, which commemorate
Stories of horrific disaster — cyclones, which lifted
People, barns, churches, livestock, pianos
Into their swirling vortex. Some are impaled with gruesome,
Memorable deaths, and some are spared through miracles
Still more gruesome. Yet, except for love, that most gruesome
Of relics, all these salvations would dissolve as smoke —
An old man sitting in a urine-soaked chair, his squalid
Voice relating why we returned and why we will surely stray.

Oneiric Scripture
Clutter 6
Written 18 October, 2015

And they took as a sign that the babe's babbling
Could be like unto prophesy, and that a child, who
Could as yet scarce walk, might, by a single leap of faith,
Establish a dawning sky in the mean cloister of their
Hearts. Suppose that the first light in the big elm trees
To the east could cleanse you with the grace and power
Of archaic speech? And that the dreary confines of Sunday's
Empty face, eyelessly staring through the week, could pull you
Into glory? Would you then acknowledge the babe as king?

You remembered upon waking your terrible vision
Of progress — that doctor in white lab coat terribly
Slicing the limbs off pure, white lambs — and you thought of children.

Jesus is so small now, swaddled in his blue mantle,
Emerging from his tiny tomb, as the sun does in the east.
They are only ordinary elms, and the sky grows blue
With blue shadows of first frost. Progress has passed you
By, and even your preterite children seem
So old, so archaic. But something inside you
Still rises from shabbiness, turns dawn's blood blue, and tells you,
In archaic syllables, of redemption for the least,
For the feeble, for the children of sleep's oldest Bible.

To Future Readers
Clutter 7
Written 19 October, 2015

——————— • ———————

I confess I am blind, and may only tell
The direction I am facing by the warm touch of the sun.
And I admit that my words are much like those of a toddler,
The intimate babbling of deep need, which only
A vigilant mother can interpret. You are that sun.
You are that vigilant provider. The depth of my need
Is the depth of your compassion. Where light pours
Through the webworks of a tree, and a Blue Jay comes
To shriek at Earth's blind children, here we both must dwell.

For my life is not of flesh and blood and gravity
And Time, it is of stillness and waiting, the hum
Of distance in the hermit's ear, the music of last sleep.

And your life is movement, articulation, meaning.
Your life is a longing for the useful word-machine.
And this place of wheeling, feathered, bright descent,
This whisper of wing-drift before the raucous
Shriek — this is the place where compassion
And need must meet. This babbling unites us.
I confess that these words are useless, and that the scant
Instant of our union will never make us complete.
But even the blind believe that a vision is coming.

A Few Involuntary Remarks on the Power of Insomnia to Destroy Rigid Habits of the Mind

Clutter 8

Written 20 October, 2015

———————— • ————————

Because the composition of nocturnes is so
Foreboding, too often they begin with the frightened
Snigger of a schoolboy, who sees nuns
Smoking in the back of a hearse. If there are any
Lights, they are hooded with amber, and they cut through
The blinds of the house, bearing shadows of trees
In trembling, ominous slashes. Sleep will not come,
But our wakeful torment does not stifle dreams, and heightened
Imaginings distort, disturb, make strange the world we know.

The words of the nocturne defeat our good intentions,
Take on a life of their own, stain bodies blue,
Shatter the self who is named, incite contention.

It is almost as if we are primed to take a journey,
A journey where these conflicted, fragment-selves
Must scatter at dawn in a thousand diverse directions,
Each dragging a heavy portion of the night through unmapped
Regions of the day. New traits we were loath to
Own reveal themselves, and the bandage is unwrapped
That hid our wounds. The hooded, amber lights run
Red with dawn, a flow that does not kill, but weirdly heals,
As the cleansed, the myriad selves, enact new dreams.

Trundling Towards Extinction
Clutter 9
Written 21 October, 2015

———————— • ————————

"Farewell" is always the last word before disintegration,
But the words just preceding this last are soon forgotten.
The drama of departure is just too obliterating.
Suppose you are a boy, and you gaze down a grassy slope
That accumulates leaf litter. You will not think of the whites
Of dogwood blossoms, or the great, green globes
Of summer's flourishing oaks, or even these crumplings
Of russets spread out below you. No, your aspirations
Will be fixed on snow, the ultimate annihilation.

All of the exhibits memorializing fire will be
Subsumed by this cold rubric, this final, brilliant white.
And the boy, no longer a boy, will leave his body.

There, there in the snow, you will see him lumbering,
A bear in a man-suit, laboring through the snow.
And the bear will speak with the eloquence of madness,
Of wilderness destroyed, of hibernation.
But the man-suit will obscure his poem's light.
You will hear nothing but grunts of consternation,
And will never imagine that a song of bliss
Is issuing forth from his too bestial chest. And so
Disintegration's wisdom will bear for you no meaning.

Primordial Temple Complex
Clutter 10
Written 22 October, 2015

Surprising how the most fantastic wonders can be
Made grey by a prosaic mind. O yes, he is in there,
That tourist of colorless habit, who claims to have an
Exotic urge to wander, but whose imagination
Is more spare than a banker's devotion in the ruins
Of childhood. This sad accountant of inhibition
Has shaved his head, yet jungle invades the bone and his bland
Mania for arranging things in columns. Is this the heir
Apparent of youth — this skull-caged codger so full of Empty?

Surprising how the rising saffron sun, which makes fine lace
From the shadows of rampant vines, can be undone
By the codes of our beliefs, which claim to have deciphered day.

And surprising too how the intricacies of aging
Can retain the naiveties of youth, yet be stripped clean
Of all youth's sensory riches, then, naked and wrinkled,
Pretend to be clothed in wisdom. I have a mind of paper
Riddled with holes, yet not yet void of elation
At the sunrise, not yet immune to surprise, when the air
That was featureless night grows bright with ripples,
Ripples all tangled with saffrons more serene
Than the forehead of a Buddha meditating.

Nuggets and Pearls
Clutter 11
Written 23 October, 2015

—————————— • ——————————

I am being buried alive. I look up from this auger-
Hole, as someone I know leans down to observe me. Dirt falls
In the hole. Has he come to finish the job? No. The light
Circling above is the pupil of an eye, and the body
That blocks it is a closing, a smothering retreat into
Deeper sleep. An odd word — *pursuivant* — repeats,
Not as mere sound, but as action. Gray men pursue me. Why?
Yesterday this same word arrived from three people
Who scarcely know me, and do not know each other.

I have wanted to find out how each heart opens its sealed clam
Into the Sea of Time. Something uncanny is coming through,
Invades the lungs like water, threatens to drown who I am.

We all live in neighborhoods where the lots are
Divided by fences. The weathered boards are scratched with glyphs.
Do these coded messages tell who loves you? Do they tell
You who we are and who can be trusted? I am trying
To break that code, to write it out in poems. Please. Please, you
Must help me. I am telling you there is meaning,
However uncanny. It pursues us all. It falls
In like dirt, gushes through like water. Please. Please. If
The gray light shifts to bright, we might know, might love each other.

Time's Feminine Fortune Tellers
Clutter 12
Written 24 October, 2015

———————— • ————————

For the novice who has already exhausted
Fifty years just in this lifetime trying to reconcile
The imponderable mystery of the trinity,
These intimations are both alarming and reassuring.
Forget the Father-Son-Holy Ghost decoy, instead
Think 'daughter, wife, femme fatale.' The fervor of believing
Is like a long sightline down a rugged coast, the sea's
Surf always roaring or murmuring, rising in swells
Or falling, but never allowing her depths to be read.

The wife, the daughter, these two are one, forever
Loved, forever separate from the seeker. But why wed
This unity to one whose passion both redeems and murders?

Under waves and waves of unruly, grey hair,
The neurons spark these inexplicable scenes,
And the rolling majesties of coastal fog give way
To labyrinths of dreams. Think of a maze
Of bookshelves, a library, books collected
By generations of novices, and under this gray haze
That shrouds the sea, think of three women with cards, at play.
One of them is a child, one a comfort, and one a deadly,
Lustful queen. They look away from you. They darkly whisper.

Royal Affair

Clutter 13

Written 25 October, 2015

———————— • ————————

You were never more sleeplessly you than on this night
When solitude gathers its voice from the moonless sea,
And repetition repeats itself with inarticulate,
Primordial moans. A minute is torment, an hour
Inconceivably vast, and the planet's population
Compounds these human insect-numbers with the power
Of one plus one equals billions. Strange how this late
To early bout of insomnia opens the bones to the pleas
Of the unsheltered, even as the surf drowns every cry.

Billions and billions of selves, every night, throw their bodies
Away in sleep, the willing suicides awaiting the sun
As a signal for resurrection, as a sign it is safe to be.

But night goes on too long, as if the limits of suffering
Will never be reached, as if the minutes, like multiplying
Bees, will sting and sting the throat of the desperate poet
With a Mantra which sings his torment ceaselessly.
And the sea, like the choirs of all Earth's sad denizens,
Will continue to stir her genetic mysteries,
And repeat and repeat the song of her restless spirit,
Because it is her voice which foments dreams. O! She is calling,
Calling sleeplessly, to lure to bed the shell of her mad king.

A Scherzo On the Doctrine of Reincarnation

Clutter 14

Written 26 October, 2015

———— • ————

Unless death really is a game of peek-a-boo, it is
Hard to fathom the appeal of happenstance.
It seems the interpolations of chance, whether through aging
Or accident or sudden catastrophic affairs
Of the heart would be inimical to that
Stability mortal bodies so desperately require
To stave off termination. Yet, we all love beachcombing,
Roaming as close as possible to an avalanche
Of towering surf merely to find a piece of glass.

Now you see them, now you don't — the game that makes all babies
Laugh, the dead gull in the glittering sand, the red that
Clings to the dainty white of the ribcage — what a curiosity!

Or this green crevasse gouged by the sea's persistent fingers
With emerald mosses on the purple rocks, and its jagged
Niche where a chunk of driftwood has been caught and rounded
Into a perfect, featureless skull — these curiosities
Tell us how everything disappears in that
Slow or quick hilarity we call "change," that blasphemy
Wherein the mother's face is abruptly covered
By a screen of hands, the bright eyes darkened, the smile that fed
Us gone, only to suddenly, joyously re-appear.

Fall

Clutter 15

Written 27 October, 2015

———————— • ————————

I know you have been promised freedom many times before
By charlatans, hustlers, grifters of all sorts, or even by
Those flame-eyed ecstatics who claim to want nothing
From you but the chance to gift you happiness. But this time,
With these words, things are different. "What things?" you question.
But your query can only be met by these shaped sound-signs,
Forming stories, or snippets of stories, because nothing
So inflated as freedom can be attained by
Straight-jacket facts, which always keep us from seeing more.

More. More today is found in the oppressive grey
Of a sky heavy with the last, damp cold of an autumn
Which has been glorious every day, but which now decays.

All these wintry corpses are slowly moving through the low
Vaults of heaven, so that their ragged feet shuffle
With the presentiment of a much needed rain, the wind
Arranging the green shrubberies into temporary
Topiary sculptings of beautiful, young women.
These glowing sirens, freely promise more, these last frailties
Of summer, saying, with wild leaf-whisperings, "Farewell, friend,
"Farewell to indolence and warmth and plenty. Farewell
"To promises, past and future, and welcome to cold sorrow."

Skimming the Surface
Clutter 16
Written 28 October, 2015

———————— • ————————

Who is this who sits in the stern of a boat and watches
The white ribbon of the wake unfurl its momentary
Record of the past? — the only luminous thing in what
Is otherwise a universal fog. The wake is a tongue.
It does not speak like the wail of a human
Child. Yet its turbulent froth begins to throng
With pictures: a screen on this undulant surface that
Hides the depth, a cross-section of humanity
Whose rabble engulfs you. They tell your tale in snatches.

This tale is mostly a confused babble of alien
Phrases, which move like bodies, wild to escape what's random.
The gist? We are all of one origin, all with clogged intestines.

I am never quite willing to wake when I do — if I
Do. I want to return to my dreams, however confusing
Or seemingly random. But this morning, I hear a child
Walking to school, wailing in protest, no mother's phrase
To scold or comfort her. I am aware of the pun
That froths from the word "wake," and also dully amazed —
In my *mourning* fog — that waking and sleeping are linked. The child
Wailing now morphs to the call of a bird, then the calm whistling
Of breath as I start to float again between day and night.

Instant Faith
Clutter 17
Written 29 October, 2015

———————— • ————————

"Weather Report" that used to prick up the ears of ploughmen
Everywhere. But who cares now, on these brightest of late
Autumn mornings, if headlines read: "Chlorophyll Drains from Leaf:
"Scarlet Celebrations Ensue!" Do not misunderstand.
I do not wish to enshrine nostalgia for bacon eaters
And egg suckers as the inspiration for a new brand
Of scriptures devoted to the exploits of hayseeds.
These propitiations of the past mean nothing. To antedate
Ecstasy is folly. Though folly is no sin.

It comes down to a question of courage. Will the nakedness
Of the spontaneous mind be indulged? Will the seer
See, the hearer hear that first spark that starts the fire of bliss?

"Now" is the word. Now is the only time that the scarlet leaf
Will draw the sunlight of this angel inward. The leaf falls,
And its vital, fantastic green irrevocably turns.
This is the fluttering limit. I am this limit. To go
Beyond me is to exit the mortal body, and enter
The bodiless ream of beauty's flame. This is so:
Time is combustable and eternity sweetly burns,
And that angel of scarlet who Oh so brilliantly falls
Gives mortals the courage to worship my brevity.

Night Fires
Clutter 18
Written 30 October, 2015

———————— • ————————

Listen. Do you hear the nocturnal voices? Composite,
Intimate, they call you from deep sleep, and in the morning
Your keepers find you, fallen at the bedside, unhurt,
Except for a small tear in the skin, which has let
These multitudes in. Henceforth, you must be as still
As the tree in the presence of the saw, and the old fit,
To which you lent your name and covered with a bloodless shirt,
Must finally grow calm — all your attention on listening,
As the voices choir, singing their golden secrets.

These voices negate that murderer of millions, whose
Harangues dictate war policy to the body, and squeal
Like a squeezed rabbit whenever Time's fang bites you.

You will never swallow that victim's meat again —
The muscles of your throat reserved for phrases
Extolled by the golden harmonies of the voices. You
Will listen before you speak to this inner music,
Whose choirs will sound like a single child, a single
Innocence donning a million costumes, a quick
Succession of sparks, which burn all bodies, but whose
Own formlessness survives all flame. In unison, these blazes,
Millions strong, will free you from the prison of one skin.

Tea with Sophia in
the Sacred Grove

Clutter 19

Written 31 October, 2015

———————— • ————————

Who has not heard the father, politician or priest
Whose voice seems strong, but whose words, like insect-ridden trees,
At the slightest touch of a termite mandible,
Break way to show their weak and rotten entrails? That was
Yesterday's bitterness. Today the sorceress arrives.
She brews their rot into her wondrous tea, and what was
Bitter becomes sweet, with properties quite magical.
It tastes of mocha, lavender, chocolate — a treat
For autumn's dying selves, a soft slide into sleep.

In the absence of external stimulation — i.e.,
Those heavy masculine speeches — the tree of I revives,
And the seasons move inside the lonely body.

But theirs is not the I of politicians, the I
That needs destruction to survive. Theirs is the I of growing
Appreciation, the tree that casts aside old leaves for new,
The Screwtape glyphs that come alive in song, the mole hill
That becomes a copper mountain, flashing the scarlet skies
Through peacock sheens — great arching prisms full
Of captive Time. Theirs is the I whose plenitude includes
All of those termite selves the father loathes. Their I sings
Though the priest's dark word of sin, to feed on satiated sighs.

By Heaven I Think
My Love More Fair
Clutter 20
Written 1 November, 2015

———————— • ————————

The common conceit by generations of mendacious
Poets is that the splendors of their lover cannot be
Described even by the splendor of words. Yet, what,
But words, is like her? Since she, like them, is as the wind —
Uncontrollable, an indivisible force whose supreme
Gift is omnipresent beauty. You may depict shapely limbs
And enchanting faces day and night, but exactly what
Have you made? A sign? A symbol? These stand-ins still hardly
Explain her magic — both common and miraculous.

A shoe worn until it cradles the foot like warm water,
Bright gem-lights spangling the chop of a sunlit sea,
The touch of lips to lips, the depth of death — these are her whispers.

And that whispering of words in the crater of absence
Or at the pinnacle of elation, tells us of surging
Oceans, exultantly fertile, yet present beneath her skin,
And ageless as affection in a child. I love her. I
Am loved. Words say this. Because to feel these silken streams
Of evanescence issuing from a throat, which shapes the sky,
Is to know her splendor as that sweet sensation,
Which touches everything in every season. This feeling
_Is_ her body — the words, whose presence sanctifies her absence.

How the Profligate
Learned Gratitude
Clutter 21
Written 2 November, 2015

———————— • ————————

"Are we going to have a problem here? I _hope_ we are
"Not going to have a problem here." That is the way
Autumn often speaks to me, with gangster innuendos,
Which I too often succumb to, identifying
Too readily with the dead and dangling leaves, resigned,
Like them, to fall, and, like them, to be sweetly drifting,
If only momentarily, on the wind. I might know
Then the pungent truths of earth, I , who have always
Lived with my head in the clouds, drunk on the sunlit air.

And when I am under or even one with the earth, I
Might then understand what my father, mother, teachers tried
To tell me — "Be practical, rooted, take hold of your life."

I might then see those gangs of trolls beneath me, their
Terrible labors transporting sun through dirt. I might
Then know how all my fluttering ways have fed
Their toil of constancy and pressure. For these have borne me
Up with their dark cries, and now, as sunlight dies,
And winter rises, I feel a kinship with their agony.
Their words — "Be practical, rooted, take hold of your life." instead
Of threats or guttural laments, seem somehow to belie
Their dreadful state, and beckon me to join them in their lair.

A Plain Wedding on a
Bright Day After Rain
Clutter 22
Written 3 November, 2015

Irregular shapes of water from last night's rain rest
Tremulously in the shallow hollows of the garden's
Flagstones. The unveiled morning sun is slyly changing them
To vaporous disappearances. The lakes are as dark as
Hematite in the center, but are unendurably
Bright round their deckled rims. The light from those edges
Transports me, as though by catapult, through a diadem
So immaculately round and blue, its heaven
Is called "heaven," while I am called nothing, but "blessed."

You may denounce as excess the license of this complex praise
Of a common phenomenon. Yet, if you were to be
As I am — flying in absolute stillness — you too might praise.

Still, it is wrong to impute my praise solely to sun
And water and this crown of high, round blue. The scene would have
No force without my praise — and your assent to hear its wild
Excesses. To listen to the effluents of my
Words is to cross through realms of sonorous ecstasy,
And — flying in absolute stillness — touch highest high.
These are the rhymes where Time's irregular shapes, culled
From the commonest phenomena, complete the half
Arc of Earth's broken rings, and join us to the circle of the sun.

Composition Without a Frame
Clutter 23
Written 4 November, 2015

———————— • ————————

This is one of those mornings so intoxicatingly
Autumnal that its clarity of light, its freshness
Of seminal breezes, makes a reversal of inner
And outer senses. Now we look across the landscape
Into sky as if we were seeing the sheathing of bright
Personas. One wraps another, stretching like fate
To form the past, while also reaching out to shape the future.
And the sheathings themselves are personas made of glass,
Each interlocked, transparent, and utterly lonely.

On days like this, it becomes more and more torturous
To maintain the fiction of separateness, because sight
And insight merge, and the simple subsumes the complex.

A green leaf on a tree, a gold one beside it, a leaf
That is crumpled, tumbling on the grass, the wind
That says everything to everyone, and fills the lungs
With visions of the sun, the total pleasure of being,
While being no one, the sound of a word which does not blight
The silence, the slightest most intimate breath, expanding
Through space, to draw the scattered galaxies back to one,
And that one, sitting quietly in a chair — the genuine
Zero, the mannequin of glass, the poet fused with poetry.

Behind the Glass of
the Candy Case
Clutter 24
Written 5 November, 2015

———————— • ————————

Once you surrender the notion of profundity,
The dream images revert to their function as curios
In gumdrop curio cabinets, that is to say,
As enticements for children. And yet the notion
Of profundity still continues to startle — a jackhammer
Bursting the sleeper's eardrum, like a sudden
Perception of chaos disheveling order, like a break
In the magma shell that cakes the hours. Snap! — you
Go down, abruptly swallowed in flames, as quick as change in dreams.

Hell is as sweet on the tongue as these gumdrop sensations
Of sound, the child's home in a hollow tree, the pied-a-terre
Of fairy tales, a fox that becomes a cat that becomes a person.

In this school where one's words are memorized and recited
By pupils arranged in rows, who have no notion
Of meaning, only order, one suddenly feels, profoundly,
The notion of nonsense, that the images make you react,
That the rhymes keep jangling, that the heat of hell grows as warm
As a mother's caress. These are the curious facts
Which rattle the ear, the jackhammer pounding incessantly
Every form with the rapidity of change. Change is the one,
The only, curio, which any child can be permitted.

The Spirit of Autumn and the Ghost in the Machine

Clutter 25

Written 6 November, 2015

———————— • ————————

Through a series of ingenious exploitations,
We have melded the entrails of mountains with certain
Organic polymers of high molecular mass
To conjure forth an entity, who chases dead leaves
From walkways. The entity is fed by the jellified
Remains of ancient sea creatures, whose collective bodies
We have unearthed from subsurface crypts. "Why," you might ask,
"Does he scream so as he toils? Is there an anguished demon
"In his guts?" But no one asks, because we know the reason.

There is something inside us that needs to have control,
And the dead leaves confront us with the chaos of mortified
Autumn. Thus the demon expresses our outraged vitriol.

But Autumn is another, mightier demon, one who makes
Magic from the shedding trees, one who breathes simpler,
Far more soothing sounds, as her desiccated liegemen
Scrape cement or hurriedly whirr while twisting through bright,
Blue air. Queen Autumn listens to these anguished cries,
These gravelly shouts that would disperse her peace and fight
Against her uncontrollable glory, and Autumn
Shakes her hair out in defiance, knowing that he who mocks her
With blustery scorn is just another heap her love enslaves.

Color Escapist
Clutter 26
Written 7 November, 2015

You might fancy yourself trapped in a space/time vector where
It is not possible to change skin color. But I can
Volitionally regulate my melanin so that
I might pass from translucent alabaster to a black
That shines like vitreous bitumen. It is not magic.
It is simply an understanding that the satiny track
Linking one illusion to another slides right through that
Richer illusion called "brain." When you say "I am
"Fixed. I am human." I say, "You could be free of that despair."

I say, "Today I believe I shall make the sky chartreuse,
"And streak it with magenta crows. I shall tune the music
"Of the fluttering leaves into harmonies that suit."

Today I shall say, "Tomorrow's tomorrow is here,
"And this skin that is no one's, covering nothing real,
"Will undulate in oscillating rainbows. I shall make
"My magenta crows a symbol of freedom, and have them
"Perch and caw among your tombs. The tongues of the cypress trees will lick
"The air — the chartreuse air — with scintillating rhythms.
"And the ghosts of your fixed, dead flesh will start to shake
"Like leaves that flutter in the autumn winds. These leaves will trail
"Long purple flames and burn the chains that chain you to your cares."

Related or Unrelated Instances
Clutter 27
Written 8 November, 2015

———————— • ————————

The weather this morning is heavy enough to drip, but not
To rain, the drops small enough to satiate a gecko,
But big enough to drown an ant. Lizard and insect are fused
In life and death as a single baffling image. A body
Is found in a weedy lot, another a few yards away.
Death was from natural causes. Yet both victims faced east
And lay on their left sides, and neither knew the other. To
Attribute linkage to these coincidences is to hope
For a single intelligence composed of many thoughts.

I should like to see how the clouds arrange their forms
In the eye of a dying bee. I should like to see the play
Of light in the drop that drips where a great river is born.

Last night I dreamed of a small, blue book marked "Travel."
This morning I hear that trees are the hair and lungs of our
Planet. The hair collects water; the lungs make oxygen.
Ninety percent of the planet's forests are gone. Authorities
In a bustling Asian port have found in its ship-filled bay
The body of a man my height and weight. Thus the sea
Accepts me, though I live far inland. I am told the sun
Will break through the grey by noon. To speak of the weather
Is to bore the aesthete. To speak is to hide and reveal.

Conversation With An Ancestor
Clutter 28
Written 9 November, 2015

———————— • ————————

One can hear the footsteps of the intruding boy, crashing
About the rooms upstairs, looking for the Giant's golden
Harp. They sound like a chain of great, blue mountains jutting out
Of a turbulent ocean, and booming through the sleep
Of the future's sleeper as the voice of thunder. Thunder
Moves through the snake bodies of the coastal valleys.
Thunder awakens the past as a sound you can smell, the snout
Of the ancestral tree shrew, sniffing the first exultation,
The first terror, in its first inkling of the Human Being.

The rain's rivulets streak the glass of the windowpane —
The rivers of the world re-filled, the snake valley's boulders
Resounding with the voices of thunder released by rain.

Now you understand why the boy is intruding, why he
Must climb the magical green stalk and steal the Ogre's golden
Harp, why he must, in the end, rise from sleep and its fearful
Fairy tales of devolution, and harmonize the thunders.
For you, it is simply one streak joining another
On a windowpane, the storm's voice tracing silvers
Across bright glass. But for the sleeper, for the sleeper full
Of the torrents of the past, this is where freedom begins,
Where the song of "Human" supplants the primal shriek.

Self-Silencing Poetry
Clutter 29
Written 10 November, 2015

———————— • ————————

A hiker on the skinny footpath carved precariously
Round the edge of this ravine, sees mostly the opposite
Steep. It slides down as russets of redwood needles,
As greens of laurels and ferns, and from a few autumnal
Oaks, as the isolation of their last leaves' golden relics.
The feeling is that of immersion, and though a stream tumbles
Through the V of the wooded cleft, excited to runnel
Blue flashes of morning sky, the hiker's spirit reflects
Something richer than movement, something more than mere scenery.

Look down the ravine of the mind — the body's puppet — needles,
Loops, spindles, arrows — thin projectiles of every kind — each frantic
To form the perfect letter — all now have swiftly congealed.

Let us call this the moment of intermingling sympathies,
The moment when movement and stillness meld, when hiker and steep
Ravine shimmer together as a single life. And let us
Not disparage this life with any inarticulate bleat.
But rather let us honor it. Let us extend its magic
Down, deep down, into the jumbled pit of the ordinary,
That place where the wooden-headed puppet makes its mundane mess
Miraculous, and proclaims light's eloquence. The hiker needs
More than forest sights to free him. He needs the gift of speech.

Sleeping Through Renovations
Clutter 30
Written 11 November, 2015

————————— • —————————

You may as well accept that your grandchildren in the future
Will be breathing under water as easily as you
Now breathe the air, or that the dog you loved most as a boy
Will bound out of the dirt and want to play. Memory —
That old house, which grows and shrinks through inexplicable
Laws — is constantly attacked. Repairs go on incessantly.
Oblivious men with hammers and power saws employ
Their furious devices to beat the peace to death. You
May as well accept the noise as silence — that lie, your cure.

These eccentric characters involved in semi-dramatic
Actions ply their trades in dreams. That we all know. That we all
Accept. But can you accept the corollary wreck … ?

That the whole of reality is a ruined dream … ? is fragments
Of dreams that are dreaming? Can you accept that this body
Breathing air is also a body breathing under water?
Can you roll on the ground in the dirt with the dog of death?
When the builders attempt to build sense from nonsense, they fill
The air with mechanical hysterics, replacing the myth
Of decay with the myth of progress, the noise of their labor
Digested by the house, its dark bowels quietly
Working. You may as well join them, content to be impotent.

Flâneur

Clutter 31

Written 12 November, 2015

———————— • ————————

Maybe you find yourself in the crumbling innards
Of an interminable city. And maybe you are
Searching for something. And maybe among the ad-hoc, seedy
Businesses, the rubble of collapsing buildings,
And the weedy vacant lots, people are wandering,
The people of the edge, the outcast hustlers, scavenging
Around to eke out dishonest livings. And maybe
You are afraid. And maybe not. Maybe you live here,
But without a home, alone, without cohorts, kin, or friends.

I have said that the city is interminable.
It is despair without an edge. But the people living
In this post-industrial dump do not seem miserable.

Here is depression, but without the depressed, without cheer,
But without self-digested sorrow. The violence here,
The hunger, is suffered without affect. The people
Are what they are. It is you who are different. Maybe
Because you are searching. And maybe your searching
Is the interminable cause of this ruined city.
And maybe you think 'In a dream you cannot dissemble,
'But remain the lone searcher of your thoughts, the searcher
'Of interminable waste, thinking you are someone somewhere.'

A Thousand Miles without the Warmth of a Hearth. Ten Thousand Days to Forget Past Troubles

Clutter 32

Written 13 November, 2015

———————— • ————————

To content oneself with imbecility is to accept
Idleness as a condition of being. One thinks of those
Old men who wander through the verses of Chinese poets,
Bent, broken, alone in their mountain huts, and stupidly
Watching frost become dew become haze become the day's high
Clarity, the afternoon's blue secrets, the night's plum dreams
Of drunken bubbles of stars. The translators of such poets
Must be Edwardian gentlemen diseased by old
Titles and the bugbear of a leisure, rich and decrepit.

The crazed hermits murmur the unpronounceable names of places
And people, dead even to them, as they recite the whys
And wherefores of their disastrous and coveted loneliness.

These imbeciles claim to be content. Oh, and it is hard not
To admire them, with the long hairs of their regal white
Eyebrows twitching like lute strings in the wind, with their devotion
To dead wives and lost battles, with their venerations
Brushed across parchments more fragile than the autumn leaves that fly
On waves of chilling autumn breezes. And those gentlemen,
Who in tweedy idleness had time to revive the mumblings of foreign
Geezers, how we do envy their erudition, and sigh
As they sigh, in their brandy snifters, for lives cleansed of thought.

Companion Animal
Clutter 33
Written 14 November, 2015

———————— • ————————

Sometimes we find traces of bile or blood on clothing
Or even on chairs, but for the most part, the effects
Of these globular conglomerations of words and nerves
Remain invisible, though victims inexplicably cry
Out when these beasts squeeze a foot, a head, a heart.
People kennel them in closets, pantries, drawers, or they hide
Them under beds — yes, often under beds — as sort of reserve
Reservoirs of pain, redundancies, as a matter of fact,
To be added to the moment-to-moment pains of living.

But mostly these pets, these animals fed on slights,
Are traded among friends, since, if they were not, then when Time parts
One moment from another, a ray of joy might alight.

And — Oh — we could not stand that. The past's regurgitation
Forms our identities, gives us stability, a name,
And keeps us from having to join yesterday's bird calls
And dew shine in the blank annals of oblivion.
We could hardly imagine a sun whose glorious art
Could exist for only this instant, and no other, one
Bling on an eyelid or grass blade, one un-historical
Beauty destroyed by the next, with no chance at all of fame,
No chance at all to lavish pain's pet with affection.

Swirling a Sequence
into a Simultaneity
Clutter 34
Written 15 November, 2015

———————— • ————————

Last night, low clouds poured over the sleepless city, bleaching
The landscape white with reflected light. Then came those specters
Whose bodies are the wind, pushing the trees about among
The buildings, like fireflakes of snow. Rain fell, rhythmically
Pattering us into deeper sleep. Then, then came the day,
Sun spangled blues and greens, in which the tumbling autumn leaves,
With spastic antics, animated space, their almost-songs
Of golden whisperings mixing with bird cries, merging theirs
And ours into one vibrant, vital pulse of living.

It is axiomatic that human beings are superb
At studying entities smaller than themselves. But this day's
God is bigger. This day's God is calendar and word.

This day's God turns poet to prospector, digging the blue
With the pickax of his speech — to unsky what? the diamond
Of the God's mysterious body? the beating heart of Time?
The peal of silence slicing word from thing? the end to
The stultification of dead thought? But the God of Day
Will not reveal His secrets, nor separate Himself through
That which splits. The God of Day is single. Our poor speech finds
No answer in sound's segments, and yet a revelation comes
When this single, sonorous One subsumes all twos.

Fishy Adaptations
Clutter 35
Written 16 November, 2015

———— • ————

You know you are walking towards the sea, and that this cement
Trough hemming in the creek has been engineered to tame
The water's aggression and assure the city's peace. There
Has been some sort of commemoration at the shore, complete
With orchestra and choir. But now you see, among dead
Leaves and oil slicks, the remains of music books, their sheaves
Of notes riffling on the wrinkled creek. A salt smell in the air
Affirms the identity of the desecrator, and blames
That entity known as The Water's Lord — as blind assailant.

But perhaps the transgressor was not The Water's Lord,
And the music was not completely annihilated
When He raised up, then thunderously crashed down, His wave of
words.

You sit. You write, yet know you have reached the ocean.
The waves are deceptively gentle, almost demur.
All human forms of music have been drowned. You are yourself
A victim. You know as you sit in your chair and write your
Sounds, that only inhuman conjurations will be read
By the future's inhumanity. These underwater
Readers will have gills and lidless eyes and bodies scaled
With riffling forms of music. All that was once engineered
Will be broken. Only the water's words will then be spoken.

Apocalyptic Humor
Clutter 36
Written 17 November, 2015

———————— • ————————

The faux-brick front of our beach house has been painted a glossy
Schoolbus yellow, which casts a Floridian glare attractive
To a tiny, prolific form of scarlet beetle.
A hundred million species of Coleoptera certainly
Prove God's whimsy. Sadly, the swarmings of this beetle
Have also attracted birds — robins — a northern variety,
Uncommon here. They break their beaks on the bricks, and flail
About on the lawn, a tragic spectacle indicative
Of an ecological weirdness, which proves man's whimsy.

At the rear of the house, the ocean is so calm, so clear
That the fish seem printed like items on a menu. Most call
This phenomenon "convenience." Most are its worshipers.

Everybody is pairing up — girlfriend with boyfriend, even
Wives with husbands. They hump like beetle-backed scarabs,
Their offspring swarming the planet with whimsical furor.
They croak like broken birds with broken beaks, and call
Their croakings "News" — another species of convenience. I call
Them poems. In any random moment, these comical
Threnodies can enthrall the prolific, beetly worshipers.
All this has certainly made God laugh, and cracked his ribs,
And filled with thunderous whimsy hollow heaven.

Identity Crisis
Clutter 37
Written 18 November, 2015

———————— • ————————

You will forgive me if I deem it necessary
To use an outmoded word like "natatorium"
To described this depression era adjunct to the high school's
Gymnasium. But the white tile, the turquoise waters
Of the swimming pool, the ghostly nature of this place —
Hollow, echoing, huge, a little mildewed — seem to require
Such vocabulary. In winter, few brave the damp, cool
Isolation to swim here — the school closed, and education
No longer needing a facility for training bodies.

If I say that reading poetry is similarly
Outmoded — like swimming in antiquated waters with weights
Strapped to one's wrists — to be immersed, to risk — you will forgive
me.

If the white of the tiles has changed to the white of snow, and you
Trudge, as you once swam, through waves of drifts, the weights
On your eyelids now, on all your limbs, as you feel the freezing
Heaviness of immersion, attempting, with no success, to
Educate, to train, with words, the soul, you will say
I have abandoned interpretation, and am flailing through
Old dreams. And you will ask: "Who is this who must sing
With blue lips — murmuring through numbing sleep — to make
"Another drowsy victim drown?" And I will say: "It's you."

Bolus

Clutter 38

Written 19 November, 2015

Whenever Mr. Typicus — whose numbers are legion —
Was subjected to poetry, he did not so much hear
The angelic shapes of air, colored richly with the bright
Hues of ecstasy, as feel the presence of slugs, gumming
Up his hairy ear holes, like so many witless squirmers.
These extraordinary encounters found him crossing
An alien threshold, wherein a third kingdom, that blossomed right
Out between fantasy and reality, engulfed him. Queer
Monsters appeared, plaguing him with queerer inner visions.

Suppose instead of the usual porcelain of a glazed
Locust tree, gold-green against the sky's blue-gold, you heard fire swarms
Of insectoid words — like Mr. Typicus — you might be amazed.

But Mr. Typicus loathed these weird surprises. He wanted life
Ungarnished by such spices. He wanted words subdued
By hard, grey facts. He wanted signs for things, not things as signs.
He feared to claim this extraterrestrial child, whose big eyes
Glued him to his narrow image. It was as if a future,
Full of crisis, wild with beauty, materialized
From poetry's intrusions. It was as if straight lines
Ballooned to volumes, which drowned him in an opalescent goo,
Digesting him as food to feed this other, larger life.

Gourmand

Clutter 39

Written 20 November, 2015

———————— • ————————

Walk down this avenue of over-arching sycamores,
Their wide, flat hands, golden in autumn light, squeezing out large
And small globules of azure. These tear-drop shapes
Are ruffled by the breeze, the counter-trembling shadows causing
Strollers to flutter away their solid forms. This is called
"Work at the Psychic Institute," where the psychics keep changing
From something to nothing, and showing you big, strange
Schematics of impossible inventions, while the man in charge —
That fat boss full of infirmities — sleeps in a chair and snores.

Look around you. The fat man is Mystery, and however
Unsavory his outward form, his inner workings are full
Of motion and beauty — of leaves floating on sunlight's river.

Look around you. Don't deceive yourself into thinking that
The fat man is an allegory. He is sitting right here —
Rank in the effluvia of his gluttony, seemingly
Inert on the outside, but inside teeming with schematics
That test the furthest limits of what is possible.
In the avenue of the sycamores there are cryptics
More challenging to read than madmen's dreams. What is, what seems
Are interpenetrating — leaves floating on sunlight's river,
All things gorging on change, and growing enormously fat.

Shapes Shaped from
a Surfeit of Surf Sounds
Clutter 40
Written 21 November, 2015

——————— • ———————

You must have heard by now of the anonymous, perhaps
Even criminal, sculptor, who vandalized Nature's wastage
With his art. Finding silvered jumbles of driftwood on lonely
Beaches, he would set to carving generic human shapes,
Polishing these proto-beings to honeyed smoothness, and leaving
Them *in situ* to be tide-shuffled and sunbaked, their waste
Joined with Nature's, but with a difference. The green sea,
And the grey sea, and the blue sea cannot read this page
Of beauty and despair. But poets can — being the scribes of scraps.

Lovers are poets … and children … and the mad. These seek lonely
Places in forests, on beaches, in books, forever searching
The wastage for nooks that can hide them, for worlds that they can read.

Great storms pound sea cliffs and loosen the roots of trees. You can see
How such violence can lead to voyages … and to destruction.
You can read the biographies of the wasted, their phrases
Jumbled and barren, begging for someone to come with their
Chisel to shape a proto-human from this mess, to bring
A generic order, even a beauty, from this despair.
You can even imagine these isolated places
Where lovers, children, and the lonely mad find consolation
From ghosts of words once spoken to the deaf and deafening sea.

He Is So Skeleton Thin, When He Turns Sideways You Can't See Him Anymore

Clutter 41

Written 22 November, 2015

———————— • ————————

How confusing these just-before-dawn discoveries, when
We realize, however nebulously, that the body
Is only a coagulation of images,
In one moment those of a city, in the next, those of a
Wood, a desert, a seashore, or a sewer. There is nothing
Like tissue or organs, much less identity, nothing a
Surgeon could cut or a mortician bury — just vestiges
Of quickly dispersing dreams, just the fleeting mystery
Of stars being extinguished by the rising sun.

Is the arm which reaches into space, the flame of space?
The swirling of murky waters? Or a stone? Is the scent, rising
In the nostrils, that of an animal, which can never wake?

The images change too quickly to finalize answers,
Though the brightening east forms silhouettes of sable —
The geometric shapes of roof-lines or of monstrous,
Shaggy trees, pretending to make that limit called
Horizon. In a moment or two, the blues of first morning
Light will steal away these revelations, and a visible
Self will return to hoodwink us, and to make us
Believe in solidities and daylight. The impossible
Immaterial will fade, as the ghost of bone re-appears.

Meteorological Cogitation
Clutter 42
Written 23 November, 2015

Today, all the urban shaman crow-clan-men will be flying
Through what weathermen call "the dirty edge of the front,"
Because tomorrow the season's first onslaught of arctic air
Will prevail, and beat today's blue haze into angry, grey
Submission. Just now you are wondering, "Exactly where
Are these words heading? Are we going to sail away
On the black wings of fancy, inhabiting a creature
Existing only as an atavistic poet's stunt,
Or are we going to hear about rain falling and snow flying?"

In the mountains, there will be snow, and on the coasts, rain.
And the crows will experience this as if their flocks were
One crow-creature, sharing one colossal crow-clan brain.

And just now you are wondering, "Exactly what is this crow brain
Thinking, flying about with the flying waters and snow,
Alive in a thousand eyes on a thousand wings, and filling
The throat of the storm with cacophonous music
To compliment the howlings of the wind? And what does the ear
Of the urban crow-clan-man hear in this song of the arctic,
Which has so transformed him?" To ask such questions is to fling
One's self through space, is to squawk at earth, so that one can go
Where this giant of shattering cold sings wild refrains.

Thoughtless Inquiry
Clutter 43
Written 24 November, 2015

———————— • ————————

Today's steady drizzle has provided an ideal
Opportunity for our entomologist of human
Post-mortem psychology to take to the field, and study
The disintegrative effects of rain on an abandoned
Termite mound. The networks of tunnels branching from the central
Chimney have collapsed. Both king and queen are dead. But the dung
Nursery walls are still intact enough to house larvae,
Untended by worker castes, and left to dream at some
Depth uncluttered by memory, in the luminous unreal.

Our scientist can see how the brain shuts down, eroding
Slowly as it ages, and after passing through physical
Life, reaching a final infancy, composed of dreaming.

Each segment of each dream is as clear, as empty, and as
Reflective as a rain drop … and there are untold numbers
Of them, more than our entomologist can tally. Each
One slated to drown some larval stage of sentience, each one
An image of the luminous unreal, each one a runnel
Of guttural sound bound to engulf the last inhuman
Remnant of the human. "These angels are beyond the reach
Of death," or so our entomologist claims, his reason blurred,
As, waxing poetic, he affirms, "Our first state is our last."

Intentional Tremor
Clutter 44
Written 25 November, 2015

Let me tell you about a cabin in the High Sierras,
Which you will never see in winter because you will
Never take this potholed fire road that sneaks past its
Inhospitable door. At night, when the kerosene lamps are lit,
You must not stare through the window where a hook in the rafters
Suspends the bow of a tree saw. It looks like a giant's
Dangling, matressless bed frame, and its chipped red paint has lent it
A murderous air. The mountains around are stupendously still,
And the red gleams from the snow like predators' retinas.

Let me tell you about a midnight call that clinically
Reports that someone old has fallen. If that someone is your
Father, you will know what those eyes mean …

And know how blood is stung by cold, and why the moon must make
A dazzling silica in this wilderness of titanic
Isolation. The thick snow has hunched the pines so that they stoop
Like armies of old men, shuffling in broken ranks, the white
Bones of lumbermen in the afterworld. These are our fathers
In their Biblical generations, braving the icy night,
Unsteady in the presence of the saw. Their cold roots
Release their ancient granite footholds, as the frost's hands crack
Them free from suffering, and the still night starts to shake.

Thanksgiving
Clutter 45
Written 26 November, 2015

———————— • ————————

No moon was ever rounder or fuller or ever shone
More wondrously on snow that ever glowed purer or brighter
On any night that was ever quieter or colder than this
One. These woods are pathless, and even the fox must leap through its
Snowdrifts with the same arching sleekness with which a dolphin leaps
Through waves. The owl waits hungrily, a hooded silhouette
With yellow eyes, hunched in the snowclumps of a fir tree's branches.
The wind weaves serpents of vaporous powder, and the deer
Exhale blue, whispering stars. I am awake and alone.

No dawn is coming, none will ever come. That does not matter.
What matters now is wakeful inwardness. The night knows this. She
Keeps all secrets. She is my mother, and the cold my father.

So I go slowly to the hearth of cold, deep in a valley
Where the black stream flows, frozen above, moving like blood below,
And carrying gently all my memories. None of this
Matters now. Motherless, fatherless, I have finally come
To the orphaned heart of mountainous, silent beauty.
I have finally come to the zero of all equations,
Where the infinite kills the finite with absolute bliss,
And the self, which has made itself out of frozen sorrows,
Slips quietly down the steeps to the depths of the sea.

Tinnitus
Clutter 46
Written 27 November, 2015

———————— • ————————

This punishment, almost laughably mild in its initial
Effects, is as excruciating as sleep deprivation
After several iterations. Think of it as the anniversaries
Of your birth, the first few, celebratory in the extreme,
But then, as a mid-point number is exceeded, becoming
Thirty-five — to choose a Dante-esque example — the lean
Wolf stalking you in the snow through the menacing trees,
Begins taking longer strides, and you feel his starvation
In your own gut, and on your bleeding lips, his eager snarl.

You know what is going to happen. But since it is not
Going to happen right away, it is easy to let your thinking
Become deluded, and believe you will never be caught.

I am a little lost, a bit deluded. The wind and new
Snow are erasing my tracks — all tracks — and it is easy
To let my desperation grow, and to hear in my ears
The ringing of a death knell — to hear it, in fact, for years
Without much alarm. I see a tree that has fallen, splaying
Its bare, broken limbs like an animal's ribs — that hunger
Of the wolf displaced in form. When I note how the sharper
Splints are softened by the clinging snow, it is easy
To tell myself: "There is no danger. Cold Time blankets you."

A Peaceful Father and Son Outing
Clutter 47
Written 28 November, 2015

———————— • ————————

Having for years cavorted with all of the fabulous
Pretenses spawned by nonsense, and having let fall the clearest,
Most prismatic tears because through all those years I have seen
My father's brain dying — now that he has fallen, and his
Porous brain swells with blood, I can tell from the voices
On the phone — voices quite disrespectful of distances,
And fraught with their kindly bedside manner — that the scenes
In the hospital are only the footage for dreams. He sits
By a lake, fishing, imagining life below the surface.

A door, perfectly fitted to its odd-shaped opening,
Closes, and one thinks of a bullet exiting a gun, our choices
In the past, all speed and violence, suddenly slowing …

So the bullet returns, perfectly fitted to its barrel.
Certainly there has been an explosive passage. It is
Nonsense to think it could end so peacefully in a chamber
All clinically clean and metallic. It is nonsense to
Think it could end. Years hence, I know I will hear those voices,
So disrespectful of distances, go rippling through
My dreams, like breezes ruffling water. I will be sitting near
My father, fishing, and trying to see through my tears his
Alert blue eyes, as they track sleek movements under fluid veils.

Joking Gesture
Clutter 48
Written 29 November, 2015

Even in warm coastal regions such as this, these sharp frosts
Hasten the fall of autumn leaves, and greatly accelerate
Their degradation to mulch and earthy fecundity.
Let us now direct our attention to human beings,
Who are likewise scythed by assassinating Time. A young man's
Strength is also crumpled by frost, and an old man, tumbling
Into a hospital bed, is likewise degraded. He
Becomes the pool of his body's basest functions, a spate
Of shit and piss and pus — and the dross of memories lost.

The autumn leaves sport carnivalesque colors, made brighter —
More clownish — by the frost's ice crystals. So a young man
Sees an old man as a clown, flailing in murky waters.

Survival of the fittest is survival of the stable —
The balanced — and nothing unhinges the stable like earthy
Laughter — the carnival celebrants dancing in wintry
Death masks, and falling as bundles of rags on hospital beds,
All of us someday becoming unwitting clowns, each one
Of us making his noisome contribution to this great bled
Pool of cess that is the Earth. Our Father who art dirt, we see
You glibly grinning, waving your hand as a tremory
Affront to the funny illusions we all think are real.

Head Wounds

Clutter 49

Written 30 November, 2015

———————— • ————————

As hard as it is to conceive of a language less
Bland than the inverted pyramid style of obituary
Journalism, still the emotion of the situation
Needs denaturing. Thus "Roy Doughty, 88, of Hot Springs,
"Is convalescing at Rapid Regional Hospital
"From a head injury suffered in a fall" seems more fitting
Than any floridly poetic concoction
As a lead for this story of fathers and sons, and the dreams
That connect and divide them. Perhaps the barest prose works best.

But the son dreams of wheels as black as ink on newsprint, wheels that
Turn smoothly through birthday memories to suddenly halt
Before a picture window. He presses his face to the glass.

Inside he sees his father on a couch — the head protruding
From a woolen blanket. The mouth is open, the eyes shut,
The skull pale, except for a blood-red lump. Everything else in
The room is small and dark. He stares at the blanket, trying
To detect the rise and fall of breathing. The blanket swells,
Collapses, rests inert. In the distance: reports of crying.
Thus, another Roy Doughty, forehead pressed to glass, his skin,
Collecting ice inside a dream, feels these long cleanly cuts
From shards of sliding tears, whose cold turns fiery on waking.

One Way Conversation
Clutter 50
Written 1 December, 2015

---•---

At this latitude, in this hemisphere, the winter's sun
Drifts so far south, that even straight up noon is sideways slanted.
Thus the sunniest of middays walk crookedly, shuffling
Towards dusk at an old man's hobbled pace, and absent-mindedly
Groping for a bed. Father, your shadow grows longer
As you grow frailer, you try, but cannot speak, your strong voice weak,
Your syllables slurred to vowels, the sun in your eyes sliding
Sideways — so softly searching for something not far ahead,
Whose dawn is breaching and dimming your sight's last sun.

All margins impose risk. And in those persistently
Darkening annals of disorder, your words breed danger —
The breathless language of the dead, infusing your garbled speech.

O! they are calling, just beyond the reach of what your eyes
Can eat or your ears swallow. Your brothers, your father, your
Mother, you scolding wife, their voices pouring a stellar
Excrement into this shuddering world, which only fears them.
But through your mumbling, we hear angelic whispers,
Like sideways words, slanted by winter's sun, and from these poems
An eerie comfort comes, like numbness clotting scars
On open wounds. The words die at the margin of your lips, your
Language flowing inward, like a sob, feeding kind ghosts your cries.

Footnote

Clutter 51

Written 2 December, 2015

————— • —————

Do you remember your exhilaration when you first knew
How the dull overcast of winter could be made warm
By writing the letters s-u-n? how X could be Y
In the language of dream, and how wearing shoes too large could
Represent your awe of your father, your extreme delight
When your feet in those shoes plus the magic of childhood
Could make you the man who wore them? Now Y
Is not X. Y is Y — not the question, nor even the form
Of a letter, but just three merging lines that do not move.

On the other side of the mind, there is a man deemed holy,
To whom all things are bliss. He can sit in a room void of light
And experience joy as swarms of energy.

Do you remember the exhilaration you first knew
When you felt the jump of atoms beneath your skin?
When the overcast of winter did not matter? and the feet
Of your father, upright as he lay in bed, the skin of their
Soles full of sores, was only a random swarming of lights,
Blissful to be what is in the instant that is? when Father
The man became only a puff of dream, a tick of speech
In the language of ecstasy? or an end that begins again
When a child slips his foot in the cosmic shoe?

On the Power of the Powerless
Clutter 52
Written 3 December, 2015

No one in this country — no one in his right mind anyway —
Would stand up and pound his chest and say "I am Shiva,
"The Destroyer," but that's who I am, or to speak in less
Grandiose terms, I am one of the god's more fumbling henchmen,
Whose chief weapon is neglect. In the grip of extreme
Senescence, my father is totally dependent on
The offices of professional caregivers, whose best
Efforts lack the one resource that I alone can give: a
Palliative love. But I am a continent away…

… I am a continent away … of sunless miles of winter
Distances, forbidding to cross, a mountainous travesty
Of snow and cost, and winds that bellow "Danger."

What is this game? If the game is about the acquisition
Of physical pain, then perhaps my father is winning,
Though the last time he spoke, he said that he felt none.
If the game is about the elocution of words, then I
Am winning, for he can do nothing that resembles speech.
If the game is about destruction, then Time wins, and I
Am the master of Time because I can waste it. One
Hour, one lifetime of neglect, is the same for Shiva, king
Of dithering, as an eternity of absent suns.

Nebulous Articulation
Clutter 53
Written 4 December, 2015

———————— • ————————

The wet trees from yesterday's drizzle have joined the houses
And the black asphalt of the streets to exude golden vapors
Into raking morning light. Now fat blue noon is whitened nearly
To the paleness of the soft, low clouds, and the haze infects our
Mood, so that we banish all ambition, and allow ourselves
The luxury of drifting. It is as if our sleep, whose hours
Were stolen last night by sickness and money worries,
Returned as boneless postures of lassitude, the languor
Of warm indifference defusing whatever might rouse us.

Suppose old voices — leaked from the ruins of words — recite
From a drifting cloud that "loss is inevitable,
And what's given is taken back," would you know if they were right?

Or suppose your ancient father could murmur only clouds
Of words. These ghosts might touch your heart, as vapors touching
Vapor, but still say nothing. Are they the messengers of
Weather, of swathes of winter sunlight after rain,
Of warmth that arrives for an instant to forecast cold?
Now suppose those murmuring spirits could steal your pain,
So that your thoughts drift back to times when love
Inhabited a will strong as itself, and not this flickering
Ember of a brain, which cannot speak its tenderness aloud.

The Weatherman's Present
Clutter 54
Written 5 December, 2015

———— • ————

A near uniformity of overcast has filtered
The morning sun so that it saturates all with a cool,
Russet elixir of winter light. The weather is always
Changing, but one can imagine the Father of Heaven
Behind these chilling veils, enthroned, locked in a meditation
That it is taboo to disturb or to sully. In him
Is the stillness of dignified royal awe, which conveys,
As symbol, the earthly father's flesh. In him the rule
Of light need never change, nor tip his justice out of kilter.

The horizon this morning is the sacred circle of
His rusted crown, within whose orbit peace is made common
As the universal inheritance of his love.

The father forever lies beyond the horizon. It is
Said that he cannot age, nor can he succumb to illness.
It is said that his effigies may die, but not himself.
It is said that he secures his domain by the direction
He turns his face when laid to rest. His many children
Are like tabooed thoughts, who will not consent to consign him
To Death's realm — although Death's mystery drapes imperial
Purple around the fissured frailty of his bones. It is
Said that his agony gifts us blessedness.

Imagination
Clutter 55
Written 6 December, 2015

——————— • ———————

The north wall of the magician's cell is a wall of glass
Pressed by the sentient leafery of medicinal plants.
The light that enters the cell is green. The sill of this window —
Like the cell's three other walls — is lined with books. These are his
tools.
With these he conjures. With these he conquers illness.
For him these opacities constitute clear crystal.
Through these he travels to realms washed clean of sorrow.
In these he transcends the psychotic human trance,
As he follows the light where he will through the crystal's lattice.

Today it is raining. For others the rain is descending.
But for him the drops are chains of channels, linked by bliss,
That ascend into the heavens, where medicines are waiting.

We need these medicines. Here, the old use metal prostheses
To lurch towards cremation, and the young are deceived by
Hallucinogenic sex. The magician is not human,
Much less a doctor or lover. The magician is who
We are when we drop our needs for anything else but gnosis —
The knowledge that all we are is a brief passing through,
A passing of rain through skies, of light through crystal, a span
Of Time that streaks without duration, a ravenous eye
On a page already read, propounding this healing thesis.

Escape

Clutter 56

Written 7 December, 2015

———— • ————

This is one of those rural highways which — where it can — snakes
Through the pastures and woods of valleys and — where it must —
labors
Up steep round hills. These crest to views of pastoral
Panoramas with exhilarating vistas of rugged
Coastlines and fog-wreathed mountain peaks. You might see anything
Here and not be sad — a formal convocation of buzzards
Feasting all afternoon on road kill fawn, the worm-eaten crawl
Of wireless fence posts over a rutted hill, a lone horse,
Head depressed, the steam of his breath stirred, when his withers shake.

You might see anything here and not be lonely. You might follow
The grey afternoon into chilly dusk, as the smiling
Thought of an earlier, brighter noon diverts your sorrow.

You came here just for this — to see a lugubrious place that reeks
Of beauty, collecting, under solemn winter skies, these scenes
Of greens and golds and tawny browns that hold the grays of day's
Soft atmospheres in peaceful highlights and in deepening glooms.
You came to find a place free of such weeping
As urban concentrations prompt you to.
It shall be night here soon, but you shall end your day
Back in the city, where the false lights, laughing, gleam,
Safe from the reach of owl hoots or the stricken rodent's squeak.

Thoughts for Tomorrow
Clutter 57
Written 8 December, 2015

———— • ————

They tell you this is your own house, and they tell you that this
Is the hallway you traverse each day to cross a threshold
Into a room where you spend all your evenings. Why then
Do you feel as though you are piercing an opening bud,
Rife with creamy pulsations and violet perfumes? Why does
Your body granulate, as if an invisible sieve had
Multiplied you into multiple buzzings? And why, when
You pass a mirror, are there golden light-streaks, and not that mold
Of features you call you? Why all this bright forgetfulness?

Yesterday, all day, you stared at a houseplant, an orchid
Without a bloom. Today that creature is gone, and what was
Leaf becomes leaf's memory — this feeling of something you did …

That you no longer do. And the feeling expresses a space
That was hiding inside you, like that houseplant's untapped
Potential to make a bloom. There is talk in this glittering
Space about remains, and how to dispose of them. The talk is
Like music in a hollow tube, like a fragrance that wafts
Over moonlit citrus orchards. This talk becomes the silence
In sound's wake, when all the waves go smooth, and all the wings
Of all the bees of speech, in unison, cease to beat, wrapped
In the glow of a wondrously apt phrase.

How Bright is Brighter When Jutting Forth From Darkness
Clutter 58
Written 9 December, 2015

———————— • ————————

Above a foreground wall of evergreen and autumn-yellowed
Shrubberies, a hummingbird rises, zips that way and this,
Flashing his tiny ruby against the lace of a barren
Locust tree. A sunlit drizzle falls. "Where is the nectar?"
An urgent question, which winter refuses to answer.
Silver foil, frantic bird — the mist of last things seen, the rain-blurred
Twirlings of a last, few locust leaves. These final golden
Survivors remind us of the last words of a loved one. They twist
This way and that near a bedside transfigured by sorrow.

Where is the nectar? You must surely have seen how the drizzle
Compounds the sunlight, how the air and the frantic bird glitter
Together in a bright cascading myriad of jewels.

You must surely have seen how the foreground and background converge
Round the ruby of the loved one's whispering, and how
The bed, lost in the mist of distance, is utterly erased
By wintry tears, so that nothing remains but this drizzle
Of beautiful grief. And as the hummingbird's humming stirs
The air, you must know for sure how the babbling of final
Words distance all meaning, yet preserve a gem-like grace,
So that such hazy brilliance may transfigure sorrow,
As glittering flight and winter's mysteries merge.

A Meditation on the Second Letter of the Hebrew Alphabet

Clutter 59

Written 10 December, 2015

———————— • ————————

Often poor supplicants ascend to my jungle cave, their eyes
Wide open wounds, and ask: "Master, do you see the sun as we
See the faces of loved ones, alive in memory only,
Their bodies having passed beyond light's reach and softened to
Perfection by our needs?" They are so pitiful
With their questions, and I so pitifully unable to
Requite them. Still, I answer: "My children, the sun shines only
As we shine. That is the secret of his fire. Our memories,
Our aspirations, create the rapture of his splendid eye."

Suburbia thrives on many levels. Where ornamental
Leaves dazzle the eye with last night's deluge: that is one level,
The level of crystal — my cave in the depths of the jungle.

Yet there are other levels, less fundamental, levels where
Worries barnacle the eyes or clog the veins with angry
Ciphers, levels where plumbing draws away life's wastes, and levels
Where a mental apparatus, old as fear, makes of our house
A fortress full of weapons — those questions that bristle
In the hermit's ear. The sun is only what I am, the house
Of light that makes my house of words. I sit in this cave and babble
To myself, recalling faces in dithering reveries,
The Perfected Master of Nothing, mumbling my prayers.

Arrested Development
Clutter 60
Written 11 December, 2015

Like the first photographers, it is imperative for
The connoisseur of the random to freeze the scene. He is
Obliged to frame his shot, to set his camera up where
The instantaneity of miracle might be caught,
Snatched from the infinite flux, and exposed as an absolute,
As when the most pellucid of morning lights light a drop
Of last night's rain as it falls from today's red leaf, its career
Making a momentary streak which, for reasons mysterious,
Ignite a flame in the heart of the connoisseur.

He knows, this seeker of an absolute, that the frame is as
Deliberate an artifice as there could be, an absolute
Necessity that his fixed stare brings to focus.

At the deathbed of a loved one, you can see just how intense
This search for the random becomes, a lifetime of staring
Is stopped in a single stare, and everything flowing can
Now speed up, and a rain of miracles can suddenly streak
The air and ignite the heart of the connoisseur. The white root
Of his passion for frames is exposed. The drop from the red leaf
Streaks back to the pregnant instant when its swelling ceased, and it ran
Through a steadier instant of morning light. This sight, winging
Its way through the random, is now impaled by stillness.

Vacationing in Paradise
Clutter 61
Written 12 December, 2015

———————————— • ————————————

Like all images that so brilliantly sear the unconscious,
These will fade quickly, and in a half an hour, will be like
A day in Caracas where your boyhood in shantytown
Was spent in brown sunshine, dodging corrupt police, and drinking
Diseases from the same street sluices where you pee. The appeal
Of the exotic remains an issue, not only during
Sleep, but every time you lose your train of thought, the sound
Of birdcalls in wealthy northern suburbia growing quite
Remote, as the pop of gunshots excite a fictional lust.

Even the most cursory study of film will make clear
That only sudden shifts of scene can make the unreal seem real,
Only these cuts and splices can create narrative structure.

But the real reels out of darkness, lights up a screen, and conceals
From you the presence of a post-mortem interrogator.
He wears the uniform and the helmet of the losers in
The last world war, and demands that you confess how you killed time.
He silently screams: "This stream of arbitrary scenes, this whirl
"Of exotica was your way of murdering the shine
"Of tear drops and dew drops. You killed the calm of your suburban
"Garden, so you could sit, lost in a narrative structure
"That you would only indulge because it seemed so unreal."

Scenes from a Marriage
Clutter 62
Written 13 December, 2015

———————— • ————————

Some Arctic Malevolence has predetermined our
Criminality and released his hordes of bounty hunters
As these wind-driven nails of rain. Hate seeks us out. All night
It slams into the house, but with that irony so weirdly
Associated with criminals, its rage only deepened
Our sleep. In the morning we wakened refreshed, a great scene
Of havoc spread all around us, the terrific fight's
Destruction only bringing to our lips the slight curvature
Of a smile. "Winter, do your worst. We will survive your war."

Science has yet to investigate the asymmetrical
Relationship of weather and our moods, but the war ends
Only when the combatants blend and become compatible …

Us with our skin, and the weather without one, us trying
To cower, and the weather trying to break in — an irony
Conducive alike to violence and sly grins. The wind's banshee
Howls, and the missiles of rain descend, and we watch white
Streaks of rain crawl on our windows — toys of contemplation.
Inside our skin, we drift through clouds of violence, white
Clouds in summer skies, languid and blue, our memories
Perhaps of former crimes, or just as probably the dream
Exploits we have, each night, to keep our waking selves from dying.

Conquistador

Clutter 63

Written 14 December, 2015

———————— • ————————

I live with this deep, somnambulant terror, that I will
Never be able to show you so much as a map, let
Alone the territory, where these green mountains tower
Over narrow blue fjords, and of whose beauty and mystery
I have only this bare symbol: two snakes in a circle
Printed in red upon a field of … I wanted to say "green,"
But the truth is that the name of the color eludes me, or
Else it is no color, but a kind of diamond inset
In the flesh of the eye, a flash that is scarcely bearable.

Among the homeless beggars who squat on corners with greasy
Hands cupped forth for greasy coins, I will be that one pitiful
Bum, waving my rag, its mute tongue pleading for release in speech.

My face will betray deep lines of grief, and my dirty rag,
With those stupid squiggling lines inside a wobbling ring
Will seem to you insanely illegible, but I will
Be pleading as you hurry by — "Read, please read. I know
"Your torment, and know that I can cure it with this symbol."
And suddenly, inside you, where your sorrows burrow,
A hollow will appear, cloudy at first, but as its veils
Disperse, you will see the outlines of a continent, dazzling
And new. It waits for you, its prodigal king — go — plant your flag.

Memoirs of a Synesthesiac
Clutter 64

Written 15 December, 2015

———— • ————

Only the most idle of psychonauts have enough free
Energy to analyze the overtones of today's
Winter sunlight. Noon. Blue shadows in brass reflections. Rose-
Greys on ceilings that a just awakened sleeper, not wanting
To awaken, sees entwining richly into lavenders.
These recombinant colors shine like sunlit snow falling
From wind-shaken pines. At this same instant, one of those
Exotic parrots in the distant tropics drags the bray
Of its irritable squawk through dense jungle greenery.

'Now,' thinks the psychonaut, 'these deviant sound-images,
Scratched on the glass of the idlest of brains, conjure
Alluring questions *vis à vis* our various existences.'

He sits in a chair, idle, drugged by sleep, yet listening
As a yellow leaf etches its parroted sound across
A flagstone. The leaf scrapes underneath it a yellow-blue
Shadow, where an explosive charge of energy, infused
With peace, is waiting to ignite and burn his brain. A roar,
Whose sound is most akin to silence, abruptly imbues
A rhythmically moving form with The Wonder of the New —
The wonder of stillness imbued with the choiring gloss
Of those hues which elude the sight to saturate feeling.

Metaphysical Cardiac Legibility
Clutter 65
Written 16 December, 2015

These remarkable close-up cameras which can reveal
The tiniest of pulsations in the most miniscule
Of molecules can only expose the red world of the heart,
And not the world that is read, the world of the transient
Image: the giant at the foot of the child's bed, holding
A rifle, the scrunched up forehead of a mother, intent,
As she rolls out dough for biscuits, the light on a wall that starts
High and then, like a golden slime mold, slips to the floor, rolled
Up like the hedgehog that the hunter, dulled by boredom, killed.

The hedgehog's blood is red on the hedgehog's snout, her little
Hedgehoglets sniffing its bubble, as the vast sky goes wheeling
Over a forest screened as a close-up on a corpuscle.

My uncle was a cruel man, who drank and smoked until
His testicles swelled up to elephantine grotesqueness,
One day his detested son found him. His heart had exploded
In his chest, all that accumulated red of eighty
Misspent years escaping its fatty pouch, and cascading
Over the laddered ribs, unfettered by any sympathy,
But bearing with it, perhaps, odd images: the eroded
Montages of dissolving time, the blood, read on the lips,
Of one who shot down hedgehogs, and had a laugh at what he'd killed.

The Poet and His Audience
Clutter 66
Written 17 December, 2015

———— • ————

After he fell on his head, the ancient pioneer would
Roam the wooded grounds of the State Hospital and harass his
Captive audience — comprised of other inmates — with lurid
Tales of his "reasonectomy," pointing to the stitches
On his shaved skull as a verification of his absurd
Observations: "The fortuitous alone can spawn our genius,
The juxtapositions we find where crowds — lit with livid
Strobes of neon — mix their fantasies in dreams. It is just this
Kind of hodge-podge from which our brilliance takes its precious food."

On other unripe occasions, he spoke of bombed-out cellars,
Full of disease, as ideal spots for sexual trysts, his words
Crawling like lice into the waxy ears of his listeners.

But the words stick, and squiggle around, wanting to live, wanting to
Eat their way into those frigid centers of the brain, where
The ice mansions stand — peopleless palaces with ornate
Galleries, bright with exquisite reflections of sea-green
Lights. Here, the walls absorb blue refractions, their cornices stirred
To glittering animation by the fleeting strobes of scenes
Inexplicable to the rational mind: Pale ghosts that circulate
On the institute's lawn, each clothed in a hospital gown, their
Airy forms tattered by pine-shade, as the wind flutters through.

An Investigation into DNA's Insensate Fluidity

Clutter 67

Written 18 December, 2015

———————— • ————————

A two-year-old boy discovering a pinecone — he tosses
It up, up in the air — ah! — gravity. It has rained. It is
Going to rain. The boy stands near a creek, grey with celestial
Conversations, green with earthly ones. The creek is widening
Here in immediate preparation for its merger
With the bay. The boy squeals in delight while abruptly heaving
His arms out from his sides. The creek slides by, making wrinkles
In a reflected egret. The boy's grandmother watches,
Standing near. She drops a wadded tissue, which the wind twitches.

The generational netting that encodes the woman's
Enmeshment with the child prevents her from hearing the water's
Conversations. The boy's squeal blocks the water's wisdom.

Who you are, who you are becoming, as you dive deeper
Than the water's wrinkles or than human relations is
A question for the Detective of Perception. He sees
The white of the tissue clumping in the wet. He hears
The voices of colors — the bright of the egret's feathers
Whispering above the scarlet shouts of the boy's rubber
Rain boots. He is the solver, the dissolver, of nets. He heaves
His arms out from his sides, squeals quietly in his spine, and is
Exultant. He is the water's grandson. She pulls him under.

Baptism
Clutter 68
Written 19 December, 2015

———————— • ————————

One naive theory is that we do not have to answer
These questions posed to us like drops dripping at the edge of sleep,
And that this brilliant sunlight on a morning following
Rain will clarify everything, and prove our innocence.
Every cell in our bodies will be sanctified as they cycle
Through the processes of oxygenation, the evidence
Against us dismissed, as if we had really been praying
At all these chemical stations of the cross. If the steam
Rising from the trees is God's golden breath, what should we fear?

Yet the dream's inquisitor is ruthless with his inquiries.
His voice shreds silence. It is a machine, relentlessly full
Of accusations inimical to naive belief.

He shows us the tiniest device, which when magnified
Is seen to form a seven-pointed star, each point also
Bearing seven star-shaped nodules, and so on, so he claims,
Into infinity. This is no drip, drop, drip of simple
Water roiling into steam. It is a corpuscle
Fraught with images, all of them stamped with that original
Guilt, which coagulates as we sleep into a name.
But when this machine of thought grinds to a stop, all that we know,
Or need to know, goes "blip." One drop drips, and we are deified.

Confessions of the Weather Prophet
Clutter 69
Written 20 December, 2015

———————— • ————————

I am hiding under the bed. I know I do not have to
Explain things to you. I am hiding under the bed. I
See a man in a grey suit. Last night the overcast seeped
In and buried the moon with all her stars. This morning it
Has started to drizzle. Small flocks of very worried birds throw
Themselves on wires and bare trees. That's how the man will have it.
I see three men in grey suits. I know you will understand me
When I tell you that their eyes are like those red discs seen at night
To mark the curves on winding rural roads. You know this is true.

I am hiding under the rainy skies. Even as babies
These men wore grey suits. I know you already know. But so
Much doubt infects us. It falls like rain. It is better to speak.

Even as babies the grey men had black hair with V-shaped
Widow's peaks dividing their pale foreheads. You know about their
Grids. I hide under the bed. You drive at night on winding
Rural roads, the eyes of reflector discs tracking your moves.
All the stars and even the moon are vanishing. You know
What is coming. You know where this road is taking you.
The grey men have told you. You know you are not escaping.
The grid is here. And even from the woods the red eyes stare.
That's how the men will have it: the rain washing color away.

Passive Tense
Clutter 70
Written 21 December, 2015

———— • ————

This shape probably aspires to the certainty of a black-
Framed rectangle, something with an electronic screen
Where the underlying chaos can appear orderly —
But it has degenerated around the edges. Even
The simple pronoun "I" seems meaningless mist, and time
Signifiers like "morning" and "winter" make so little sense
That they are dispensed with. Nonetheless, in the vicinity
Of an upper-left-hand-corner a neon spiral is seen.
The spiral is red, the neon unlit — a strange artifact.

Specificities like this abound. A tiny yellow
Label, arrow-shaped, appears, disappears, a shrunken sign
Affixed in a bland corridor, printed "No where to go."

It is no longer permissible to say "I see people
In nineteenth century costumes, warding the halls of a
Sanatorium, taking the cure for consumption." It is
No longer possible to imagine what is not contained
On the screen, or to think of a word like "people" or to find
In this jumbled cabinet a thing called "meaning." A brain
Exists, yes, but it no longer collects random tidbits
Into mornings or mists or these odd simulacra
Which chant "Me. Me. Me," as if to be were inevitable.

Timid Explorer
Clutter 71
Written 22 December, 2015

———————— • ————————

As he aged, his wildest treks confined themselves to smaller
And smaller circles. But his tentative steps and uncertain
Sight involved him more and more with what he called "The Vertigo
Of the Image." It was enough for him to see the random
Distribution of leaves on his rain-slicked sidewalk, and he
Would slip right into amazement. "The rebellion of the common,"
Was how he put it, a bit of inadequate farrago
That invoked swimming Siamese elephants in North England,
Using their trunks to roll half-naked, half-drowned immigrants ashore.

No more Romeos fumbling with their Juliets — youth's suicidal
Passions paled compared to these more wondrous incongruities
Dropped by the trees — these yellows, reds, and blacks scattered pell-
mell.

Mixed leaf fringes, veins, stems seemed as weirdly unpredictable
As the sight of angels in the Sahara jockeying
Giraffes — sometimes he wanted to laugh. But the absurdities
Were so linked to his infirmities, so ecstatically
Spawned from the shadows of raven wings, so absolutely,
Incontrovertibly common that he could not shirk the belief
That he was crossing a threshold. Another reality —
One magically devoted to chaos — was awaiting
Him. He was striding to heaven with steps that were slow and small.

Unwise Expression
Clutter 72
Written 23 December, 2015

————— • —————

These sages from the subcontinent claim that our speaking
Is polluted, and that is why at these latitudes
The sun grows so small in winter. Sri Know-All says: "Words are like
"The small golden fish suspended in mid-air. The fins beat
"Like the wings of bees. You must hold them in the mouth, and release
"Them only when you find water." His words make me feel the bees
Stinging and the fish wriggling. What could he mean but this fight
To incorporate the sweet waters of silence into
A vibrating urgency? All reticence is agonizing.

Of course, when the light returns after the solstice, one finds
The metaphoric torturous. It is the intimacy
Of sunlight that one craves, the golden stillness that calms the mind.

An oceanic grief has been gathering during sleep,
Days and days of darkness and low clouds, mothers and fathers
Drowned in those deep waters which bring decrepitude and death.
And we are helpless against this violent flood, our tongues
Polluted with inexpressible feelings. And yet to weep
Affords no comfort, unless this includes those frigid songs
Of winter. That we have a life, that we suffer, that our breath
Hangs like a fish out of water at the graves of our mothers,
The bedsides of our fathers — these silences cry out for speech.

Reckoning by Underwater Phosphorescence

Clutter 73

Written 24 December, 2015

—————————— • ——————————

While I sit and watch this rainfall, there are embryos in
The millions which have yet to form eyes, or yet to decide
If they will be human or rodent. Each drop makes a sudden
Crown, which widens into a rippling ring. I watch for hours.
The clouds move slowly, their colors deepening as subtly
As rain glazes an albino ivy leaf buried under
Its own vine's multiplying shades. A Polynesian
Navigator, the last man who knows how to read the sea, dies.
Henceforth no canoe without instruments will cross the ocean.

If you dream of a bright white space where poets are assembled
From golden lace, and hung head-down like bats, you will start to see
The magnitude of this task — the monolith must be scrambled.

It is time for your therapy. They will take the rails down
From your protected bed, and holding your tremory arms
On either side, they will walk you slowly to a porcelain
Commode. Up to now the goal has always been translation —
To move the unknown to the known. We thought lucidity
Would be possible if mystery were expunged. We believed the men
In lab coats who murder mice. No one took time to see what rain
Was doing — opening and closing circles, from storm,
Extracting calm. No one could hear how words devolved to sound.

Disappearing Deposition
Clutter 74
Written 25 December, 2015

———————— • ————————

"If you try to pick up one of these tiniest of colored
Sugar sprinkles, it will dissolve on your fingertip before
You can retrieve it." That is what the sun says of the frost
Crystals. I feel a child's first bitterness at discovering
That sweetness is unattainable through the application
Of will. "Ejectum" — a legal term for that which Mother flings
From her protection, "flotsam," "wreck," that which was utterly lost
At sea, yet the sea vomits forth the dream where our dead mother
Returns, making unreal demands, the frost's broken mirrors.

I misspoke by a single letter when I used the word "sun."
How flippant I have become, resorting to the lowest pun
To extricate myself from these elemental emotions.

To speak of the mere human with ultra-human terms is
To violate the Law of Proportion, the sea's hand moving
Over the land, leaving these frozen and untouchable
Crystals, the sweetness dissolved before it can be tasted,
But living in regret and in anticipation, the son's
Unreal persistence in feeling that death could not have wasted
Or turned to dreck a mother's love or that age would not fell
The father who's strength was the strength of fire. This miniscule
burning
Is a bit of sugar, a tongue-tip word of vaporous mist.

A Common Catalepsy
Clutter 75
Written 26 December, 2015

———— • ————

In the mornings, while you are gulping or sipping your coffee,
Busily planning for work or, on weekends, even
More busily planning for idleness, that's when we few
Celestialphiles climb our spindly towers, and skinny
Sloth-style across our high suspension wires to faithfully view
Clouds. Clouds move, but not this one, which has been stationary
For hours and hours, as fixed as a fingerprint on the blue
Sky's skin — white ridges and whorls without a finger. I can
Imagine that for you such oddness must beggar belief.

Doubt, however, is passé. For we creatures who were born
To die, only such miracles may recompense our pain. To
Believe only the believable is to fix death as the norm.

Pour a little cream in your coffee, and watch the convection
Currents swirl milky veils of stratocirrus. Those fires
Cooling there are deeper than ocean trenches. Dive in. See
A Goliath Grouper whose massiveness dwarfs your tiny
Comprehension. The Grouper is steam-white, the coffee blue,
And you no longer plan for work or idleness. This sea
Might be a sky for all you care, cloud-watching now with me,
With all these fish, suspended like a sloth upon your wire,
As fixed as sparks inside of quartz, lost in light's contemplation.

Accepting Simple Simon's Burden
Clutter 76
Written 27 December, 2015

———————— • ————————

Certainly everyone in the middle desires to remain
In the middle, to buy what is being sold, and to repeat
What is being said. The trite gray troll animated
By the savvy advertisers totes away those stone portions
Of reality intolerable to bear. Last night,
The moon was full, and Christ was born again, and once again
A small wheel of the solar system turned, and the fated
Event repeated its trite exultations with the same trite pleas
To the round young virgin to cleanse the common, primal stain.

Tonight the round of the virgin moon has lost the edge of its
Edge. She wobbles a little as she wheels her light, leaving night
Tremors in her silver wake as little star-tears crushed to bits.

But what extravagant and wastrel beauties populate
These dangerous frontiers! Insomnia, frost, eccentric
Revelations, the excremental ecstasies of visions
That see the babe as babe, and not as savior, an infant
Like all others, who, this night, descends into the teeth of Time.
Just like the moon, the common flesh must wane, its fullness spent
Just as it reaches its prime. The small wheel of the solar system
Turns, and returns, as does the Christ child's birth. And the heretic
At the edge shoulders this great stone weight, and is not desolate.

Movie Pitch

Clutter 77

Written 28 December, 2015

—————— • ——————

Storyline and theme: the most dangerous violations
Of unspoken taboos. The scenes: quickly changing, multiple,
The exterior/interior interface of the mind/
Emotion configuration. Night. Sweeping aerial shots
Of a place like Venice … California. Jump cuts. Sudden
Zooms to close-ups. Little footbridges laced with colored dots
Of holiday lights. Post-Christmas intimations. Snake lines
Of electrical reflections in black, black waters. The swell
And fall of surf. Creamy breakers. Dimpled, deserted sand.

Deep shadows. Movement in docked canoe. A dog? No. What then?
A duck standing on the rower's bench. A lone, hooded man
Transfixed in Gibbous moonlight. Pulse-spike. Calm fascination.

Scene shift. Noon. One day previous. Stretch of rural interstate.
Traffic backed-up for miles. Frustration. Close-up: median.
Car parts strewn. Long pan of thousands of cattle standing in
Filth of feedlots. Cow eyes. Gummy hooves. Crusted hind-parts. Tails
Swishing, hanging limp. Flies. Cut to close up: child in car seat. Pan
To acid-green sprigs sprouting through black shoulder cinders. Calm
Fascination. Inquiry into nature of dreams. Questions.
Word and image streams. Harsh juxtapositions. Smooth blends.
Victims of accidents. Child in manger. Water pictures. Blood. Fate.

Superfluous Commentary
on a Quote from Plotinus
Clutter 78
Written 29 December, 2015

———————— • ————————

Difficulties abound. Can such feelings be described in
Terms of color? Or in terms of sound? A rube from rural
Podunk — never been off the farm — walks to the end of a pier
In the swankiest city. He sees how cerulean
Ocean slides in an instant to indigo, then black, the black
Of the pre-dawn cry of a crow, sharp-edged, almost human,
Like the cry of their new-born to first-time parents. The splendor
Of thousands of highrise glass façades in the copper thrall
Of sunset. An eye-blink. Night falls. The lights in the windows dim.

From deep sleep, emotion's theorist mumbles: "The senses
Denied are the senses deified. The purity of lack
Is an incredibly serene emporium of bliss."

The mysteries of metal clanging stone — the aftertones
Ringing, an octogenarian's cough, the myriad shapes
Of hair disturbed by sleep, the various geometric
Plasticities of humans, plunging through dreams, the pronoun "I,"
An elusive science excluding the cancerous facts,
Night's final, loneliest hours intensifying moonlight,
The blues in equatorial island lagoons, the arctic
Clarities of shattering ice — this is the condensate
Poets form from smoke: "the flight of the alone to the alone."

Multiplicitous Motet
Clutter 79
Written 30 December, 2015

When you come to the end of the world, as I have, as you
And everyone must do, it will at first seem the usual
Four or forty or four-hundred lanes of traffic, all taillights
Heading west, at night, in drizzling rain, all in near stasis,
With just enough inching forward to frustrate hope. You will
Think 'This is IT, the end of the world.' But of course, this is
Not IT. There is still the passage through the tunnel, its white
Ceramic sides rippling with light, its hollow filled with the growls
Of rumbling motors, all moving, like cold sludge, as they must do.

This "it" is bad, yet familiar. You trust in the narrative
Links. But this is no story. The bones of the prey animal
Are scattered by the predator, so that the grass might live.

Now the tunnel is changed, and is made of crude, thick timbers,
Its dirt floor scarred where muscular draft horses once dragged
The logs of those forests cleared for highways. That work is done.
The tunnel opens to an ocean cove, enclosed on either side
By walls of jasper, high walls of jasper cut by rills
Of gold. The water breathes and breaks with turquoise lights,
And vivid scarlet kelp wafts through its depths, as voices drone
With glutted tidal boomings. You know these ragged
Songs. And you, and everyone, join in, singing "Begin" in choir.

A Brief History of Photography
Clutter 80

Written 31 December, 2015

———————— • ————————

I am fighting for my life. This all began honestly,
Even innocently enough, the sight of the corpses rotting
At Gettysburg, the Little Tramp milking a cow into
A teacup. People were horrified, delighted, hungry
For more. There were things inside of them they could not see. There
Were jokes in coatsleeves, and birdshapes quite unlike the letter V.
There were intricacies of twigs, and shags of ice, and truths
In the random postures of milling crowds, forms without feeling,
Bodies without pain. It was magic framed. It was heavenly.

I am fighting for my life. The sun came out and released
The frozen dew, and music declared itself in drops of water.
I tasted sonatas arising from deep inside me.

But everything now is converted into image. I do
Not feel the face inside the picture. Even the foods I
Choose are images of sunset faces eating slabs of meat,
No pulse that beats without a teleprompt, no horror, no
Delight, just these pre-packaged dreams, only these lights that stare
Immortally out of the camera's excrement, so
Beautifully devoid of any presence, so utterly
Free of burdensome existence: only these sights for un-sore eyes,
These flat, dimensionless grins that always ask "Where are you?"

Windblown

Clutter 81

Written 1 January, 2016

———— • ————

I find it hard to believe that most people are not shocked
In the least when they read a sentence which mashes up rude
Words and ends with the phrase "butterfly corridor." Seen
Fluttering at a height of fifty feet above an urban
Garden (beautifully decimated by frost) a solitary
Monarch instinctively hones in on that current of wind
Which will guide her on her impossibly long migratory
Reading of un-Proustian forgetfulness. Yes, Chance, that crude
Usurper of meaning, still speaks where Lepidoptera flock.

I find it hard to accept that most people do not believe
That the cell mutations of cancer or of senility
Are not part of Nature's capricious, adorable psyche.

"Stochastic" means "noise," the resonance of the utterly
Random. At the threshold of chaos (the phone call "Father
Has fallen/Mother is dead"), living organisms become
Alert to slight perturbations of informational
Pulses. Orange wing-beats in the sky above a city,
These are cocoon enough for their capricious, adorable
Transformations. The cells go wild and change configuration.
The words hatch out from random webs of sound, as the wind's career
Makes currents where migrating spirits write their crazy stories.

Ice Sculpture
Clutter 82
Written 2 January, 2016

———————— • ————————

We see no expression at all on the bright faces of
The mesmerized. Except for their eyes — perhaps fixed, perhaps
Abruptly saccading — they do not indicate that they
See, let alone feel, how the morning's overcast has left
A thin citrus strip at the eastern horizon. They seem
To be jailed in a catalepsy whereby the whole rest
Of the world is negated. Think of those films that portray,
Or try to portray, the lives of poets, where all that crass
Footage parodies with action the stillness that they most love.

Instinctively we know that the mysteries of cloud motion
Will never be solved. By midday, the skies show the most serene
Masses and rolls of stratocumulus congregations …

And the inert-seeming-one remembers how in a dream,
He tried to give numbers to the swift sequencings of spinning
Wheels he felt along his spine, and how the street that he drove
Down, arched with autumnal trees, and lined with the venerable
Houses of distinguished professors, had, coincidentally,
The name of his grandchild. The citrus strip somehow recalls
All that, and he stands a long, long while as these heavenly hosts
Merge inner and outer worlds, their mysterious roilings
Roiling inside of him, and causing his body to freeze.

The Homeless Sorting Through Trash
Clutter 83
Written 3 January, 2016

———————— • ————————

Tee … ta … tee … taaaa, a motif of three brief notes and a long one,
Sounding in quick succession, and repeated, again, again,
Until a dreamer leaves Main Street of a small Texas town of
A quarter century ago, where a green, humped-back Ford,
Circa nineteen-forty, fades to a shuttered window.
Fog: a cold gray start to the day. Sunday: when the good Lord
Awakened in a world without form and void. A number of
Frozen twigs show through the slats, trembling as a bird springs from
them,
A sparrow, perhaps, whose fall is numbered, his song foreknown.

Somebody's mother — whose? — was born eighty-eight years ago
Today, according to an arbitrary count of once slow
Yet now fast days, which the sparrow that has flown would not know.

Time: Always. An obese grandmother with dyed black hair posts
An electrified picture of "my first Mandela." The woman
Takes drugs to lower her blood pressure, and coloring,
As her black hair shows, calms her. She lays claim to a body
With diabetes. So far, three strangers have "liked" her post.
These are the friends she will never meet. Their dendrites all feed
From a screen that puts them to sleep. The symptoms keep repeating,
Because repetition calms the organ sack, improves its functions.
All parasites need hosts. So the bird repeats its set of notes.

A Case Study without Precedent
Clutter 84
Written 4 January, 2016

This is a pit-of-the-stomach feeling, one which retired
Lawyers continue to refer to as a "misadventure,"
And if it rains, even a "malfeasance." It is raining,
And the weather, which is the great bodiless paramour
Of both sexes, declares that true love is not a point in
Space, but a dispersal of affection searching for form,
A man, a woman, wandering through a city while dreaming,
A city composed of the translucent flesh of a creature,
In darkness, like those in ocean trenches, all rainbow fire.

In this city, this love, both law and lawyers are moot, or
Rather, their presence is as ubiquitous as ants in
An ant mound. There is no she, no he, just a together.

The case baffles our retired lawyer. These drops now falling
Everywhere at once, pose no adversarial positions,
No feminine or masculine distinctions, just this vast
Pointillistic sparkling of faces, each featured like its
Lover, each one a rainbow fire, each one a violation
Of the Law of the Separate Person, and each a spirit
Of transparency, brilliant in its descent, whose feelings cast
No shadow. The lawyer watches the rain, and his visions
Stripped of judgment, flit through his gut, like bats with silver wings.

Counting the Ineffectual
Clutter 85

Written 5 January, 2016

The total number of ants on Earth is equivalent
To the total number of angels which might dance on the head
Of a pin. Oh angel, why am I telling you this? Is
It because the acquisition of an exoskeleton
Is the first step in achieving levitation? To fall
From the great heights of life, and escape damage — a common
Occurrence with ants and angels — is a prerequisite, is,
In fact, the prior bad act that precipitates flight. How sad
That the small and the many are considered unimportant.

My ancient father, my angel, you are as heavy as one
Of the insect-numerous raindrops that this morning fall
And fall from those low, cold clouds of wounds, which are your heaven.

You fall because the lead of eighty-eight years is weighing
Down your bones, and though you are too weak to walk, you believe
You can fly or, at the very least, float, unharmed, and in
Defiance of gravity and time, to an unearthly place
Where each life is singular, each angel indispensable.
Your skin is so thin that the slightest touch precipitates
A blossoming of blood. You need an exoskeleton.
You need to become one of the multitudinous beings
Which are immortal. You need the drone ant's set of paper wings.

Babysitting
Clutter 86

Written 6 January, 2016

———————— • ————————

In the morning we awaken again to this persistent
Rain, which for days has alternated between drizzle
And deluge, and has finally cured the devastating
Drought that has left acres and acres of orchard as gray, dry
Sticks fixed in the heart of every farmer. Their last words were
Coughing prayers for water. And our first thought, as these green skies
Finger, with multitudes of drops, the cracked skin of our aging
Imaginations … 'Have these children returned in time?' To be healed,
We now feel, is to be drenched or drowned by what is innocent.

All such awakenings, and especially these restorations
Of authenticity that come with second childhood, are
Bound to breed hideous and miraculous contortions.

Just how on earth does the sunshine of a grandmother's face,
As she watches her grandchild at play, equate to these fields
And fields of sterile orchard, where our hopes lie staked with our past's
Most fertile dreams …? (So many corpses on the battlefield
Of sex.) This morning, rain falls, and the cold, dry sticks of winter's
Depredations runnel with brilliant drops, which plump like fruit, full
Of the juice of youth. The dogs bark and the child runs and laughs,
And the face that survived millenniums of drought is instilled
With the thrill of summer days, where the dead past lies, effaced.

Pregnant Philosophy
Clutter 87
Written 7 January, 2016

———————— • ————————

It is not, my dear, as if life were some auditorium
Presided over by that ultimate professor or
Guru lecturing on "The True Nature of the Self." Suppose
You are transported back to the town of your childhood, the place,
Much decayed, the school, the bank, the feed store, the church, the
diner,
The one hotel, even the meat packing plant, have all been made
Into junk shops: brass ear trumpets, buttoned shoes, moth-eaten hose,
Those glass insulators once gracing telephone poles, toasters,
Taxidermied ducks, thimbles, spoons, cracked-glass aquariums.

So what, my dear, if some stuff happens to grab your attention?
This tin lawn ornament, rusted, of a conquistador,
Or this bronze owl heavy enough to be a murder weapon.

It is all wastage. It is all the chaff of trashed memories,
The sharp fragments, my dear, of smashed mirrors. There is no brain
Inside the skull, no heart inside the ribs, it is all image,
Corroded and mixed by the acid of spent emotion,
It is all the afterage of living, the infertile core
Of an argument for our existence as corruption,
As seed husks randomly scattered around a ragged edge
That never had a center. It is all that has been named,
But never loved. A baby, my dear, is not the past's debris.

On the Road to Damascus
Clutter 88
Written 8 January, 2016

Between yesterday morning's rain and this morning's fog, a
Clarity intervened, like the golden veins of the channels
Showing at low tide on the sunset bay, or the silver
Tangles of resurrected streams that brilliantly emerge in
The clefts of the newly greened steeps, their gossamer shining
Like mercury, as if the spiders had died in heaven,
And their patterned webs had fallen, scrambled, to awakened earth.
Grazing deer are silhouetted on the cusps of the hills,
And auroras of buzzards pray round a road kill mandala.

The magician will now draw your attention to the maggot
Mounds comprising third-world cities, where the makeshift housing
Of the slums teem with the dreams of the permanent have-nots.

All pray to the altar of fortune and fame, to the singular
Monolith rising from the heap. The rains, or else orders
From an invisible monarch, have driven ants through the walls
Of the bathroom, where they search the sterile tiles for meaning.
They are not silent. If you put your ear to their mound, choiring
Sounds are heard — magic without a magician! — the poor, singing
Poems in anonymity, while the god of roadkill,
The reader, hovers round. A lone car makes the buzzards scatter,
And a clarity ignites the shadow driving the car.

Alarming Savior
Clutter 89
Written 9 January, 2016

———————— • ————————

Courage will do you no good in traversing these moonscapes
Leading to the essential self. Rather, a certain floating,
Warm detachment is needed, wherein one can witness scenes
Of primal shame without evasion, even to the final
Drawing of the crepe curtain when the kaleidoscope goes
Dark, and the word "Awake" is heard. A premature child
In a shoebox cradle, as blue-skinned as Krishna, is seen
As a breathless object of fear and pity, a wriggling
Clot of suffering, too weak to ever propagate the race.

And even when you find the big book of nomenclature
With all those flowers on the cover, the heavy folio
Will be too dense to lift, and scrawled in illegible ciphers.

No intimate knowledge of neurology will help you
To expunge your uncertainties. Can counting raindrops ever
Satisfy thirst? All your bodily necessaries will
Be performed in public, and your poetic excursions —
More precious to you than your bones — will be seen as waste, and thrown
Into the cold waters of anonymity. There, no sun
Will touch them, and no crow laud their relics. But still, there will
Be that word, stronger than fate, too red for shame, and far, far
Too bright for sleep — and it will be a clarion call for you.

In Old Age the Painter Switches from Nudes to Seascapes

Clutter 90

Written 10 January, 2016

———— • ————

At last you see me, not as the saint I am, but as the man
You fear. That my body is all of one color, including
The spiky hair, and especially the pinned-back ears —
What the Old Masters called a "Naples Yellow" — that attribute
Only heightens your humiliation. I can satisfy
A woman with my tongue, make her climax in a wild spew
Of laughter, and all I do is speak. This is what tears
Your heart. This is what swells the sack of your understanding,
As you once swelled with pride. This forces your confession.

When does poetry cease being art and become confession?
Answer: When it becomes too easy. When you read and say "I
Understand. This is mine." When you hear, but need not listen.

The music that changes you, and strips clean your outer sheathing
Of flesh (which is never mortified by your arrogance,
But only by your humiliation) lies much, much deeper
Than that. Imagine hearing what once you could only see:
These slowly rippling architectures of waves, these allies
At the calmest end of day. They can so beautifully
Stir two hues together, blue sound and yellow sight blurred
In one oceanic life, as a climax of pure happenstance.
It is in these chance ripplings that you feel the woman laughing.

Real George*
Clutter 91
Written 11 January, 2016

—————— • ——————

If I could just find someone with the patience to track these bright
Conflagrations of images in memory's brief puddle,
I know they would understand my fondness for rocks and flies.
My grandfather had a place in the Black Hills, and as a boy,
I would visit in summer, and after my chores were done,
I would sit patiently on a granite rock to enjoy
Catching flies. I would make an almost-fist and when the flies
Crawled in — double-quick — close it, and trap them. How fine to feel
Feet tickling and wings buzzing, when the flies were out of sight.

Later I learned that the granite outcropping was of a type
Called "pegmatite," a pink wonder packed with crystallizations
Of quartz and mica stars. These chips toyed with the crisp mountain
light.

If I could just find someone with the double-quick grasp that
Catches the correlations of rock-shine and fly-shine, someone
Whose mind is much like both the fly with compound eyes, and the
rock
With granite patience, I know I could tell them what these mountains
Still mean to me, and of the hard man who always "rolled his own"
And smelled of tobacco and sunlight. I know I could say: "Friend,
We are kin. This is our grandfather, this one made of rock
And words and silence and double-quick violence, this calm one
Who waits, as a corpse that catches flies, this one my heart's fist traps."

*George was my grandfather's first name, and the phrase "Real George" according to *The Dictionary of American Slang* is "an expression denoting the speaker's awareness of any extraordinary, remarkable, or attractive thing or person." The phrase was much in vogue in the 1950's, but probably originated much earlier than that.

Seeds in Dirt
Clutter 92
Written 12 January, 2016

———————— • ————————

You get up in the morning and the sun collects these fragments
From the disintegrated muddle of your dreams. You seem
To be a unity. Let us examine that assumption.
Let us suppose that the story that you heard of the orphaned
Mother of a dead son is true. The woman is a painter.
Suppose on her garden wall, her mural of her garden
Stays green all winter, while the garden collapses in ruin.
There will be this collision of the false and true, a story,
In brief, whose unity is only a pastiche of fragments.

All night the mother of the dead boy grieves. Suppose she dreams
Of disembodied hands in black gloves, which are the murderers
Of the sun. When she awakens, what new world will she see?

It will surely not be a garden in ruins — or so
You would assume. It will be the perfect garden on the wall.
In brief, a face she has painted, not the one on the pillow,
Which grieves. You get up in the morning and you go to your
Easel. You apply your make-up. But as you get older,
Your paintings get more weird. The sun does not see its mother
On the wall, but in the earth, among the seemingly fallow
Ruins of the story, the parts that the author cannot call
His own, the buried fragments that the muddled reader grows.

Cannibal Kin
Clutter 93
Written 13 January, 2016

———— • ————

As much as the urban shaman might want to pierce the septum
Of his nose with the hollow bone of a bird, or to belt
His waist with a sash of Philistine skulls, he has had to learn
To conform to social morays. He reads. And so he enters
The jungle of the antiquarian bookshop, a green
World of dangerous, disembodied spirits, whose fires tear
At his mortal flesh, yet leave him ecstatically burned
By what the erudite call "The Omnific Word," That he felt
Harrowed by vultures, there is no doubt. They feast on such odd men.

In the guts of various vultures (they can digest anything),
His various bits fly to the first rungs of heaven. Dream
Images become real. He is fitted with leaden wings.

He meets a beautiful woman, who tells him "Fly!" But his lead
Wings plunge him down to the depths of babble. There is nothing he
Can say to win her love. She is the spirit of water,
The queen of tears. His ashes are scattered on her milky
Sea. Now he is back in the bookshop — again: the jungle scene.
He dons his mask of wooden calm. The shop clerk is not deceived.
The brilliant plumage of parrots ignites the stifling air.
Their screams stream through his nose bone. They pour through the
Philistines'
Sutured lips, and fill with music the reader's shrunken head.

Praying to Ganesha
Clutter 94
Written 14 January, 2016

————————— • —————————

Explain this mystery: Why are there so many love poems
In the world, and so little love? My hands move tenderly
Over your effigy, like a mind that seeks the meaning
Of a dream. Yours is the bedroom of the house that grows or
Shrinks according to the law of hope and desperation.
You sit with your elephant's head and rodent's feet in a chair
In a corner, smoking your pipe. The smoke wreathes round in rings,
Which smell of springtime rains. When your pince-nez glasses drop, I see
The golden ingots of your eyes, then hear your lovesick moan.

You say: "You cannot find clarity in the fogs of sleep,
Or in the mists of love. Nor can you proclaim what my golden
Gaze might mean. You can never fully waken from love's dream.

There will always be obstacles in my realms of riches.
That is why every poem that was ever written exists
In a mist where dripping, drooping trees must erase distance
And inflate intimacy. That is why my words must beckon
Logic to ruin, and why love annihilates ruin.
That is why my pachyderm head must lift its golden ton,
And make love's moan. That is why my feet, like the rat's, must chance
All mazes, and why so many baffling poems insist:
'Love is mysterious, impervious to your wishes."

Diver

Clutter 95

Written 15 January, 2016

———— • ————

The sun is up, but the room is still grey, and you can hear
The other members of your household stirring. They are eager
To depart. They are all going on a long, long journey,
A journey of genetic transmutation that will lead
Neither to death nor to sensory annihilation.
But you are not ready to leave, or even to rise from sleep.
The dream you are having is not complete. You have a need,
A languid need, to see what this man has dropped upon the floor.
What is it? … the ribbon spool of an antique typewriter?

Ghost letters pierce the ribbon, negatives punched out of purple
Ink. You think of creatures in the breathless depths of the ocean.
You say: "First there must be this obscurity — this punctured soul."

You wade in the shallows, the shadows, a total honesty
Your only means of breathing. But you are dishonest. You
Are lazy. You know these things about yourself. You know how
Journeys, how departures and thresholds upset you. How are
You supposed to survive when everyone you know has gone?
The house is empty now, and so is your skin. On the floor,
The ribbon has unspooled, and those tiniest ghostly rows
Of letters lead out of the house to the sea. Reading, you
Follow them. They appear to be the names of the deceased.

The Rainman's Confession
Clutter 96
Written 16 January, 2016

Yes, officers, I freely confess that I am to blame
For the unseemly outburst of gratitude that occurred
This morning during the rain storm, and that occasioned the
Saturnalia in Sector XXX. I am to blame,
But I am not guilty. Let me explain. Unseen ecstasies
Roam abroad. Their silver glitterings possessed me. The usual pain
And torpor of sleep became inflamed. My whole groin, and the
Inner thigh of my left leg, leaked plasma, and I heard
The sounds of angelic choirs distributing bliss as rain.

I know that such happiness is as outrageous as it
Is infectious. Children trapped in houses saw jeweled drops gleam
On the tips of winter twigs, and collapsed in laughing fits.

People stopped worshiping their devices, and actually
Looked at each other. Some even spoke without the benefit
Of their electronic prostheses, and became enamored
With the intimacy of direct communication.
All buying ceased, and the Sector's entire economy
Devolved to the pristine barter known as speech. When
One spoke, the others listened. It was almost as if words
Mattered. It was almost as if the rain had brought a gift
That was shiningly, criminally shared as poetry.

Unfinal Judgment
Clutter 97
Written 17 January, 2016

———————— • ————————

Mayhem at the breakfast table — a crowd of imps follows
You from sleep, your silent accusers, each robed in a little
Scarlet cowl, each as justified as the blood of children
On foreign battlefields. Your violence is pure because
Your body's wastrel lifestyle is not negotiable. War
Is always impersonal, as is all blood loss, because
Guilt is a shared commodity. That is why your dreams run
Red with corpuscular metaphors, their surreal
Tribunals forever dogging you wherever you go.

Let us be blunt. The purpose of these words is not to make
You understand. You understand too much as it is. More
Clarity only hurts you. The dead have not bled for your sake.

Your lungs fill, and oxygenate the blood. In Greek temples, there
Were little cowled figures who stood near the statue of the god,
Their fat stone fists gripping unread scrolls. The blue corpuscles
Turn red as do spring's greens each autumn — and you are not, were
Never, responsible. The mayhem of this ceaseless war
Was never yours, but Ours. We are the Gods, the Metaphors,
The wounds that bleed from your human hearts. Ours are the wastrel
Images you dream, the beauty of winter rains, the odd
Tear-shapes that haunt you in misty, impersonal weather.

Lurching Yonway
Clutter 98
Written 18 January, 2016

———————— • ————————

… May God us keep
From Single vision & Newton's sleep.

William Blake

Again, the once handsome but now aging actor is jarred
Awake — the presumed cause: a violent cramp in the calf
Of his left leg. A steep is furred with trees contorted
As the prevailing westerlies have tortured them. The site
Forms green leafy waves too wooden to quite break. A barren
Crest is toothed with jutting cairns. Bell's palsy sags the wrong side
Of a face. Whole sections of cities lie depopulated
By vast deserted mansions. Happiness — the presumed cause: half
Of a gross asymmetry, sleep's silence enlarged by words.

Sir James took tea at his club. He writes of those tribal kings
Whose left thighs bore ritual mutilations. Sir James, when
Walking, leans on a cane — a golden bird with a limp wing.

Writer, reader, speaker, hearer; long summaries that are
Incomplete; emotionless distance, intimate confessions;
Brain aneurisms drooling poetic speech; balloon hats
At a birthday celebration; the you's and I's who circle
Round a we; a galaxy hid in the ink of a pen;
The fame of a bumpkin; an evidence bag with a curl
Of the murderer's hair; a woman who keeps her dead cat
In the freezer — the presumed cause: a glitch in God's strange plans,
The aging actor again where the city's lights blur stars.

Reflections of a Drowned
Ventriloquist's Dummy
Clutter 99
Written 19 January, 2016

———————— • ————————

This is what I want to say. At the rear of this property
A wooden pole has been erected. It has six sides, each
Of which has been affixed with a white ceramic plaque that
In six different languages sport the message: "Peace on
Earth." The rains fall so heavily that the lawn is a lake,
The lake rising steadily round the pole, its surface bombed
With little explosive splashes, whose beauty belies what
Those explosions mean. I am alone in the house, and each
Passing moment intensifies the danger of this siege.

This is what I want to say. There is being together,
And there is being alone. There is this face, my own face,
The face of the other, and also the face of the water.

It is the face of the water that reflects my speaking.
Like the angels, it shines from the heavens. Like ascetics,
It sleeps naked on the earth. Its singularity is
Plural. This is what I want to say. That the multiple
Babbles of languages on earth explode on a rising lake
That is many, many things, but is never quite peaceful.
It will always seek to overwhelm the tongue. It will blitz
With equal furor singing angels and silent ascetics.
It will say what it wants regardless of who is speaking.

A Refulgently Inexplicable Paradox
Clutter 100
Written 20 January, 2016

A sky-crushed undulating plain, where you can walk for miles
Without finding a live creek or a live tree, where destitute
Gentry grow too fat to leave their trailer houses, and make
No better use of their voluminous acreage than
To breed and graze the obsolete mule. My mother was raised
Here, and here, with my ninety-year-old uncle, I now stand
To muse on houseless cellars and the craters of unmarked graves.
This dirt grows only grass, and holds no seed, but the dead and soon
To be dead, which is to say, this dirt is glowingly fertile.

The brain stows no memories, but this hummock tells a foot
That a brother, dead of a tonsillectomy, once played
Here round a kitchen table. Now his bones lie wound in roots.

Zeno asked questions that got him murdered. How can a thing
With an infinite number of atoms be as finite
As a finger-length blade of grass? The Pythagoreans,
Uneasy optimists, did not like that. One level beyond
Understanding is inspiring, two levels, and the way
Is paved towards sleep. At level three, there suddenly comes
A gust of choking rage. Beyond that, the optimists' hands
Itch for nooses and knives. To say that the dirt is alive
With infinite longings is to pray where mules are grazing.

Inflated Gimmick
Clutter 101
Written 21 January, 2016

———————— • ————————

Perhaps you were born too late to have witnessed the comic
And sad phenomenon of the balloon man, which was a huge
Puffed up, smiling abstraction that for a time businesses
Would place near their establishments to attract customers.
Full, full of air, he bobbled about in an atmosphere
Of fame. Some merchants trade in gold bars only, but the Masters
Say "If one comes for rat droppings, these are my wares. If he searches
For gold, it is gold I give him," the parable of the moon
And the finger inserted here, like dog dung stuck with a stick.

I wave about in the element of buffoonery,
My empty, empty air, swirling, swirling about where
Eloquence should be, a bloated expeller of lunacy.

The Masters say "To talk about Mind or Spirit is defiling.
To brood on such is defiling. But to gouge words on paper
That puff on about life's mysteries is especially
Defiling." But what could I do with those masterful turds
Expelled by wise apes with physical bodies? I am air,
A man of air, more abstract than an advertiser's words.
I wave my arms about and say "Look here! Look here!" silently
Smiling smiles without a care. And yet, they come, my customers,
My readers, pawing for gold in piles of rodent droppings.

Remembering What Was Mist
Clutter 102
Written 22 January, 2016

---•---

The conversations of the rain drops on the roof are swished
Together as smoothly as the sound of circulating
Blood when you are drowned in sleep. One drop might talk of a
One-night tryst at a youth hostel in the mountains. The girl
Had a soft, unfashionable body, short-waisted, with a wide,
Full face — eyes that invited and refused. A distant girl,
Like the snow on the peaks in June, only the one drop in a
Medley of heart-thumps, a sparkling nostalgia pit-patting
Into a world behind the eyes, a world of bait and switch.

One loves the commoner idioms while fishing in the depths,
The bright lure that will flash out of the darkness, the silver light
In the deep, green stirrings that softly wash through the breath of sex.

This, this ... this is the music that one must tenderly forfeit,
Like the talk of one drop in a panoply of drops, like
Wishes, in a tribe of wanderers, for a home that does not
Slide on wagon tracks, the horses in harness, heads drooping
In a caravan of sleep, the gypsies who move in the night
Among rain's thin curtains, the hearts that love for an hour, and sing
Of this girl with the deer-dark eyes, whose breath forever gasps, stops,
Gasps, stops, alive with those passions winding in vaporous flight
Through heaving ghosts of pine tree silhouettes, sighing: No regrets.

Absorbed

Clutter 103

Written 23 January, 2016

———————————— • ————————————

One could hardly imagine brilliance being more brilliant.
The multiminded Celestial in one moment drapes his face
With silver veils and in the next flashes his great golden eye,
Sun showers and water dazzles alternating with equal,
Though contrasting, splendors, to say "day," "shadow," "rain," "light."
The lonely house is lifted from its moorings, and, with a calm
Assurance, drifts with our hearts to heaven. So, our delight
Comes simply from sitting still, and watching this intricate lace
Weave water and sunlight into this most domestic trance.

If a widow sits in her house crocheting doilies, are
We to call her "My Angel of Molten Glass?" And will he cry,
Her husband, from his dirt, to see her bone-hooks stitching flowers?

The dirt grows sodden and the coffin floats, suspended in
Her thoughtless occupation. She looks out the window, while
Her hands keep working. One could hardly imagine a longing
More profound. The bevels of the cross-sash of the window
Distribute their fragments of rainbow through the room. They shine
Like the bodiless eyes of the dead, probing the shadows
With celestial splendor. The widow is simply sitting,
Yet disappearing, because the stillness bids her go. A smile
Hangs in the air without a face, as the weather's grace flows in.

Outcast Cast In

Clutter 104

Written 24 January, 2016

———————— • ————————

Lately, conversing with the changeable weather, deepening
My contact with those drifting-intensity techniques well
Known to urban lunatics and Siberian shamans,
I have arrived at the electrified membrane between
Sunny ease and winter storm. Let me illustrate with an
Analogy: Hansen's Disease, known metaphorically
As leprosy. I do not mean that scourge which ate the skin
Of those victims jailed in their colonies of pain. No. I dwell
On the lone leper, because he is poetry's skinless king.

All this talk of social networking, of microtubules
In neuronal functioning, of nonlocal vision that scans
The interiors of atoms, I spin into one word: Soul.

Not your great-grandfather's Presbyterian soul, that vapor
Floating in the cave of the body, but the soul that clings
Like a slime of jellified fire to the leper's unheard
Words, the words at the shifting membrane between sunny ease
And winter storm, the words whose drifting intensity can
Stick in the brain like a vision of peace, or else a disease
That isolates the eccentric in the privacy of bird
Chatter or water whorl, at those contested borders that wring
From colliding clouds a bliss that stuns the lonely listener.

Awaiting the Messiah
Clutter 105
Written 25 January, 2016

I have spoken before of the crippled surrogate, he
Of the mutilated left, with the night-cramped tongue, who wakes
Us from dreams with a mutilated scream, who clogs the drains,
Who sequesters us in hospitals, whose desperate talk bores,
Who breaks the door from its hinges, who damages the car. I have spoken
Before with a breathless evangelical fervor
Of the metaphor hidden in his pet dog, who brings the rain
Right into our houses and hearts. I have tried to make my case
With babbling scriptures of the dangers smiling in his teeth.

The surrogate says: "Your neighbors are aliens." That was to
Be expected. He repeatedly speaks of the dark wisdom
Lurking in women, who, when they see him, say: "I love you."

And I love the surrogate too, I who have made my body
The museum of childhood's shame, I who have spoken
Rashly, and clothed crepe in bright insight as if it were public
Lewdness, I who have made a surrogate of the loved one,
Who wakes at night with a cramp in his leg, and I, who when
The rain falls through the roof, add up the incalculable sums
Of my indiscretions, and say to myself: "You are sick.
You have caused this disaster," absolving innocent heaven
Of all blame, and telling the night, "The surrogate will save me."

Flighty Harmony For
Patricia Keel on her birthday
Clutter 106
Written 26 January, 2016

———————— • ————————

These are common bird calls, faintly seeping through the cold walls
Of the house on a drizzly winter morning — probably
Sparrows, the winged equivalent to Christ's poor, scavenging
For sparse fodder, much like the lover, who awakens from
The dungeon of sleep, seeking the last seeds of meaning. I
Miss you, faithful and absent one, not so much, I think, from
Loneliness, because I burrow in solitude, like seedlings
Under snow, but because your joy is my sun. It warms me,
Stirs me like brassy trumpet calls that pierce through prison walls.

I believe that an occult chemistry binds us, untouched by
Distance, where entities in egg-like forms turn round as an I,
A you, and vibrate our bodies to the pulse of one song's sighs.

These are only common bird calls, but the little bodies
Of such musical searchings recall me to our hidden
Chemistry, our ultimate atoms spinning in one sphere,
Though the whole globe of the planet is spinning between us,
You on the warm side, and I on the cold. I miss you. I
Feel you. These are not two separate things. I feel you. I miss
You. Hear how the rhythms of those simple words sound like the aires
Of the sparrows in the distance. Six little pulses that spin
Two hearts together, as though they sang within one body.

On the Devolution
of a Bodily Form
Clutter 107
Written 27 January, 2016

———————— • ————————

The Master exhorts me: "Awake!" But when I try to, I am
Mobbed with terrible images of myself, the dark core
Of a conniving animal known for its lust, hidden
Within the deceiving nimbus of a proto-human.
A smell engulfs me, like that of refined old ladies whose
Heavy, sweet perfumes attempt to mask the stench of decay. Can
I be candid without showing you the dirty strand
Where the bodies of aspirants lie bound, helpless, near the roar
Of the encroaching sea? Can I confess what I fear I am?

I am always on the verge of a journey, for which I am
Ill prepared. My clothes are too tight, or else they are far too loose,
And my heart is shamefully naked. Do you understand?

The Masters claim to. I devour stacks of books with weak eyes,
Trying to clear a shelf where I can rest, and escape the
Exhortations. I uncover a pipe full of lint, blue,
Like old rags of sky. I remove the obstruction, and out
Crawl a litter of beautiful mammals, of a type unknown
To taxonomists. They have silken red fur and they look about
With dark-eyed Kuala faces that never would presume
To exhort or accuse — and yet — I am afraid of them. The
Time to depart creeps nearer. I read that in their human eyes.

Leaving the Cinema
Clutter 108
Written 28 January, 2016

On grey days, one lives inside the story as though one were
Trapped in some black and white post-war film, where the director
Has made everything bland and dangerously enigmatic,
The print washed out, the music seesaw dissonance, the shots
Claustrophobic, the characters crowded into shabby
Apartments, engulfed in bombed-heaped rubble. There is no plot,
And the relationships are skewed and distant. One hears the click
Of the film running through the gargantuan projector —
One feels so anxious, so desultory in the theater.

At some point one recognizes this as a form of prayer,
We have been so intent constructing one personality
That we failed to notice this prevalent collective despair.

The meditator discovers that the war is over.
He discovers space, and a majesty of lavender skies,
Where a smiling quietude of sunlight breaks through the clouds,
And traces the flight of a pair of birds across the face
Of immensity. The film is not going to end sadly,
As one expected. The film is not going to end. The pace
Of time is going to expand, and the dissonant sounds
Are going to subtly, beautifully harmonize
Into heartbeats. On this grey day, one lover finds another.

PHASE TWO

Caught in the Storm
Clutter 109
Written 29 January, 2016

———————— • ————————

Think of an infinite scroll repetitively printed
With the templates of business cards. On one of these, you
Must hurriedly scrawl your name. Of course, the rain is falling
Thickly, drops blowing that way and this in great rippling sheets
Of vital ephemerality. Your name says "I am here
To compete for a job that I will hate." If the committee
Chooses you, you will write scripts for comedies, illustrating
The ridiculous lives of anonymous people — like you —
Worthless, but lovable, masked actors, laughed at by the dead.

How could you have guessed that your individual survival
Would depend upon your speeding species' extinction? Here,
Quick, here, write down your name — remember how the rain falls.

If you are one of those funny people who read ancestral
Poems, you would know that the scripts you are paid to write are
Lies. You would know how the deserts long for one drop of rain,
How the name you sought in the annals of the dead had nothing
To do with your survival. Your job here is simple: Care
For the anonymous people — like you — care for the daring
Way each rain drop grips the light, makes special anonymous pain,
And cares for ineffectual caring, for the instant which bears
Its bright reflection through the skirmishes of this mighty squall.

Alone Among

Clutter 110

Written 30 January, 2016

———————— • ————————

This kind of precious information is hard to come by.
Fortunately, I am awakened by a pre-dawn phone call
Where a nurse says "Your father has fallen again." There are
No beginnings, I know, only continuations. He is
Very old, and cannot stand alone. But every night, he
Is on the move, going through some fragrant pine woods, where his
Own father awaits him. I go back to bed. At this hour,
It is not clear what the sun is going to do. I fall,
But not asleep. I fall where silence makes my muscles cry.

Without me hearing it, they have been crying — they have been
Crying a long time, clenched in unending anxiety.
I know there are no endings, only continuations.

When dawn comes, it is bluer and brighter than it has been
For days. I am on the move, going through a noisy city
Where I see thousands of anxious people, as stiff as trees
Turned to steel. They roll on fiery wheels. They must use motors
To move their paralyzed muscles, and they must use phones to speak.
They are very, very old. They have out-lived time. They are
Mad to escape that Ancestral Father. They believe machines
Will feed them. They believe what begins, what ends, appears on
screens,
And I, I so long to join their frantic continuations.

Sugar? One Lump or Two?
Clutter 111
Written 31 January, 2016

———————— • ————————

The neighbors across the way shine great klieg lights into our
Bedroom in order to infiltrate our dreams. They wear white
Shirts and work on complicated "Adultery Machines,"
Those "libido stokers," as they are colloquially called,
That tempt us to cheat on our legitimate reality
With this strumpet, Imagination — ex-wives, girlfriends, all
Seducing and spying on seductions in scenes that teem
With coinciding, colluding emotions: guilt, shame, pride,
Lust, filling our nocturnal world with bright, conflicting stars.

The sage, having transcended such galactical mental
Aberrations, denounces these stars, which recite to night's deep
Listener odd love poems. He has one central eye: a pool …

And when the exhausted lover reaches this lustrous pearl
That reconciles all jealousies, all betrayals, what is
He to do with his past loves and love poems? Is he to drown
Them in this slowly swirling silence, be one with these neighbors
Who work on the machine? Is he to smother every
Word with this single, all-luminous, coagulated purr
Of sagely quietude? Or should he cleave to star-sounds,
Conflicted as they are, cling to his lie that suffering is
Bliss, and fall for the come-hither eyes of another girl?

X-Ray Imagination

Clutter 112

Written 1 February, 2016

———— • ————

Lord Weather, that ancient, changeable adolescent, whom we
All talk about, but whom no one understands, does every
Thing he can on sunny days to substitute his dream theories
For our dreams. A flowerless flowerpot shining with her eye
Of rainwater blinks and dances where a quick sparrow bathes
His head. Our eyes watch this on their day-trip to paradise,
Where we find the two mountains of crystal. True — poets' plead
With us to see these common miracles. But since they lie, we
Always take some lump-coal theory in lieu of diamond dreams.

To see these mountains, the first thing we must learn is how to
Speak sentences about sentences, since to differentiate
One crystal from its twin, we need this convoluted voodoo —

Otherwise known as "The Magic of Inscriptions." Mountain
One is inscribed with a few simple directions, cardinal
Virtues, easy to understand, impossible to do.
Mountain two is a palimpsest of poems, the unscrolling
Stories of dreams, as changeable as Lord Weather. Today
You have seen a bird-mosaic in the blinking, dancing
Eye of a flowerpot. You have spoken words about words. You
Have looked inward and read the crystals' secrets. If you tell
Yourself these, you will see light vaporize a pair of mountains.

Prequel
Clutter 113
Written 2 February, 2016

After a good night's sleep, nourished by rich, yet happily
Forgotten dreams, I like to imagine I am God, lounging
In a winter apple orchard on a sunny morning,
And watching the frost steam into azure haze. The trees will be
Twisted, old, and jacketed with lichens, some red leaves
Still clinging with vestiges of wrinkled fruit, the twig-tips deep
In winter's slumber, and a long, long way from fertile spring's
White, blossoming pregnancies. I will not yet be thinking
Of Eden's pruning shears, or of Adam's chatty company.

The trees will not be in rows, but will arise like fountains
From the flop of languidly milling cloven-footed beasts,
And from where raccoons in moonlight have left sweet cores — half-
eaten.

And the grass around the trees will lie in matted pallets
From where the deer have slept, and where the serpent, still with feet,
Has wandered, a millipede making esses as he slithers,
More blameless than the serpentining vapors. I like to
Imagine The Word inside my mouth, not quite yet ready
To make a friend with speech. I know I am — which is enough to
Know. And the trees, as the sun bows down for evening prayers,
Will stretch their twisted shadows towards my feet, and I will lean
Into this fiery peace, poised to make flesh from spirit.

The Mime Before the Mirror
Clutter 114
Written 3 February, 2016

———— • ————

The retired and disappointed mime, having dispensed with masks,
Wigs, make-up, false phalluses, and his box for collecting
Donations from people in the public square, cries to himself
"Can we not create in vivid sounding words delights
As rich as those probed by the eye?" To which he answers (to
His disappointed mirror), "No, we cannot." But the eye
Of the ear in the depths does hear the Here, the vivid pulse
That sounds when the mirror goes smash. The eye of the ear sings
Sight to the eye of the mind, when the mime removes his mask.

The eccentric silhouette of a locust tree cuts through
The azure foil of the horizon — the closed eyes have no clue
As to how the wind goes clicking through the mute and vivid blue.

It is our talk that kicks the sleep from hearts, and makes them beat
With quicker, with slower, and with deeper rhythms. The eyes
Make only public comedies, the open boxes for
Meager donations … and yet down here, we hear the broken
Glass, tinkling in the pulsing bag, with shards of morning's blue,
And locust shadow-branches. We hear, but cannot see them —
Except in cutting fragments. These fragments are the comic lore
Of mimes, the stage directions for a silent show, which cries
For captions for its public clowning, in acts of private speech.

Dropping Nuggets of Wisdom
Clutter 115
Written 4 February, 2016

———————— • ————————

Boredom: the absence of emotion in the presence of
Miracle. The Cedar Wax Wings have returned to pillage
Whatever remains of the tiny purple berries in
These wax-leafed trees brought to the West from Asia because
The oaks and madrones and redwoods did not wholly satisfy
The suburban landscapers. The beautiful Wax Wings buzz
Frantically about with whistling appetites in
The fluttering thrall of forces that bore us. We take umbrage
Also to both birds and trees because their mess drops from above …

It sticks to our driveways and cars — white and purple excrement
That was manna to what lived here before we arrived.
I know you are bored with the tenor of these comments.

Frustration: the presence of emotion in the absence
Of satisfaction. Imagine an entire civilization
Built solely for the purpose of feeding fatty foods to
Bored people before lit screens. No. I know you will imagine
No such thing, because those circuits have been anesthetized.
What you require is the grotesque served to you like manna in
A frantic shit-fall called "Entertainment." Please, do not construe
These comments as criticism. What good is criticism?
We only do what all birds do: perfect incontinence.

Color Circle
Clutter 116
Written 5 February, 2016

———— • ————

Even in these most stable light conditions of spotless
Blue morning skies, the evolution of colors on so
Much as a single blade of grass is dazzlingly mutable.
Let's try to keep emotion out of this. Why should it matter
That the dew-shine moves from blue moments of industrial
Steel — chromium bright — to slide into that green where water's
Surface has turned sky to shore in a movement more subtle
Than the in-and-out slither of a serpent's tongue? One stows
These changes where dream fingers can pluck them forth in crisis.

Let's try to keep emotion out of this. "But the light,"
The light," you say, "keeps changing everything, How can we stall
These impassioned refutations of our poor pronoun "I?"

How can we be one thing in this avalanche, where a simple
Blade of grass foreshadows death by shattering its serpent form
In morning light? Let's try to keep emotion out of this.
Recall those fingers of our mutable dreams, how busily
They work without our knowledge to dizzily weave these tangled
Wads of thread into their dazzling symbols. In a great city
Of dispersing selves, in a sidewalk crack, a single grass
Blade grows. Its shadow worms across the white cement. The more
The shadow squirms, the more light spins emotion on its wheel.

Surviving the Deluge in Dirt
Clutter 117
Written 6 February, 2016

———————— • ————————

Imagine a ring-shaped stadium stuffed with hordes of people
Who shout at an empty field, a field as silent as the slide
Of one moment into another. Is the field green? Yes,
It is green. The composite roar of the crowd is a saw-tooth
Jumble of linguistically hostile hooligans, all
Trying to affect the center with a different tongue. You,
In one moment or another, are every person here. Yes,
It is confusing. But there is that green emptiness inside —
That swirling drain of a ghostly, silent circle.

If you spend enough of these draining, silent moments, watching
One image slide through another, all of these boisterous people
Choir a kind of hush, which merges with the songs of grass growing.

The I that says "I am here, in the center, not at the fringe,
"Shouting," has neither arms nor legs nor torso nor head — nor heart.
It has only this sweet, deeply entwined, and quieted
Majesty, twirling its pale roots down into sunless soil,
And spinning its green shoots up to suckle sun. This I crawls
Almost silently through Time, as it slides its multiple
Languages into one. The raucous stadium is quieted,
Covered with vines, and broken down to soil — ah! — the soil — that Ark
Conserving these inhuman shapes, safe, from the dissonant surge.

The Above Within

For my friend, William, who loves flying

Clutter 118

Written 7 February, 2016

——————— • ———————

Probably you too have sailed through sunny Sundays, swept high
In the groundlessness of flight, because you have thought for far
Too many years about how to get off the sharp tip of Time's
Arrow before it hits Death's target: Thump. Or whatever
Sound Death makes — a church bell, a crow's caw, the mindless
hysterics
Of a crowd as it flees a fire — or maybe, a water
Sound: first still, still, and smooth, then "plook!," the swallowed sigh
Of a pebble, disturbing the paralyzed mind. But where,
Exactly — where have you been, when you made this groundless flight
… ?

… probably not at the tip of Time's fiery arrow.
Maybe the smell of this smoke of speculation has wicked
Into your stalled brain, a scent, not a sound, your cure for sorrow.

It is certain that what the Sunday sun warms is not this
Heavy bricolage of flesh, disintegrating as the
Arrow accelerates, nor is it this shadow
Cast upon the lawn, changing the dew-shine of the grass-tips
Darkly — white-blue to black-blue — with momentary magic.
It is certain that when the arrow tip finally hits,
It will not destroy this magic. It is difficult to know
How this Now that is always Now could ever end. What could the
Arrow hit that would stop its flight? … unless it is flight's bliss?

A Brief Experiential Organic Excursion into the Current
Machine Phenomenon Known as "Deep Learning"

Clutter 119

Written 8 February, 2016

——————— • ———————

No amount of surface calm can convey the urgency
Of these words. The portals of paradise appear just where
The first rays of sunlight wash over the dreamer's face. Look: there
Are celluloid segments of increasing transparency spliced
One atop the other, six strips of film, which suggest under-
Water movement. The surface layers — the portals — are ice
Crystals prickling from leaf mulch. They are the dawn's frost gloss that glares
From rot, their hue like that of aged varnish on an Old Master's
Painting, a skin that you see through, like these letters as your read.

Here, you are suspended, and the rate at which sound propagates
Waves under water is four times faster for the sea creature
You have become. Before, it was you and waves, now, only waves.

How deep is the bliss engendered by these transmissions! No
Amount of surface agitation can betray their calm.
The paradox of urgency and stillness is the novel
Vehicle which transports you through the layers, thick brain mulch
Transformed into fabulous spikes of crystal, where leaf litter,
As common as death, builds a palace of ultra-natural,
Compacted glory. Quickly, calmly, you speed through the portals.
This is insight without eyesight, the spirit's light in the realms
Of diamond ice, by which the dawn implodes in dazzling snow.

Musical Cryptogram
on a Moral Theme
Clutter 120
Written 9 February, 2016

———————— • ————————

The sunlight imparts joy to everything and gives a jumping-
Out-of-the-skin happiness, as though, born deaf, suddenly
We heard birdsong. Then comes the transposition, a dark shift
To a lugubrious minor key draws us through the rainy
Heart of sadness. Slow lines of chords move like the poor at a rummage
Sale. They buy useless trinkets simply because they are cheap.
The mood reminds us of handling cast-iron figurines, odd gifts
From the dead — a bat, an ant, a crow, a horse — the theme
From the initial letters infused through what the birds sing.

Both happiness and sadness seem necessary in
Order to give meaning to our indefinable rage
For diatribe, a noise required for the self's composition.

In the end, the most indefensible, the most immoral
Positions must be the most rigidly maintained. The master
Must have slaves for his plantation. His eloquence must turn
To vitriolic denunciation, to spurious
Claims in defense of a spurious honor, to outrage
At the mere suggestion of emancipation. That bliss
Might be had on all occasions, that music in the minor yearns
Also for unfettered ecstasy, which, among the poor
Sparrows, will still sing — such blasphemies would kill the trinket self.

Memorial Perfume
Clutter 121
Written 10 February, 2016

———————— • ————————

Once you dispense with even the idea of simulations,
Those common events — let us call them "Prima Materia
"Category A," as say these white tulips wilting on
The kitchen table — are seen to be only the fascistic
Grandeur of an indoctrination, a political
Edifice with red-veined marble pediments and slick,
Funereal, granite columns, a kitschy Egyptian
Anachronism meant to interpose the fantasia
Of appearance between spirit and spirit's creations.

If the body is only a machine of computational
Capacities, its out-put can be bested by greater falls
Of cascading algorithms: Niagaras of numerals.

"Tulip," from a Turkish word meaning "turban," one of whose bulbs
The stock-jobbers of Amsterdam could trade for a fiefdom,
A fine carriage, a brace of prancing horses, rich harness,
And the immortal Calvinist soul of its purchaser,
This is the name some brains give to these flowers on the table.
They are wilting. Exotic plant volatiles whose scent-trails stir
Pheromones through your pleased nostrils, cry: "Distress! Distress!"
And for a moment the simulations cease. A revelation,
Let us call it "Prima Spiritus X," comes as death's sweet smell.

Baring the Teeth
Clutter 122
Written 11 February, 2016

———— • ————

Having broken all four upper incisors while making
An arrest, the detective wore a partial plate, his smile,
Or grimace, or snarl, pleasant enough in situations
Of repose, but libel to become bestial during any
Rough and tumble action. People did not know what to make
Of him. In the middle of the night, an arresting dream
Violently jerks us awake. We lie there in the dark, in
A rubble of broken teeth, broken images, a vile
Beast roaming the brain, the body frozen, the heart racing.

Dishonest people, remaining frozen in bed, go back to sleep,
And do not confront the criminal inside them. At daybreak,
They fake a smile at their neighbors, with artificial teeth.

But the crime, the crime is beyond perception — immobile,
Then thrashing, reposeful, then violent, it violates
All laws of time and space, and makes this persona whom we
Call "detective," an enigmatic searcher of bad dreams,
A questioner waking at night to watch the stars create
This larger self. Blasted apart by darkness, the history
Of this artificer is strewn like teeth through the heavens. We
Watch this as we would the constellations. We know it is late,
That the mouth is choked with night and pain. We know this, yet we
smile.

Bioluminous Diver
Clutter 123
Written 12 February, 2016

———— • ————

Not all departures are sad, but most are poignant. Winter
Departs at spring's approach, and the grandfather fails as
The grandchild arrives, the whites of dogwood blossoms negating
The whites of snow. Last night I dreamt of you. Already you
Were with another man, as I was preparing to leave,
Never to see you again. In the dream, I was glad for you,
Happy as always to be. In the dream, I felt that seeing
The sea would relieve some of my sorrow, that the pain that was
Might depart while facing the infinite Is-ness of water.

The history of any life is inevitably
A history of arrivals and departures, but love seems
A sea as perpetual in delight as in agony.

In the dream, crowds, cities, fears, my opaque memories
Prevented my seeing the ocean. But already I
Knew, I know, that the sea is like love, an infinitude
Surging inside me, the presence of depth, beyond the restless
Glitter of life's surface, a belief in you as a sea
That will always be. I leave, you arrive, yet what is this
Motion, if not an affirmation of our love? I love you,
And I am always drowning in that darkness, a creature whose light,
Though tiny, glows through the depths of delight and agony.

The Birth of Eloquence
Clutter 124
Written 13 February, 2016

———————— • ————————

When he looked, his eyes oozed a kind of batter, which could turn
The object of his gaze into an edible griddle
Cake digestible by a grosser sense. He made summations,
Bitter or sweet, of the whole, complicated entity
Of the weather, his simplified binary reactions
Analogous to those of a single-cell animal. He
Did not do nuance. This approach evolved a moral sense
That allowed him the powerful freedom to embrace or kill
Without empathy, never burdened with having to learn.

Suppose you and he lived "in one taut skin," and saw the same
Sunlight with the same transfiguring gaze. Your lizard reactions
Would be those of a tongue, tasting bitter or sweet with names.

Once my heart was calm — like night. And my gaze was blank and
simple.
But I woke in the morning and reached my hand into sunlight,
And felt the day in its palm. The weather was full of nuance,
Full of lizards — and uni-celled, binary perceptions,
The bittersweet climate of a tongue that tasted the sun
In the most intricate entities of speech. "In one taut skin,"
No longer meant a name, nor the muck of a summary glance.
My heart was calm once more, but not with the dullness of night.
The taste of "human" filled my mouth, and I spoke like an angel.

Inception in a Quiet Grove
Clutter 125
Written 14 February, 2016

———————— • ————————

Tiny petals, four, white, tinged with pale rose or lavender;
Upper leaves, three to five lobes, basal leaves, compound; leaflets
On stems, sharply toothed — these virgins lie scattered through
woodland shade,
Flitting their stars through the russet-green gloom: *Dentaria
californica,* although we call them "common milkmaids — "
Perfect miracles of condensation, consummate Sutras
Requiring no grammatical key, and loved, not for the sake
Of their symbology, but for their being. A light breeze flicks
Its fingers, the stars lose focus, and the milkmaids softly blur.

The odor of grass, of dew, of an ancient female ritual,
Of lowing, of haze, of heavy, swaying udders. First rays
Of sunlight, golding new green grass, stirring mammalian smells.

The trail to the barn threads through a small copse of trees. The voice
Of the girl shapes a song, three to five bars long, a phrase that
Softly rises, softly falls through a shade where her mother
Came to meet her father. From a soft mattress of needles
And leaves, a few small flowers tremble. It is here that the milkmaid
Stops, and gazes, and tilts her pretty head, and slyly smiles.
Tiny petals, four, white, tinged with pale rose or lavender —
Perfect miracles of condensation, they speak of the past.
And like mute Buddhas, their brief Sutras, revive spring's coital joys.

On the Mysterious and Sad Disappearance of Zest
Clutter 126
Written 15 February, 2016

———— • ————

At last you glimpse this face, which could be that which was once addressed
As the soul, and she is not angelic-looking at all.
She is a square-faced Slav, with a sallow skin, and with hair,
Once blond, but now graying, unkempt, an ornament disheveled
As her determination fights her despair. Her eyes,
Though, are the focus of attention, glacial blue crackled
Glass cut by square leaves of polished brass, eyes that might disappear
At the next blink, but do not, eyes through whose pupils you might fall,
As you would through the words of a poem that soothes your distress.

She tells you of a journey: a man with two children, who
Beginning far inland, aspires to reach the sea. Does she lie
When she says "Only one child survives … but not the one called 'you.'"

What happened to the other child? Why were there two? Who is this
Man — their father? their captor? and why do they make towards the sea?
Her eyes do not answer your questions. Instead, they paint a scene.
When the man and the boy reach the sea, they see a fire.
It fountains from a golden strip of strand, and shoots blue light
Into a bluer sky, while backdropped by a slash of bluer
Ocean. The two, in the flames, see a shape, a shape that is green
And wavering, gesturing to them. The soul's eyes blink, the scene
Evaporates, and the child in the flames dissolves in mist.

Navigating Blind
Clutter 127
Written 16 February, 2016

———— • ————

Stunning how the electrical excitements of the bustling
Cities collapse into a small rusted box when Boredom
Slumps through the nerves. The box lies among weeds. Neglect has filled
It with sand. In the box are the half-interred bodies of bats.
They are right-side up. We must be upside down. Abnormal
As this is, it feels quite normal. Because the pulse is flat.
Perhaps the bats are the brown seeds of future flames, which will
Rise in the darkness, their trembling flight, like flutterings of chrome,
Weaving through cities with electrically sparking squeakings.

Some say the bats are the souls of minor characters, far
Removed from the protagonist's heroics, their role
In the drama to gossip about his moral failures.

A good poet — a poet of the soul — is endowed with that
Same sense, which guides the bats through darkness. Their biosonar
Can flit through an intricacy of gossipy echoes,
And hear the delicate footfalls of dream insects. The cities'
Excitements are dull in comparison. They make abnormal
Flights through the nerves of Boredom. Imagine a box in the weeds,
Rusted and small, but filled with grains of sand, each grain aglow
With the drone of dense sound wounds, inversed stalactite barriers
Jutting through cavernous night — now imagine flying through that.

On Walking Through
a Wall of Light

Clutter 128

Written 17 February, 2016

———————— • ————————

To be what the walls experience in the color called
Magenta, to feel what the wind feels as it slips through a shaft
Of sunlight, is to be an is, not a me. The Is says: "All
Learning is unlearning." The truth or untruth of this, is
Not the question. The issue is in its fermentation.
The letters fall apart into sounds. The whistle hisses
Through a larynx. A cloud of selves is born. These are the selves
Of eternity's blink: magenta paint on a wall, a shaft
Of sunlight sliced by wind, the calm theorem in the blood's squall.

A jay squawks in a pear tree swollen with unburst blossoms.
The flames which drive machinery lift a city. The din
Of ten trillion voices rumbles with untranslatable alarms.

Never is always speaking in absolutes: "All unlearning
Is learning." The sounds coalesce into meaning. The wall
Tastes a color called magenta: its red the skin of speech.
A light crawls down the wall, twirls, as wind goes twirling through fat
twigs
That a jay is squawking into bursting blossoms. An organ
Of utterance flutters in a throat. Machines croak as they dig
The city's roots. In the wall of a fictional me, a breach
Occurs. No one has made the breach. Half-truths become a wall.
A red tongue sloughs these whistlings: "All learning is unlearning."

Lazy Illusionist
Clutter 129
Written 18 February, 2016

Mother has been dead seven years. "All things swirl in mutual
Sympathy," so say our current theories of gravity
And electromagnetic radiation. So say those
Delirious rabbis meditating on the Cabbala
In their medieval ghettos. Mother harangues her son:
"Why aren't you doing what I told you to do?" There is a
"Life-field" that shapes the organism, just as one of those
Cook's molds shape the bread. The rabbis say: "To pray, kneel between
The Glow above and the Good below, here, radiance falls."

Mother has no truck with the sophistry of illusion.
To read is to loaf. To loaf is an abomination.
Her words pulse an electromagnetic radiation.

The condensate of dreams is one-hundred times less
Dense than the condensate of the loafer's head on the pillow.
Mother is closed in medieval armor, the mystical
Mold of protector. The number seven is a magical
Number — the mold that shapes the bread. The psychical surgeon,
Death, has removed the brain. But the life-field dutifully fills
Another skull. What is a son to do? What spiritual
Task is being demanded of him? Between the Glow
Above and the Good below, where is there work for a sophist?

Among the Galaxy,
Eggs of a Moment
Clutter 130
Written 19 February, 2016

As she got older, the mother and photographer of our
Emotions became less interested in the surface of things,
Although she was quick to remind us that the mysterious,
Harsh bitterness revealed by the shapes of pillows had as
Yet no adequate chronicler. Now, the filtered rose or green
Light that touched the fine wrinkles of the white cotton case was
Passé. Such beauty was still wedged in the very narrowest
Slice of time. When the head, with its disheveled hair, lifting
Itself from slumber, disappeared, the hours became smaller.

What she sought now was that species of total neutrality
Which would reveal time's spherical dimension, not the sheen
Of the sun, but the expanded instant's luminosity.

At sunset, the long crest of a round, green hill culminates
In the silhouettes of tiny, distant deer.
They seem transfixed in palest saffron. A mammalian
Bliss of kinship, safety, and togetherness spreads its odor
Of slumber through the air. The head accepts the balm of sleep.
But deep in the folds of the pillow, time's magical sphere
Shows sights beyond day's thin imaginings. Ovarian
Bundles of compacted color float in an atmosphere
Of wrinkling white, each dot a trillion instants' aggregate.

The Devolution of a Non-event
Clutter 131
Written 20 February, 2016

———————— • ————————

Spring sunlight washes across the lounging suburbanite's
Face and washes away those thin films of perception, which makes
Him think that his garden is comprised of strips of lawn and walls
Of shrubbery. A sparrow bathes in the birdbath, shaking
Jubilees of droplets into the morning calm, the jewel
Bright spray falling like ingots from a midnight fire. A dove calling
Completes his avian transformation. The opaque walls
Of color grow translucent. That dove's "who?" evaporates
The film. He floats in a body that has somehow jellified.

He is the medusa, a drifting creature at sea in waves
Of light, his neon inner organs shown to visibly pulse
In intricate crewelworks of ever brighter enclaves.

Yet nothing has changed. The garden still drapes its veils of green
Against the veils of blue. The birds still flit about in birdy
Shapes. And yet the medusa has swallowed everything, its
Glassy tentacles capturing all perceptions to glut
Its inner workings of pulsing light. This is the flowing realm
That drowns the lounger, and turns the russets of his sluggish blood
Into the crimsons of crushed rubies. This is the spirit
Of the ordinary, the suburbanite's eye in the sea
Of the great sea-change that makes what seems to be what seems to be.

The Flailing Aspirant Hears a Dove Call in the Distance

Clutter 132

Written 21 February, 2016

———— • ————

You wake up in a glowing world into another glowing
World, eyes glued shut by sleep, but seeing through and through them,
hoping
To catch a glimpse of turquoise sea, a Mediterranean
Mythology to nix the pewter of a northern winter.
You seek the ultimate release into an ultimate
Coherence, a final focus into a safe blur
Of grey that yet escapes the average. You seek the sun
In the sky, and your stomach's sun, one, as the golden king,
The other as abject subject, but both your playthings.

Seeker, you are yourself a plaything, whose aging body peels
Off its molecules at an ever more alarming rate,
Each spec an incoherent monument to dispersal.

You see these departing planets of former yous as twirling
Light-beads strung loosely on these quivering, wavering strings,
Connecting you by ear to a feathered form: flight in a song
Of ultimate disappearance — and, Seeker, you are gone. You
Are lost in light-borne sound, shot through and through and through
that spate
Of sensory de-coherence without mythology. You
Are a turquoise sea, a winter slate, a bird call in that long
Glow of extinction, which pulls you into silence. Nothing
Remains of the sun whose light you sought — that zero, vanishing.

Radical Ineffective Homeopathic Surgery

Clutter 133

Written 22 February, 2016

———————— • ————————

Even on the most radiant of spring mornings, like this
One, the sun cannot radiate enough health to make healthy
The chronically, wintry sick. No, it takes another
Kind of sickness to do that. It takes the sensuous pleasure
Of a recitation, the commission of lungs, tongue,
Larynx of a leper to engage the diseased listener's
Engrossed nervous system and blur the boundaries of ear
And I. His words alone inject that fantastic panoply
Of scenes and characters that can bleed the grays from grayness.

Whatever is happening in there in the corrupted heart
And brain, whatever is impervious to the healing sun,
Might still be stuck by the prod of this most infecting art.

And that is why the Muse chooses the sick to touch the sick.
Sometimes a word like "yellow" is enough, the jaundiced dullness
Flushed, by adding another word — "blossom" — to the potion.
Sometimes the patient, in his pain, becomes the lively
Character in the work, a misanthrope added for the fun
Of seeing love, bounding through a pinched and scabby psyche:
A madman on the run through daffodils. This second sun
Of a phrase has launched the sufferer into laughing fits.
Thus the son of the sun, the poet, cures with his leprous tricks.

How Lovers Search the Vaporous Depths of Time

Clutter 134

Written 23 February, 2016

———————— • ————————

Even if yesterday were a journey through the grandest
Of landscapes, drives through ancient forests where the canopy's
Shadows stretched and tore their taffy mesmerizings across
The windshield of the car, and the forest changed to the greenest,
Steepest hillocks of pasturage, till we finally arrived
At the sea, a wide horseshoe bay, blue, in the very bluest
Sense, the high surrounding cliffs so brilliantly embossed
With gold, they seemed the spirit's wedding ring, this would still be
Only background for today. The present says "Here. I insist."

No matter how rich the lovers' nostalgia, it is, in this
Instant, only the briefest shadow of a wing in flight,
A crow's wing, too close to the ground — the moment's mesmerist.

But there is, as all lovers know, and most wish to suppress,
The constant chaos of the present's background, that glance behind
The focus of the eye, in the depths of the scene, where tiny
Squares of sky in the curve of the orb, reflect a circling
Vulture, or the corner of the house reveals that bumbling life
Persistent to bring nectar from the hive. There is that something
In the bluest ocean trenches, that grunts its primitive bleat
From the arctic depths — and the crowds of lovers come to find out
why.
But nothing appears when they focus, but yesterday's mist.

The King and the Corpse
Clutter 135
Written 24 February, 2016

———————— • ————————

The relationship between this politician and his
Public is that of butcher to cattle. His speeches are
A plant which corkscrews from cement, its blooms exuding
Poisons. The one who says this wears stacks and stacks of masks, the last,
The thinnest, the most deceiving. The old masks were feathers
And wood, rooted in blood and dirt and dancing and dreams. The new masks
Are toxic cosmetics, troweled on by advertisers. These things,
Compositely considered, create rage. This flower,
A lily cup with carnivorous stamens, is now what is.

The one who says this wears a mask of dew. One touch of sunlight
And his talk is naked. He is inhuman, a feathered
Mass among massed branches, a dew of dreams that forms at night.

At noon, the one who says this is taboo. He may not wear
Nor touch a mask. He may not eat the flesh of cattle. He
May not speak nor move. He must sit in the dirt, still as a corpse.
He must wear white, like a lily — carnivorous white, and smear
His face with red. He must make no claim to courage or fear.
Through these devices he becomes a ghost. He slips in the ear
Of the butcher. He softens rage. He weakens poison's force.
Like sunlight, he must nourish all. Like silence, he must leak
Tabooed refrains. He must show no emotion, shed no tears.

Adding Zeroes to Zeroes
Clutter 136
Written 25 February, 2016

———————— • ————————

The outward shapes of chlorophyll will always hold the gaze
Of botanists, gardeners, stockbrokers and other part-
Time sight-salesmen, who drown their dreams with coffee every
morning,
Seeking relief from the mental anguish of genetics.
They do not see the radiating lines around the membrane,
Grains of light forming scarlet dunes with white stripes where dawn licks
The blue-black strips of night, and where gigantic monoliths spring
From ancestral earth, and erosion's rock holes sing. At the start
Of any such journey, they balk, refusing to be amazed.

No one will say that the lake of dew in a leaf is nothing
Less than the blood of the ancestors— the old times, where the brains
Of the minute peddlers, like beads of eons, hang strung on strings.

No one will see the tree shrew humans, squeezing the chemical
Greens out of the landscape, and mixing them with the azure
Weavings of birdsong. No one will test the horizons. No
One will use words to disperse walls. The tree shrew shrieks in the
night,
And no one hears. No one will leap from the surface and claim
This no one, or live as the colors that scream from the eye
Of the shrew. No one will be who I am when I say "No
One," and claim to be nothing and sing that my sickness is cured,
Because I find in leaf veins, lines pressed into Time's bright pearls.

A Happy Occasion for One Whose Face Removes All Blemishes of Sin and Confers Purity of Mind

For R.D.

Clutter 137

Written 26 February, 2016

———————— • ————————

The dying tantric slumps on his seedy upholstered throne,
While his coterie of aging sybarites, with sinuous
Seductions, cavort around him. They are all old now, their
Bodies devolved to grotesque parodies, all loosely bagged
Slabs of fat and knobby bones, their king a blob of melting wax
From a spent, extinguished candle. Now they all sadly sag
Into this funeral rite for the almost dead. For sixty years
A social cancer has been exposing their souls' torturous
Descent into flesh, and now they know: We all die alone.

I must admit that I find it difficult to pair this scene
With the friend I know, the pure seeker, who was never lax
In his eagerness to serve, and who constantly honored me.

I must admit that the old Puritan fear of the body
Defiled me more than any debauchery. The king is
Dying of cancer, which has moved from prostate to bone, and his
Hanuman-monkey smile is softened by morphine. His feet,
Bare and swollen, are propped on a cushion, while the pain that wracks
Him leaks out to taint his dancing lovers' hearts. The drum beats
Serve, as they have for sixty years, as proclamations of his

And his lovers' longing to be touched, to feel that spirit is
Something more than mist, even if pain corrupts the flesh with grief.

Celestial Transaction
Clutter 138
Written 27 February, 2016

————————— • —————————

We are so used to not looking at the sky that whatever
These soft swathes of haze, these dappled stratospheres, these sliding
Low armadas of billowy galleons, are saying
Is only a matter for the rods and cones of the eye,
And not for the abstracted mind. Shades of white in subtle
Variations diffuse against equally subtle dyes
Of blue, air making itself visibly mobile, raking
Its motions across a field of elongated cells, reminding
The mind of a swaying field of wheat in a vast interior.

Our tribes are not linked by kinship, but by marketing schemes.
Our tribal territories are not proximate, and all
The touch we require is that of fingertips to flat, lit screens.

We like to stay inside our houses, not inside our eyes.
What do we care about the biology of seeing?
What do we care about the poor homunculus fallacy,
The orphaned little man inside the head, awash in feelings
About the teeming heavens? If the little creature's diurnal
Exultations are murdered by the myth of his dark being,
The skies are only packaging, things to be abstractly seen
Through window panes, the same as any two-dimensional bling-bling
That shines from screens and makes our sheltered tribes go sell and buy.

First Things First
Clutter 139
Written 28 February, 2016

First thing Sunday morning, the billionaire tech-magnet rose from
His porcelain throne, wrapped in the pungent shawl of an odor.
The shawl belonged to a woman, old at forty, who peddled
Her body as a laundress, and, unclean, died from drinking
Brown water from a culvert. First thing Sunday morning, the claws
Of a sparrow are heard on discarded pasteboard. He sings
As he scratches, but does not find his seed. Words that are filled
With sadness are emptied by death. This strange legacy of poor
Women and poor sparrows peaks through low clouds as Sunday sun.

A talent was once a unit weight of gold. What it is
Now is a calling, a creative vocation, whose law
Is: Grab what can save you when drowning in waters of bliss.

First thing Sunday morning, a Chinese merchant sips green tea
In a land far from the tombs of his ancestors. A plum
Blossom, loosed from its plum tree, drifts for miles, and the words of
A poet, dead for centuries, talk of plum wine. Reality
Has a talent for exposing anomalies — the raw
Facts of existence, weaving together, then tearing the seams
Of the shawl. First thing Sunday morning, the sun, high above,
Dissolves the cities of low clouds. The sparrow finds his crumb,
And the corpse of the laundress gives off a smell that is sweet.

Verdant Pulsations
Clutter 140
Written 29 February, 2016

———————— • ————————

Certain bright mornings, certain wild angles of freely growing,
Uncut grass appear to us as texts, accounts written by
One of the more exuberant of Nature's devotees.
We quote: "I began to imagine vivid paintings on
The immaculate blue sky. Bright sprays of hallucination-
Flowers, in jungle colors, leapt with pulsating profusion
About the day. It was warm. I was calm, as though a sweet
Sleep had enveloped me. A black, purring cat slept beside
Me. The cat and I dreamt the same dream. All that was was glowing."

When I say "we," I mean you and I: me speaking, you hearing,
This act a synergy where two neuroses make one
Psychosis: a jungle-drum rhythm innately pounding.

The grass keeps growing, the texts keep expounding. This is so
Very ordinary. Again, we quote the devotee: "In sleep,
A feeling of falling with helical speed. A cat purring.
A black warmth, then a white release. I enter a space filled
With wild simulations, a world of pulsing information,
Void of matter's encumbrances — only these visuals,
These swirling, vortical energies, only the whirring
Colors of common grass. Greens, the multitudinous greens,
Are growing with jungle heart-beats —They never cease to grow."

Man's Beast Fiend
Clutter 141
Written 1 March, 2016

————————— • —————————

The lamentable barking of one lonely dog can enrich
The green prosperity of a whole neighborhood. How so?
Are these not the houses of millionaires, impervious
Alike to the quick laughter of crows and the slow imprecations
Of doves? Are these not people with careers? Yes, but their houses,
Swollen with architectural splendors, have no doors. The sun's
Light warms both coupling sparrows and mobs of ants. But in this
Locale, such currency has no value. O poet, tyro,
Who would be master, hear that dog, who barks: "Not this. Not this."

The *via negativa* — path of the perverse to heaven —
Makes this world's diamonds broken glass. Its poet arouses
No envy — a dog, neglected, whose laments make dark the sun.

The *via positiva* turns poets to millionaires,
The laughter of the crow, quick to mock, the imprecations
Of the dove's slow call, the coupling sparrows, the furious
Mobs of ants, all coalesce around this lonesome dog. His bark,
Repetitively poor and rich, makes doors in all our houses.
O poet, tyro, master of shattered senses, if these dark
Opacities are to be your treasures, render them precious
By your fragile words. Be vigilant to catch the bits of sun,
Shining from fragments, and let your lonely barking grace the air.

A Sudden Satisfied Sigh
For Patricia Keel
Clutter 142
Written 2 March, 2016

———— • ————

A woman scatters withered rose blossoms from the cut bouquets
Of the house back onto her garden plot. Today began
With fog. But just as she straightens from her stooping posture,
The sun comes out. Her roses have started to leaf, but not
Yet bloom. The bouquets were greenhouse flowers. I watch this as
From the balcony of a remembered church, a place in thought,
Where a joyful wedding occurred. If it is the Nature
Of memory to fade, why does the sun act as it does, fanned
Out across heaven and earth with its celestial voice of praise?

Among the less celebrated expatriates are these
Spirits spun free from the senses, to make the common joyous:
A pink petal on a patch of ground grown brown as withered leaves.

What is so splendid about the sunlight's touch as it comes
Filtered through silvers to rest as gold? The years, as I watch
Her, disappear. She is not now, nor never could be, old,
Nor ever fade, like her blossoms, from memory. The wedding
Is always now. Her gesture, so momentary, exists as
Something more than the momentary. Her gesture forms a ring.
In timeless calm, this sweet diffusion, this scent that love unfolds,
Is a perpetual homecoming to that lone exile hatched
From the egg of time, who sings soft hymns of jubilation.

Ambiguous, Nourishing Repetitions
Clutter 143
Written 3 March, 2016

———————— • ————————

On such a day, when the house is wrapped in mist, and the horizons
Besiege us with their ubiquitous hordes of droplets, we
Retreat into an inner windowless space — that secret room,
Which holds the revenants of our dreams. These duplicate statues
Haunt our waking lives as one archetypal figure: the slave,
The one who succumbs to the everyday legal statutes,
And is thus declared invisible, and consigned to the doom
Of anonymity. On such days, the poetry we
Birthed returns, made captive again in a room without the sun.

If we are to speak of the kind muse or the cruel muse,
Of the birth of an interior marble figure, of the cave
Surrounded by mist, we must reject the archetypal ruse.

The marble permanence of a sought-for fame is a mist
Where all the captive fugitives run free. The marble words
Are pulverized — white bits — the dazzlements of a dazzled brain,
Fog in the inner room where no one speaks, silence alive
With a music of ground bones. The poet is never enslaved
By a marble name. Look! Look at the droplets, those silver hives
Of light, whose myriad rainbows swirl all their brights through rain —
All that is common, ephemeral, fluorescing in words,
Is like the one who's speech is always only mist in mist.

A Transcript from the Planning Committee on Domestic Suburban Architecture
Clutter 144
Written 4 March, 2016

———————— • ————————

Today, we must consider our growing housing problem.
We can no longer afford delay. We must expand our
Vision, and view the issue from every possible angle.
From below, we encounter a dark realm, where our esteemed
Guru, the slippery *lumbricid*, or earthworm, must guide us.
Here, our angel without eyes eats through a dense marl as he reams
New pathways of revelation. Tide waters flood his tunnels
With knowledge of the sea. Through the work of this legless master
Agricultural civilizations rose. We need his wisdom.

From above, the problem shrinks to the size of a bird's eye.
The sparrows claw through the gutters, turning the moister crusts
Of leaf mulch to extract tiny seeds. Their visions do not lie.

Inside the house, are two sleepers. One dreams of a lover,
Long dead, his mouth full of soil, the other of a dirt road,
Where horseman pass by, lichens filling the letter grooves chiseled
In a poet's headstone. Sparrows alight from on high, pecking
Road apples for rangle. The trees, which have formed the house's
Skeletal supports, swell and creak in the rain. Puddles, ringed
Round the garden's flagstones, fill with reflections, which tremble
With continual transformations. Today, this abode
Of time's decay becomes the other skin we must consider.

A Note on the Transpersonal-Personal-Historical Nature of Desire

Clutter 145

Written 5 March, 2016

———— • ————

Sharp winds drive the rain sideways and backcomb the high waters
Of the estuary creek counter to the runoff's fierce bayward
Flow, but in galloping harmony with the incoming
Stormtide. A couple of intrepid anglers brave the flood
And wade to the verge of disaster to catch a run of striped
Sea bass, which are instinctually drawn to the rich food
Sources provided by upheaval. The scene makes one think
Of a past lover whose stormy eyes hid vast treasure hoards
Of subsurface enticements, and the stormier drops of tears.

Tears drive sideways through the flood of years, and our past grief picks
Off bits of flesh enticements, leaving the spirit to cry
From its exposure. Heart's pain subsides, but the soul's pain sticks.

One thinks of the stormy tides of symbolism, of the fisher
Of men, who was also Pisces' fish — and O! the enormous weight
Of tears, tears that flow from every direction with incarnation,
With history's floods of words and floods of blood, with crosses
And crosstides ripping away beliefs, and stirring up strife
With emotion, and of the scrapings from nightmares one washes
Through currents of longing, which rise from the simplest vision
Of two waders, in a storm, along a creek, testing the sideways
Missiles and warring waters, because their thirsts, unslaked, require
more.

Atlas Shows Us the Difficulty of Grasping Our Ecological Situation
Clutter 146
Written 6 March, 2016

———————— • ————————

Last night's furious winds howled derisively, but only
Dead, small twigs and remnants of autumn seeds this morning litter
The ground, which is polished to mirrored brightness by the rains.
The resurrected sun now bursts from shallow lakes and broken
Bits of glass, making the flats one, and the new foliage
The other. Great, white billowing towers of cloud ascend
Through voids of limpid blue. The planet does not show her pain,
But we hear of mass extinctions, shrinking forests, leaden air,
And of continents of plastic, making dead zones in the sea.

In an alien country, on a dusty road, you meet a man
More ragged than poverty, who labors to drag the dredge
Of one huge stone. He coughs. He says his name is " Your Horizon."

We carry toys which have atrophied our throats, enslaved the air
In our lungs, and made us whimper. The stone we drag is immense,
But we hardly notice. The stone has no weight, though it is as
Voluminous as this morning's clouds — and — like them — its talk
Means nothing. Yet the ragged man roams the ragged edge
Of vision, makes dead zones of our feelings, lifting the rock
Of his pain into that space of limpid blue vacuum. It is
His labor, his alien consternation, that benumbs us.
We cannot feel the weight of his despair, nor grasp what is not there.

Maternal Ghost

Clutter 147

Written 7 March, 2016

———————— • ————————

Subtracting for a moment the import of our personal
Involvement, we might begin to comprehend the heavens,
Along with the prevailing temperature of the air,
As a dual projection, two screens that flicker brightly,
Softly, their various shades of whites, grays, bleached Prussian
Blues, ghosted yellows only just faintly
Offering traces of imagery, some hint of affairs
Reminiscent of trees, yet no categorization
Of any object quite appears. Here, we confront The Real.

Or is it The Unreal that invades, while the trees, futilely
Trying to involve us, make claim to our distanced emotions,
Announcing themselves as kin, come to rejoin our family.

Subtracting for a moment the import of the role we
Are creating, which is now retreating from its physical
Form, like a vapor of breath that slowly evaporates
From a sheet of glass, we see the dual projection coalesce.
An owl-like apparition fills the screen. The soft demon
We so loved, with Mother's eyes, blinks from the trees. She tempts us
To abscond from human life, and for a moment, link our fate
To hers: An unreal presence breathed on the real, trying to feel
An instant of involvement, and break free from eternity.

Cold Mirror
Clutter 148
Written 8 March, 2016

It is clear that I am witnessing a quite deliberate
Subconscious intervention as couple after couple,
Caught in *flagrante delicto,* are stopped in mid-stroke by
A cross-armed female figure with frozen glance and knitted
Brows. Finally, there is no one left to love, and yet the skies,
When I wake, have returned to blue after yesterday's mad
Storms. Yesterday, I could not stop myself from weeping as I
Read aloud an aging poet's protesting verses, full
Of Love's insistence to repeat her crimes against spirit.

"A charter to commit the crime once more," that was the phrase.
Question: How many loves do I have to lose to be saved? I
Try to ignite that woman in my dream, and melt her icy gaze.

But it is clear, as clear as this morning's skies, that the fiery
Progress of the passing years has caught me in *flagrante
Delicto* and shamed me to impotence with a dream. Was this
The poet's cry against the spirit? To be alive
In the spring, to celebrate the coupling sparrows, to cry
Hot tears when ice sticks in the throat, as the terrible crimes
Are repeated in Judgment's sight? Or is this some new abyss
That can only be stopped when Death arrests the passionate fray
Of sex — just as a wall of ice reflects warm bodies?

Gray Clouds Passing Above a River
Clutter 149
Written 9 March, 2016

In times of stress, even meditation cannot entirely
Appease the heart. A slow, persistent rain saturates rocks,
And draws delusion deep into the bones. We have mothers
Whose graves are unvisited, fathers, who are dying, old,
And alone, their memories gone long ago. We try to keep
The specter of annihilation before our mind's eye, hold
To a purity of Non-being, since Being is a master
Whose discipline is too harsh, and his cruelty unlocks
The door of concentration, loosing distraction's furies.

The illusions of perception are so intoxicating,
The attachments of family, of lovers, of the simply seen,
Heard, felt … we cannot easily embrace the zero's lightning.

The mother, who was our mother, not Mother Earth, the father,
Not of the sky, but of the flesh, the perished generations
Of thoughtless birds, however bright their plumage, rich their singing,
These join with the anonymous drops of rain in one
Long river whose toils find no sea. No prayers, no pleas,
Can slow our ceaseless plunge through ever-flowing oblivion …
And — that is why, in the end, we must be poets, because words wing
Their way as whirls of air, as blank as air, void of ambition,
Futility's legacy that leaves its heirs no tears.

God's in His Haven.
All's Rot with the World
Clutter 150
Written 10 March, 2016

——————— • ———————

"Hell" means returning to this little acreage five backroad
And twenty-five highway miles from the mirror-gleaming Oz of an
Inapproachable city where only the mosquitoes
And fleas have yet to be tamed. Who is living in this squalor
That multiplies as the city's sleekness grows? Ragged children,
Feral dogs and cats, snakes, marginalized adults. All harbor
Rampant diseases and grotesque mutations. All corrode
In one devolving menagerie, landlorded by an
Old, toothless cackler, who lies in dirt on stinking mattress mold.

Who is to say that Death, like sleep, is not simply another
Catalepsy where the deceiving mind confusedly blends
Our perceptions through a present dystopia of past fears?

In these terrible Bardos of the suburbanite, horror
Is not an active pain, but the painful realization
That deterioration trumps, in the end, all progress, that Oz,
In all its mirrored-gleamingness, is only optimism's
Ruse, and that Time's passage, or Death, or the blood-and-sleep-sodden
World of dream, show only the gathered filth of realism's
Eternity, a junkyard of decay where the Uncaused
Cause is an old man with the vilest gift of laughter, drunk on
The follies of fermented youth — and we, his drunker squatters.

Great White Father's White Lies
Clutter 151
Written 11 March, 2016

The essential desperations send us, impoverished,
On to the ghost-roads of forgotten aboriginal
Stories. These are mostly the stories of cannibals, terrible
Political men, who impale the vulnerable on their
Spears, and climb these tallest trees, which are the veins of earth, there,
To devour their prey with the black fangs of deceit. To hear
Such stories is to be dismembered. Their old infernal
Words burn the tongue with fire's legend. The tree where Death dwells
is tall,
Taller than twelve trees. In its roots, the hardest gemstones are crushed.

Our Mother-Reality, our Child-Reality,
Are the mild deities of mere allegorical fire.
Such sops are no defense against Our Father's policies.

The ghost-roads are ropes that tie the callused feet of seekers
To a journey beyond desperation. That the tree had
Become a city of cannibals, usurping the veins
Of Earth, we pilgrims, impoverished, could not doubt. We walked
On lies as though we traversed a desert of stormy waters.
That our hearts had become a wound as our heads became dense rock,
No one could doubt. Father, that cannibal with inhuman veins,
Was the chieftain of politicians, his tongue turned all speech bad,
And yet he remained so vulnerable, impaled upon our spear.

Tiny Vampire
Clutter 152
Written 12 March, 2016

———————— • ————————

A red city of colossal forms hewn out of living
Stone, mountainous sculptures of otherwise anonymous
People, immense architectures with interiors as
Unimaginably vast for human beings as a domed
Stadium would be for a flea. Here, the tourist loses
His way, walking up and down the same street, and feels as alone
As a sand grain in intergalactic space, although his
Body is a corpuscle in a stream of corpuscles, the compress
Of the crowds engulf him without ever really touching.

The perfidious methods of emotion to get "at" you,
Get "in" you, in spite of all isolation, and in reckless
Defiance of even coma or sleep — they are the issue.

There are two colors you can see in the womb. These, then, can be
Considered primary. That is why the city is always
Red, and the mysteries of its gigantomachias —
Whether we call them lovers or memories or money
Or diseases — are always black. The cities of our losses,
Of our near-triumphs, of our smallness lost in enormities
Of undifferentiated emotion, these Omegas
Expunging all Alphas, resist compression, and tempt each phrase
Into hyperbole, to tell of feelings suckled by a flea.

Puddles Atremble with Raindrops
Clutter 153
Written 13 March, 2016

———————————— • ————————————

From space, the storm looks like immense strands of vaporous ropes
That twirl and knot right over our neighborhood, the knots squeezing
Drenching rains. Broken trees, flash floods, and roof damage — the signals
In the gut that flash: Danger! Danger! But the drought that was
Killing everything has ended. The trees with desiccated
Roots have fallen, and a giant under the Earth sprouts
A million shades of green, and bellows: "Spring!" These are simple
Irresistible trials — as vast as the trauma of an infant crying
Cries no mother ever hears, the knotted cries, which choke first hopes.

These drops that kill us to save us defy representation,
The fear inside a bereft infant, when tears cease, does not end.
It gathers turbulence, weaves nerve ropes, makes future thunders drum.

An old man will still see a big, bright picture of his mother's
Face turning away in all the rain's reflections. But what he
Will not see, until he himself accepts his averted pain,
Are his mother's aversions, her hurts that gleam from each puddle's
Impersonal pall. A tree falls, its rootball desiccated,
But the tragedy belongs to no one. A million simple
Spring-green proclamations flutter their painful thirsts, and rain
Pours down to quench them. The old man sees the skies of a baby's
Eyes, reflecting their brutal needs in the gaze of his mother.

Celestial Balm
Clutter 154
Written 14 March, 2016

————————— • —————————

After days of merciless storm, the morning began with a blue
Promise of redemption, but the skies knit shadows again,
And the inferior man, crippled by his own shadow,
Finds a closed room in the house to tend his wounds. From above, night
Pours in through a secret oculus in the dome of the skull, low
Moaning following. My father is an old, old man, the night's
Moans coming, not from him, but from a generalized shadow
That streams from every pore in his skin as relentless pain.
Somehow the inferior man has escaped from his room.

The relationship of father to son, of son to father,
Has never been well understood. There is always that "somehow"
Mysteriously lurking, its torment eluding a cure.

If the joy of one was the joy of the other, the one's pain
Is the other's pain as well. We age together, you and I,
My Dear One, you in your body, and I in my grieving,
And both "somehow" escaping from our skins, and storming wildly
Through the stormy skies — and yet a calm comes too, a calm so
Different from the calm of sunlight, a calm that breaks my grief,
Your pain, in two, and shares both in one heart, one tranquil pulsing
Underneath the storm, one blessing made of mystery and night
That cures your superior, my inferior pain.

Seasoned Insight
Clutter 155
Written 15 March, 2016

Among the more sagacious philosophers abiding
In the sculpted jungles of our suburban topiary
Are not the people, nor even the dogs or the birds, though
You might assume as much for all their combined commotions.
No, they are the plants themselves. In the Amazon, there are
Medicines that require dozens of precise operations
To turn them from lethal to healthful. The Yanomano
Shamans when asked how they evolved these marvels, will say simply:
"The forest told us." Our hedges talk, but are we listening?

Once Rosemary let me see what she sees. She turned my body
To glass, so that I could see to read my own mind. Such clutter
Was there! that I was ashamed, and pleaded with her to save me.

I am aware that this magical athlete is also
Merely a seasoning for cooking, but having ingested
Such knowledge, my dreams have changed. So majestically, so
Slowly they come, these green images of the wiser ones,
Showing shapes as tastes and smells, showing me the lover
I have always longed for — although I live inside her, one
In a million, but *her* one. And I see that the thoughts I so
Cherished as exclusively human have come through my glass head
From vast Beyonds as near to me as my garden's need to grow.

Vernal Exhortation
Clutter 156
Written 16 March, 2016

———————— • ————————

The sun today pours his fire in the mouth of an animal
Whose tropical appetites demand the thrill of chasing
Or being chased, of eating or being eaten. It is spring.
The objective spaces of green growth are full of the weedy
Exuberance of emotion, sexual in the extreme,
But so generalized and spread out, their extremity
Is made mild by a community of hosts. Yet everything
In the morning light is touched by one love, a fruitful blessing
That subverts the grey cold with viridian's fresh, warm bridals.

I want you to think back to a time when you were a child,
A time when you ran for the sake of running, a time when streams
Of sunlight moved your limbs with the greenest rage for the wild.

I want you to believe in an objective confluence
That burns much deeper than the ego's winter. This is the chase
Of raw appetites through our general lust for the sun,
A sun who chases round and round those years, which beat all bodies
Down to wintry grey, only to make them run and rise and gleam
In the gold ring of his afterlight. I want you to believe
That the sex that mates your breathing to all that breathes — and runs
The race of spring — is the only self you have, and that this chase
Of death through life is your one best chance to feel exuberance.

A Pauper Confesses His Theft of Emeralds and Black Diamonds

Clutter 157

Written 17 March, 2016

——————— • ———————

Of course, the piratical world of the open seas, heaving
In great green concourses reminds us also, when we sit,
Relaxed, in the green shade of a high wall of shrubberies,
Of the research that tells us that these two different brains
Inhabit a single skull. Why do we continue to
Nurse the fanatical need for unity? The bounding main
Still carries the ships of bandits, and the walls of shrubbery
Are far from solid. They are threaded throughout with the flit
And flitter of birds. Always there are waves crashing, throats singing.

Relaxed, we can sit in a shapeless moment in a green
Freedom, where the cerebral molecules float in a solute
As vast as the sea, a night sea, where a million stars are seen.

An impersonal hand has been grinding enormous jewels,
And the glistening powder falls into the mind. A million
Colors float on a sea of black, a pirate's sea, imbued
With a pirate's hoard — the teeming treasures of disunity.
I sit in the shade in the great green glass of a solitude
Threaded throughout by flitting, twittering birds. If a leaf
Should chance to twitch, my brain divides, a part of it pledged to
Villainous piracy, where the wrath of the dispossessed can
Find its blood, where mercy can still find peace inside a jewel.

Dizzy Formulations
Clutter 158
Written 18 March, 2016

———————— • ————————

In constructing soul-images from leaf growth patterns
Of the English Ivy, one must combine aimless, idle
Doodling with computational mathematical forays.
First attempts are invariably anthropomorphic —
Eyes, mouths, noses, chins, hair, providing a rather too easy
Access, which precludes a much deeper entanglement. A flick
Of breeze, the movement of a bird, can quickly change the arranged
Deity. An eye blink, and these seeming Elementals
Are seen as merely infantile — deep lessons still unlearned.

Any appeal to force must be abandoned, and rational
Polemics composed of declarative sentences must be
Seen as but one turn on an amorphous, vernal wheel.

Everything is growing! Coupling! Not under some compulsory
Dominion of rules, but as a consequence of a secret
Telepathy, whose meditations are the assignations
Of the Ivy's English, and the imagination's passion.
Some see in the leaf-shapes heart shapes, and some see a species
Of interdimensional mutants, the combinations
Born from human-plant coituses, whose springtime infusions
Spin from the unreal something all too real. To call them spirits
Is logically absurd, 'though the wheel spins on hyperbole.

Native Emotions
Clutter 159
Written 19 March, 2016

———————— • ————————

Maybe you are one of those men who think the voices in your
Head are the only ones that are speaking, and when the Spirit-
Women gather behind you, following, whispering, often
Enough, laughing at your obtuseness, you think 'this must be
A memory of my mother,' or some such silly thing,
Because you read a book on psychology. And maybe
You think it is only the wind, having a little fun
With the new spring leaves, or perhaps birds or insects
Are squabbling behind you, noise that means nothing, sounds without
words.

And maybe, after you wake to see three women, standing
At the foot of your bed, you still do not believe. Something
This strange must be a symptom. This cannot be happening.

And even when one of the women, with a face that glows blue
In the darkness, laughs, and says: "I am Scrub Jay Women, and this
Is my purse full of sweets," you bury your head in your pillow,
And pretend to be asleep. But all night you burn with a
Triple vision: Scrub Jays flitting through shrubbery, shrieking
With piercing mockery, a swarm of bees in your head, making a
Hive of your brain, a honeyed daub of sun, showing your sorrow
On a crumpled pillow. And all day, you feel a nameless
Bliss, as if the air were speaking, and saying "I love you."

Buried Muses
Clutter 160
Written 20 March, 2016

In the interior spaces of the head, there exists that
Which is much like weather. Last night, what you heard or did not
hear,
Begins to bring pale billows of cloud over the crown of the
Mountain, the vapors rolling over and under themselves,
At last roiling round a waxing half-moon, surrounding the night's
Half-closed eye with blanketing clusters of reddening veils.
As a consequence, you did not sleep well. And you dreamt of the
Ruins of a house, the roof collapsed, cratered under layers
Of vines, the windows broken, or clumsily boarded shut.

This morning, the skirmish lines of the storm have swollen, and turned
Into a full-scale invasion. The rain is unleashed, the light
Of day is dimmed to greenish grey, and everything is obscured.

It is best in such cases to remain as circumspect
As the old Taoist court ministers in the Forbidden City,
Whose ceremonious demeanors appeared murkily
Illegible, but whose deeper wisdoms could be clearly
Read. Today, what you hear or do not hear, can never pry
Into the brainhouse, and the jade treasures hidden there might be
So strangled with vines, so disheveled by intruding stories,
Like this one, that the beautiful concubines are never seen,
And the palace's splendors lie hidden beneath a wreck.

On the Royal Fate of Anonymous Crimson Arborists
Clutter 161
Written 21 March, 2016

———— • ————

Nothing deflates one so as a triumphant declaration
Followed by a rain of dreary defeats, the deposed prince of
Dreams, ever-fitful during sleep, spending the drizzling, grey day
In a half-coma, bereft of attendants, and with his tiny
Jeweled comb, combing the ideas from his eyebrows.
The prince says: "In the funnel of events, I will spin green leaves
Red, and make a day of purification." In the heyday
Of princes, such august pronouncements were honored, loved
Even. Now the prince has a vile skin disease, and is shunned.

Salvation requires at least one Spiritual Master,
Speaking in each language, or the words will die. No tomorrows
For this mute outcast, no poems in the falling of his tears.

This Master will be clogged with multiple personalities,
Each with its own body, its own deposed princeling. And mobs
Of them, each in their own bubble of isolation, will
Wander the clogged streets of our cities, muttering their private
Prophecies. They will be as numerous as raindrops, and blow
Across the mind like flakes of dandruff. Their fiats
Will always be deflated, and reduced to an utter swill
Of nonsense. They will sing about events, funneling their blobs
Of red. They will blot out grey, and pop the fire from life's dead leaves.

Echo
For Steve Doughty
Clutter 162

Written 22 March, 2016

———————— • ————————

Yesterday, the cousin I hated, died. We played together
As boys, and did things that our mothers would have cringed to see.
They said his heart exploded. He was only six months older,
But that "only" mattered a lot when we were kids. He used it
Like a weapon. He was big for his age, and I was small.
He was a bully. Once he tied a rope around the throat
Of a younger boy, and tortured him all day. He craved danger,
And cried when his dog, Sandy, died. He shot birds with his bee-bee
Gun, yet loved animals. He joined the Marines, and went to war.

That was Vietnam. I fought a horrible two-year legal
Battle, and almost went to jail, protesting. He went to kill
Or be killed. I've been shot at, but can't imagine his ordeal.

Once he tied a gunnysack to a little wooden chair,
And jumped from the loft of the barn. The sack was supposed to act
As a parachute, but he fluttered to earth like a stone.
The chair splintered, and the sack covered his screaming head. I
Laughed and laughed till I cried. I suppose this flawed memorial
Of words, these insults and reminiscences, are really my
Way of dealing with mixed emotions. They say we die alone.
That is not true. After I heard the news, I moped all day. That
Same heart had burst, which once beat close to mine — that death we
shared.

After the Dream, the Bliss of Deepest Sleep For All Our Deceased Kin
Clutter 163
Written 23 March, 2016

———————— • ————————

The road winds through and around great humped forms that swell and
hollow
With hallucinatory green grasslands, shadowed by groves
Of oak and madrone, fir and redwood, with eucalyptus
Or cypress avenues or windbreaks near lone Victorian
Houses, weathered by sea fogs and summer sun. The way crests
Hill after hill of vineyard studded vistas, then dips through vast spans
Of yellow and orange and purple flowers. Cows, in jackets
Of black and white cowhide, munch placidly in the patchy glow
Or gloom, the car passing moments, like posts, blinking now, now, now
…

Megalithic outcroppings, assembled from jumbles of basalt,
Flow. Cherts and muddy sandstones stir puzzled geologists
To meditations, which bring the trudge of eons to a halt.

The sage foretells that when we are moving on that road within,
Through its inexhaustible country, we need not attend to
The body's physical work. These tasks, however complex,
Complete themselves automatically. The eye on the winding
Road sees only the blandness of an asphalt ribbon, bereft
Of any vision of the land. It looks, and yet sees nothing,
Although, beneath this Nothing streams a question: "What is next?"
What is this that does not stop unfolding beauty, and cuts through
The Rocks of Time? And why is black the color of the question?"

Mindless Joke:
A Few More Words for Our Dead
Clutter 164
Written 24 March, 2016

———————— • ————————

The ubiquity of green walls, whether of mountains or
Molds or shrubberies or trees — these monuments busily
Photosynthesizing, turning the sun's intelligence
Into earthier energies, have fused their colossal
Intimacies into a dream. So, here is the mystery,
Permanently unsolved: the image of a porcelain wall
Of a single composite shade of green. In a world where chance
Occurrences stretch to infinity, eventually
We had to have this dream — of the great, green wall — with its door.

As we grow older, more of our friends and family members
Die, walk through that door into a space, undefined, and free —
We suppose — of all these shades of green. They go beyond this Earth
…

Or so we imagine … facing the face of the zero sum,
A sun without shape, heat, or color, a sun of tremendous
Sleep, composite, silent, where all the green occurrences
Of chance defuse their densities. Here, the dearly departed
Look back through the opening, where a tiny spec of green
Can still be seen, for a moment, before its blink goes dead.
With nothing now to see, nothing to see with, they feel the bliss
Of a massive intelligence, the stillness's genesis
In the wake of explosive laughter, where all their grief's undone.

Fertilizer

Clutter 165

Written 25 March, 2016

———— • ————

Among the crazier cognoscenti, there are those who
Collide with the soul in different guises, and in places
Far removed from the sunny lawn chairs of suburbia —
An infant of supernal radiance, skin the brown of soil,
The proportions of an adult in a body that could be
Cradled in a shoebox. This baby The Crazy holds has a full
Set of teeth, and articulates his glossolalia
As if he were spitting galaxies of stars. Light vortices
Spun from sound swirl round his head as poetic ballyhoo.

This seems mad, random, "non-computational," as the saner
Scientific seekers say. The antique relevancy
Of a poem is only the stir of neuro-transmitters.

But the crazier cognoscenti persist: the random,
The mad, the cycles cycling mistily through mist, for them, arc
In their inward spin, not just through the computational,
But also through unformed space, where galactic vapors
Spin out of infant spittle, and babble the phrase: "To be."
This is the accident of suburbia, this sunshine poured
Through The Crazy in his deck chair, this burst of supernal
Light in the drowsy head of the poetic maniac —
His words of the sun and soil, excreting gold from the random.

Audianceless Antiphonal
Clutter 166
Written 26 March, 2016

--- • ---

No doubt you thought it was an accident of fate, but there
Is, in fact, a secret cabal, which handles these matters.
A child is heard, her body invisible behind a wall
Of spring-rich foliage. That is part of their code. In a tree,
High to the left, a goldfinch sings, to the right, a sparrow
Calls. These are their cryptographies, their messages interleafed
Through leaves. They have passed sentence. You are declared invisible.
People will walk right through you. You speak, but a fold occurs
In your vocal chords, your words aspirated — lost in air.

We have come to the question of identity, which is what
The cabal assigns, and its symbols control. You say you know
These symbols. But do you know their power? Can you sing: "No
Thought?"

For a long time you have been talking as if the bird calls
And the child's voice were superfluities, as if the leaves,
In their billions of flutterings, were negated by the one
Leaf of your tongue. For a long time now these secret mutterings
Have been stealing your heart away. For a long, long time now,
The cabal of these unheard voices has been deftly changing
Your flesh and blood into silence, a silence that only comes
When you are gone. A singing from high to the left falls free
From its source, while another note, to the right, augments its call.

Finding My Familiars
Clutter 167
Written 27 March, 2016

———————— • ————————

I decided I would go to the tallest mountain on Earth,
And bathe my emotions in the sun. The air is thin up here,
Cold too, but my emotions are sturdy animals, and they
Breathe an inner fire, and warm themselves with an inner heat.
Some are herbivores, which may herd together in stupendous
Numbers. They browse on peace as though it were the vast grassy
Plains at the foot of my mountain. These warm creatures are prey
To lonely predators, intense with beauty and rage, the masters
Of solitude and motion, of fear, courage, death and birth.

My emotions deify dead places and fit their opaque
Camouflages with transparent symbols. These are the lists
Of totemic, limbic animals: the predators, the prey.

Because today is today, and no other, and my mountain
Is taller than any structure, either of rocks or words, I
Have made my decision. I have decreed that each species
Of emotion, whether antelope or lion, should be
Felt as an indelible symbol. And, therefore, its lust,
Its exultation, its vigor, its pain, should, by this heart's decree,
Be consecrated to the sun — the crux of all symbologies.
I know that my thought of these monstrosities cries
Each day in each creature's blood, and that my ardor makes them kin.

Death by Water
Clutter 168
Written 28 March, 2016

———————— • ————————

How astonishing it is to realize that this mighty
Compendium of disparities — sunlight and leaf rustle
And dirt and dreams and distant dog barks and traffic and skin
And houses and oceans and idle brains — are all only one,
One only notional entity, who speaks from heaven
Of heaven's diversities, the Void of Meditation.
Facts, which do not exist, except for one, are airy capons
That are easier to digest than these finer vittles
Of inward emptiness — these closed-eye wakings, which devour sleep.

One day, today, emerging from the less-astonishing
Delusion in which I take my I as fact, I fell in
(Or was it out?) of the compendium, and I went sailing.

On the prow of my ship, there came a constant wind, alive
With the finest spray. My horizon was near or far, as walls
Of water married to bobbing skies rose high or, dipping, fell,
According to a rhythm much like breath. The sea and sky
Were indistinguishable, and both as fickle as this wind,
Which calmed or gusted in arrhythmical pulses. Whatever I
Felt here, it was not mine, nor anyone's. It was The Real,
The is that never was nor yet will be. It was the roil
Of air and sea, the instant's puff of mist that drowns the I.

Lazy, Listless Sagacity
Clutter 169
Written 29 March, 2016

———————— • ————————

If you are one of those who sits naively in your chair,
Enjoying what you believe to be a warm bath of photons
From the morning sun, you might be surprised to learn that these
swarms
Of light contain the crystalized past and the vaporized
Future. You must know that the hearts of unbaptized children
Have made this ointment which glistens on your skin, that the eyes
Of the unsatisfied dead and the unrealized unborn
Are infused entirely through these rays, which warm you. The sun
You think you know is not the sun, and the air is more than air.

The poet, of course, is notorious for his indolent
Indulgences, lolling incessantly on his pyre, the sin
Of wasting time, for him, the very nadir of indifference.

And yet there is a point to his dissoluteness. By being
Insolidly mystified, he tastes reality at
Many misty points, the air for him, a panoply of flowers,
All swarmed about with honey-making phrases. Upon sky-glints
Of soapy blue sateen, the poet, the mummified pilgrim,
Steals his unearned rest, the bees of his perceptions so persistent
In hovering through his idle hours. His words steal power
From the sun for artificial light, as his thoughts grow fat,
Like some great, snow-bright cloud, adrift on a painted ceiling.

A Few Clouds on
an Otherwise Clear Day
Clutter 170
Written 30 March, 2016

On cloudless mornings, spring sometimes so permeates the air
That the blank blue aerates the mind with a like blankness,
Prompting us to naively believe: "I am happy." That phrase
Arises quite automatically to the lips of one
Who would believe anything, except that he is asleep.
The sky seems as stable as the term "firmament," until one
Wisp of vapor drifts in from the northern horizon, some stray
Thoughts accompanying, so that quite naively, we confess,
"I was once happy," those threads of breath presaging our despair.

Sadly, these mornings remain untroubled, in spite of the thin,
Unstable wisps of white. But why sadly? Because the fresh breeze
Destabilizes our naive sense of having ever been.

"I was once happy" is the unstable breath of yesterday's
Illusion. There is no — never has been — any such being
As "I." That firmament was always only air, the deep,
Unfathomable sleep of things that are without the need
Of anyone's belief. Happiness is, without a naive
Thinker to control it. Happiness has no boundary properties.
Its firmament absorbs all wispily drifting worries,
As easily as sleep absorbs more sleep. I am nothing,
The essence of spring, in the ultimate blank of the day.

A Walk Through Unmown Grass
Clutter 171
Written 31 March, 2016

On that terrible day, even in the midst of spring's most
Prolific engenderings, the child, no longer content
To grow, to discover, to be, says to his mother,
"I'm bored. There's nothing to do." On that day, the heavens fall,
And the magic center dissolves. The child's astonishing
Inner world is usurped by something both shallow and cruel:
The purchasable object, the obtainable outer
Surface that adults must worship because its mirrored glint
Seems to supply that astonishment, which the child has lost.

That glint which ignites the glass is the last moment that spring
Remains incarnate, the last spark of innocence, departing,
The final blink when magic is synonymous with being.

As the rational purveyor of critiques, I seldom
Laugh or shout because a tangle of grass entangles my
Feet. But sometimes, my judgment collapses in ignorance,
And for that instant my mirrored adult face is swept away
By a fire in the glass. Nothing remains of me, but spring,
A vigorous splurging of greenings, engendering day,
As if for an instant, childhood returned, and the boring trance
Of the adult was negated. The deceiving outer blight
Is cleanly purged, and I revel in the magic of the sun.

April Foolery
Clutter 172
Written 1 April, 2016

———————— • ————————

The ragged clown in the corner now contemplates the realm
Of silence. He says, or meant to say, "Absolute statements
Are too porous. They leak contradictions." Everything, for
Clowns, at least, is impersonal. I was born premature,
A blue baby, not yet ready to breathe the outside air.
No one held me. No one touched me. If you seek an answer,
Cry. I could not breathe. Therefore, I could not cry. The mother
I sought was someone other, grieving. To circumvent
Disaster, I probed silence. The realm of the impersonal.

In poetry, a much-equivocating intelligence
Seeks to harmonize catastrophe, as if the very air,
Infused with portentous silence, spoke from its primal trance.

These words are the saturated pronouncements of an infant
Too immature to speak, too breathless to cry, constrained in
A tube of oxygenated pressure, grieving, waiting.
And in that heavy silence, a mother comes, a touch of air,
Purer for its containment. One is expressed by the Other,
The totality of the impersonal, the blue air
Of the fairest noontide sky, serenely enveloping
All that is clownish, ragged, immature. The Mother-Heaven
Breathes. She fills the lungs, and prompts the spastic tongue into this
rant.

Dying of Exposure
Clutter 173
Written 2 April, 2016

The fog this morning is my inspiration to deepen
My ignorance. I will film my inner cinema in
Black and white, using a filtering lens. I will fill the frame
With grainy mystery, and extract from the blurs only
That image I most need to see: the virtuous, naive,
Heroically justified me. In the background, hazy screens
Of movement, perhaps a wall of trees, the flickering stains
That hide a memory — a mother is weeping somewhere in
That murk. A catastrophe befalls her infant son.

A garish light flares with a jagged cut: She sees her son
As a pitiful object of shame, and the infant sees
His body, in that instant, as the burden she most shuns.

In the mind, a line bisects the body's center, on one
Side, a bony infant, on the other, a flabby old man.
The two are sutured together by a lifetime of fear
Of being seen by others, of being scorned, of being
The wrinkled apple of mother's eye, the fruit of the tree
Whose spoilage spoiled Eden, and placed the coiled, poisoning
Serpent there — there! — in the belly's distorted mirror, where
No one, I thought, could see. But everyone sees. "This is the man
Who is nakedly ashamed, the fool who is fooling no one."

Guidance System
Clutter 174
Written 3 April, 2016

———————— • ————————

The hallmark of knowledgeable ignorance is revealed
First as infant appeals to the mutually exclusive
Allures of liberation and control. The little birds,
Even in the midst of my greatest human disasters,
Still fly unerringly into the thickest foliage, their
Tiny feet instantaneously grabbing the slimmest perch for
Safety — while all the while they sing. To speak the fabulous word,
An unerring psycho-physical flight, explosive
With an infantile ignorance, must pierce through all such veils.

The clouds of depression do not lift, nor are they
Disintegrated by effort, however cunning. The more
I work and work, the more and more and more they congregate.

They thicken like foliage, a tanglement of intricate,
Useless knowledge, which promises me safety. I use them as
My camouflage, but they are the prison bricks amassed for
A baby's needs. Until I recklessly throw my words through space,
Accepting all the vagaries of chance, the very air
I breathe must freeze to stones, choking, and utterly opaque.
Day after day after day, the weight of depression gathers,
As if something inside me has grown gray and dense. I stare as
A bird shoots through thickets, and grips a fragile, little stick.

The Littlest, Hottest Loves
Clutter 175
Written 4 April, 2016

———————— • ————————

Even if we knew the name of their species, we could hardly
Divine it without the aid of a microscope or some
Shamanistic supersensual penetration, so,
These two insects, tiny white motes in a shaft of morning sun,
Whirl round each other in perfect anonymity,
Whether joyous or compulsed, we cannot guess. The sun,
Their father, and the air, their mother, as far as we know,
Along with their revolving round and round, are attraction
Enough for their risking existence and expressing beauty.

Emotion leaps into an extremity of sympathy,
Then subsides gently into its own anonymity,
Some species of feeling as fleeting as wind through leaves.

There are huge objects in space, whirling with such velocity
That should they slam into our planet, all species, even our
Own naming and famous one, would disappear, and a perfect
Anonymity would reign. But the sun, our father, the air,
Our mother, would survive, holding material memories
In the unnamed elements of their attraction, their cares,
Unseen by anyone, but poised to birth into being — specs
Of essence and precedent hatched from extremity and poured
Into existence, because they burn with mutual sympathy.

Son Salutations
Clutter 176
Written 5 April, 2016

———— • ————

Photosynthesis is working its conversion magic in
Green rustlings that sing with insect and bird chatter, echoes
Of the sun's intelligence, announcing, with energetic,
Albeit, circular reasoning, the crazy wisdom
Of an animal's mitochondria — Hurrah for the ghosts
In the burning machine! Hurrah for this snow of powdered sun
That the bones become as the fictional hollow ego click-clicks
When it revolves. I am a chattering matrix, an ego's
Citric acid cycles, a social construct's wordy din.

"I am." That is the key piece of fiction, in all these fictions,
That is the poem, which the clown, from his mask that masks the hoax,
Must boast — "I am. I am. I am" his mindless repetition.

In our relentless spiritual probing of surfaces,
This mindlessness turns scriptural riches into chemical
Linkage. The sun is shining, and the body is its robot.
So God Himself becomes an atheist, whose deified
Illusions teem with glory. How strange that in the throes
Of trillions of intelligent explosions, the author should lie
About his own existence, and announce, through his product —
The poem — that all this talk means nothing. Hurrah for this ball
Of fire in the throat that sings the day star's complex messages.

Unconscious Meteor-music-ologist
Clutter 177
Written 6 April, 2016

———— • ————

How ironic that this large fair weather system, which has
Brought such springtime splendor to a thousand miles of our coastline,
Should be accompanied by mysterious breakages
In the emotional body of a man named Bird. Mister
Bird would awaken from inside an Artic Circle's cold
And darkness, indigo icebergs cracking booming thunders
As they slide into raging seas, and the foliage
Of a geranium would be seen fluffing sublime,
Nappy greenness around blossoms arranged in a crimson mass.

Something inside him would go "Crack! Crack!" and fissure lines would bloom
Random shatterings in rings of jagged heartbreak, his hurt soul
Showing hosts of interior black blossoms, glinting through the gloom.

Neural filaments finer than the splay of capillaries
In an infant's sleeping eyelid would play these eeriest
Of melodies in Mister Bird's weary imagination,
And the high pressure dome of a cloudless day would provide
An echo effect, encompassing a continent. Great folds
And plains of music would ripple along the jagged coastline,
Resounding with foam breakages of surf, geraniums
And icebergs and all spring's nappy greenings, singing palimpsests
In layers of mysterious feeling from Mr. Bird's deep sleep.

A Fabulous Echoes' Echo
Too Distant to Be Heard
Clutter 178
Written 7 April, 2016

———————— • ————————

Spring's clumps and clusters of burgeoning green, even amidst these
Angular geometrics of our insignificant
Corner of suburbia, speak only in summaries.
"The details," they say, "are inconsequential. What matters
Is life is renewed." But a few ornamental locust trees
Are slow to bud and leaf. In them, the skeletons of winter
Linger. Their silhouettes show delicate filigrees
Of broken nettings, intruded on by insignificant
Blobs of birds, a dove or a finch without the cover of leaves.

Who grieves for winter's passing? Who grieves for the silence
Of veins tangling under the ancient father's papery
Skin? Who longs for the tough persistence of the naked branch?

For hours last night, I lay awake in agony — no thoughts, no
Images in my head or heart, just a grey persistence
That did not wish to persist, a terrible awareness,
Alert to nothingness. This morning, I shared a conference
Call with the staff of my father's Senior Care Facility.
He cannot stand, eat, or "toilet" himself without assistance.
His old grandeur is as lost as the continent of Atlantis,
A mythic splendor, void of any semblance of remembrance,
A last, too delicate branch, where shadows perch on shadows.

Totemic Lament

Clutter 179

Written 8 April, 2016

———————— • ————————

Sometimes it does seem as if the sky is sloping down at
The horizons, and that these masses of grey rainless clouds are
Slowly crawling — like smoke — up towards the crown of a glass dome,
This idea, like a small blue light, similarly arching
From ear to ear on the inside of the skull. All is calm.
In the Clan of Dream Bearers, concrete fact is a being
As easily transformed as is a bear to bear fat, the lone
Criterion for this God's existence being change. Our
Minds dislike such Gods, and firmly say: "I will not stand for that."

We want a rule for how the Cloud Bear Clan names its warriors —
Tracks-On-The-Prairie, Claw-Marks-On-A-Stump, Honeybee Balm —
Or how ten-thousand generations of dreams could disappear.

On the night I was born, the umbilical was cut too soon,
And I found the outside air too thick to breathe. I turned blue,
And the priest from the Clan of the Dream Bearers came to me
And asked "Do you want to be?" And I said, "Yes." And he said,
"The poem can never escape its vision. Live this, and all
Will be well." But this has not been so. Inside my sleeping head
That blue light roams, and I suffer for want of certainty.
The clouds do not move within the skull's small dome, and there are
truths
Harder than poverty, and facts for which my dreams can find no room.

Who's Afraid of the Virgin Wolf's Aqueous Humor?

Clutter 180

Written 9 April, 2016

———— • ————

You can test this yourself, taking time into your mind, as hands
Might ball or stretch a wad of taffy: the time-mind condensing
Into points of interest, a single raindrop swelling
At a leaf tip, a view into distance through wooly veils
Of rain. Our views of culture are hierarchically
Layered veils of semantic memory, encoded neural
Circuits that create timed moods of rain. Why am I dwelling
On this? Because it is by delving into such mundane things
That eyes are alerted to wonder in the seemingly bland.

You can test this yourself. In the near and in the far,
There are colors in the rain, which vivify the normalcy
That children complain about. There are toothy bits of stars.

When one passes through habitual perceptions — one's rainy
Moods — one sees a landscape of cosmic animals, the globule
Shapes of shapes reflecting shapes, beasts of the subtle,
Uncultivated brain, sporting through a perpetual
Wilderness of predatory wonder. A drop on a leaf
Makes its own cosmic incisions. You can test this for yourself.
The taffy-like, elastic opacity turns to crystal,
That crystal jangling in the savage brain, tuning celestial
Time to timelessness, and biting through the muffling wool of speech.

New Start

Clutter 181

Written 10 April, 2016

———————— • ————————

The sky at noon today seems little changed from earlier
This morning, the ubiquitous overcast having defused
The rays of the traveling sun, so that light seems to fall
On us as a dreary uni-directionality,
Which puts a stop to time. The palettes of master painters, wiped
Clean of all their colors, all their struggles and discoveries,
Take on a silvery patina, their surface's subtle
Smearings so much like these low skies, so much like these weary moods
In us, wherein ambition dies, and the mind grows dreamier.

Perhaps it will rain — the failing parents will fall, and the tears
Will change these monochrome calms to green. Perhaps the sunlight
Will kill grief's subtleties, and blue the leaden atmospheres.

Probably there are festive crowds assembling somewhere, and
Sunlight to celebrate a royal marriage, or so the mind,
The dreamier mind, supposes. Probably a man beneath
A blossoming apple tree drowses in bee-hum, and silently
Recites poetic vows. The clouds for this dreamer would be white,
And the bees in the boughs would shake pink petals down. A breeze,
No doubt, would be stirring sweetness about, perfumes that would ease
The drowser to deeper sleep. And here, in the depths, he might find
The primal pair, enamored father and mother, hand in hand.

Orphans Adopting Orphans

Clutter 182

Written 11 April, 2016

————————— • —————————

While engaging in my usual indulgence of poking
Holes in the sky with words, the cloud-cover thinned, and while the sun
Did not break through, nevertheless, I caught a glimpse of faces,
And thought, 'These must be the famed bodies without inner organs,
Who are creatures, much like ourselves, but formed entirely
Of legend.' It is not as if the clouds, their forms all too common
In their suggestive volumes, had evoked angelic races,
Only as psychological projections. I had often
Seen such things in dreams. No, these were another order of being.

If these celestials are some clan of aesthetic hucksters
Bent on tempting me with the escapist sin of fantasy,
I am a willing convert. What could I possibly fear?

Mothers, hide your children. If you want them to be doctors,
Lawyers, or brokers, or even decent husbands and fathers,
Don't let these vaporous aesthetes get at them. They will break
All social conventions and turn into idlers. They will
Fritter away days with unprofitable thoughts. They will read,
Not only books, but the faces in heaven. And they will
Embarrass your families by caring too much for the fate
Of clouds as they drift through lead-gray skies, claiming these roamers
As kin, and saying: "The shapes of air are my sons and daughters."

Post-Atomic Fall-Out
Clutter 183
Written 12 April, 2016

————————— • —————————

Perhaps some words to address this preference of our children
For the dissociated titillations of video
Presentations might be in order here. The ordinary
Arrangements of three-dimensional space bore them a bit.
Yes, it is spring, and the heavy-blossomed boughs now strummed by
bees
Will do for the commercial's background shots — they are unfit
To capture any unfocused attention. Not that focus seems
To count one whit to the way their predatory vision roams.
They look around, but nothing's there, until the camera runs.

Of course these observations are more irrelevant than
The spent petals of that even less relevant, nameless tree.
No fruit could come of them —or it, for these unearthly children.

The uncapturable scent of spring's perfumed exhalations
Has formed an alien from an ancient, far more primal
Dimension. He asks the children to join hands and form a ring,
And to play a rosy game they do not know. The children
Go round and round, as the alien bids them ascend. The tree
In the breeze waves them on. What do you think will become of them,
When they pierce the sheathe of spring's sweet atmosphere? Will they
sing
From the vacuum of outer space? And if their voices call,
What will we hear from these black clouds, which rain no consolations?

On the Use of Rodent Models In the Decipherment of Prophesy
Clutter 184
Written 13 April, 2016

———————— • ————————

Every winged-seer is incessantly baffled and ambushed
By the mutable nature of cloud shapes, especially by
These wispiest, white brushings that haunt the more immaculate
Blue expanses. These assassinations, in which the eyes
Kill reason, and destroy the arduously assembled
City, turn the seer into a dead bird that a rat spies
Under the hedge where the mower does not reach. It is the rat's
Prerogative to squeak, as the disappearing clouds drifts by,
More silent than hunger. The rat's teeth gnaw and gnaw at the hush.

The tongue is a tooth made holy by its enemy's precious
Blood. But the enemy is not silence. What trembles
In the seer's gut is the city's insatiable lust …

Its lust to destroy all silence with its noise. The engineers will
Never stop whining about progress with their terrible need
To make the wondrous hush of clouds completely irrelevant.
This worries the rat that eats the bird's lean corpse. The seer
Finds hope in that. If the bird is dead, and the cloud uncrumples
Its vapors, and leaves only blank blue behind, if the air
Can remain undamaged by the noise, and curb the seer's rant
Against the city, than even ratty hunger might be
Appeased, when these beautiful silent citizens unravel.

The Obsolete Hymn
of Robin Dead-breast
Clutter 185
Written 14 April, 2016

———————— • ————————

It is taboo to speak of this extinct volcanic crater
Filled with crumbled lava and sea salt as if it were a
Suburban paradise, taboo to speak of these amputees
With their hingeless, golden prosthetic legs, as the pillars
Of the community. And if the archeologists
Of spring find the charcoaled remains of an ancient sycamore,
A mummified robin stuck in its final twigs, to speak
Of that vanished life as if it were life will betray
One as an outcast beyond the scorn of outraged mothers.

Beyond the crater, high up, and far away, where golden,
Hingeless legs can never climb, the outcast hears a murmurous
Stirring. He whispers the word "bird," and the pillars ignore him.

I will admit to thinking indecent thoughts, and even
Confess to perching on my branch in paradisiacal
Suburbia, and making a desert solitude with my
Curses. I will confess to loving the sticks of my legs
Better than I love gold. I will even own that my curses
Are really sad boasts. I am stuck to my charcoaled bit of twig
In the museum of antiquities, where nothing I
Say from my Plexiglas case can be heard. Stern mothers will
Point to my bones, and say: "Write poems, and this is what happens."

Contrasting Bleached
to Saturated Scarlet
Clutter 186
Written 15 April, 2016

———————— • ————————

Inquiring after the fact, I asked a stone: "When did I
Die? When did the overlapping blankness of too many
Compassionless skies cease to refresh my pulse?" And the stone
Was silent. How could I know that symphonic roses were
Blooming inside the taciturn granite, and that the soul,
Which had fled my corpse would keep on singing in there
For heaps of millennia? Before the fact, had I known,
I might have felt compassion for the mineral poetry
Flowing in my blood, the words in red that were never mine.

Suppose you had the sensitive soles of your feet pricked by
A needle. You would feel something. You would react. And the cruel
Click-clack of the cicada might prick compassion from your sighs.

The cicadas crackling irritations sing from the cover
Of new spring growth, alert in funereal ivy, while the
Stone broods in the midst of its solitude. After, before
The fact, an in-between has left my compassionless flesh
To sing, from these secondary homes, my primary soul.
My pulse is as firm as any poetic corpse would wish,
But my feelings now flow through the overlapping layers
Of the blue on blue of these emotionless skies. Is this the
Stone's answer? That granite roses, compared to blood, glow redder?

Compass-less Voyage
Clutter 187
Written 16 April, 2016

———— • ————

If you want to see the inside of the eye, look intently
At an immaculate blue sky, and soon, along with the
Intermittent bird, the debris in the aqueous humour
Will appear — swirling dots, squigglers, floaters — with bodies more
Transparent than the tiny creatures in deep sea canyons.
The analogy is that of delving a green corner
Of your own back yard. Here, you discover both pirate treasure
And the gap-toothed skulls of pirates. You take a tour of the
Imagination, the sea where poets sink their imagery.

I speak of the deep sea canyons, the darkest, coldest trenches.
Here, the remains of ten-million poets drift. If you want, you can
See them — dots, squigglers, floaters — in Death's most cleansing
embraces.

Days go and come, nights come and go, yet insight is forever
Going. To stare into the immaculate currents of this
Or that image, that or this phrase, is how the pirate unearths
Both jewels and corpses. To look, to really look, to read, to
Hear, to plumb both zenith and nadir, these occupations
Of lawless, high-seas' assassins require something from you.
They require an outcast life, and an ignominious death.
They require a burial, a drowning, in Time's quickest
Instant. They require that you set sail through your own dark humours.

Demolition
Clutter 188
Written 17 April, 2016

———————— • ————————

My friend's body has become immense steel girders, fitted
With the gargantuan rubber tires of an earthmover,
A monstrous mechanical rigidity that is the City
Transformed to image through the contextual insanity
Of nightmare. He is an artist, a pianist. I have seen
His hands set ablaze with Lisztian virtuosity,
A cocaine madness of unleashed appetite, where pity
Retreats to die, like a small animal consumed by the roar
Of a machine, and bent to wreckage by its own mental fit.

O the terrible catatonia of this sleep that makes
Us stiff with inexpressible fury, the metallic spleen
That enflames the forge of night, and paralyzes us awake.

My friend's face has become the frantic busyness of insect
Populations, caught in the circuitry of a relentless
Capitalism that sells us the commodity of need
With diabolic virtuosity. The night goes plunging
Through debauchery, and my friend's humanity careens
Into a mass of perverted I-beams, this destructive thing
That is urbanity's nightmare. My friend bares his lustful teeth
With a smile, which portends a sick entertainment, his reckless
Music corrupted by this fact: He is the City's addict.

Regional Ware-fare in
A Universal Capitalist State

Clutter 189

Written 18 April, 2016

———————— • ————————

Morning sunlight falls with a joy peculiar to this angle
Of fall, this light on the river, on the leaves of the trees,
Striking with cruel irony on to the soldiers bivouacked
There — the breeze passing among them like fate, issuing blank
Death certificates, awaiting a name and date. You try
To tell your father about a strange creature that roots the bank
Of the river, some weasel-like thing with long, red fur, its tail thick
And hairless, forked like a snake's tongue, pricked with spikes. But he
Says, laughing, "This is just poetry, the first sunlight's fable."

Work. Sell. Work. Buy. Many of the troopers have already
Died marching, many slip quietly into the river to try
To find a sleep that does not bleed, as your father's words bleed.

An art historian tells us that "The most beautiful
Animal of the Middle Ages never existed,"
And now you claim the unicorn was mythic. Only a
Virgin could capture its wild whiteness. What then of your red
Weasel, not even gifted with a poetic name? You write
On the blank certificate, and father laughs, your phrases fed
To his derisive stare. Your airy blood is mythic, a
Sunlit angle of joyousness for trees, or else for misted
Rivers, but not for the soldiers who see that weasel's snarl.

Devoured by Rush Hour
Clutter 190
Written 19 April, 2016

One bird chirping at midnight is so different than one bird
Chirping at dawn. If the catastrophe of sleep were only
The revelation of a single contemplative figure,
Alone in a beautifully eroded desert, sand,
And the volutes the wind carves in it, would be the sepulcher
Of the ego's stagger through day, and the pillow would not stand
For oblivion. The last bird chirps, and the daylight hours
Disintegrate into granulations. The thing called "me,"
Is swept into a rhythmic storm of breath, yet nothing stirs.

The last strobing fragmentations break into star-stuff, and scatter
Grains of light through ebony silk, the blip of the final chirp,
Finding a home in the mouth of a disembodied master.

The master speaks to us in sleep's deep silences. His is
A silky speech, which might, just might, have guided us, egoless,
Into his desert enclave. And there, where the contemplative
Fathers of eroded faith subdue with peace the demons
Of the day, we might have awakened to that second chirp,
The one that rains the desert back to green, and sings of gardens
In our arid lives. What is it that these silences now give,
Which only rain their gifts when one bird sings? What busyness
Is so important, that it must talk, and kill this singer's bliss?

Stark Icon
Clutter 191
Written 20 April, 2016

———————— • ————————

Lives change. Time changes them. And there are few today who can
See what the priest of our ancestors saw in the full frontal
Charge of a bull. Namely, a shape like that of a uterus
With its pair of fallopian tubes looped to the side. The bull,
Enraged, and the mother of all, engorged, these two, enflamed,
Are one. You recall how the flower artist painted as well
The skull of a cow, a work called "Red, White, and Blue," showing us
An abstract portrait of her vagina, in a full frontal
Confrontation: the door of birth, the bone of death, weird twins.

The flower artist found a place in the desert where colors
In convoluted desert cliffs so silently made
Such secrets clear. She put them on canvas and made them ours.

There are poems that are the offspring of emotions held
To be important simply because the author feels he felt
Them. But the old priests sought insight in the immediacy
Of charging terror, and in the revelations that showed
How extreme situations made serene, but abstract, portraits
Of a hidden female power. When it is all stripped to bone,
Horned head and pelvis, rich blooms and eroded desert paucity
Are one. It does not matter what the poet feels he felt,
The Muse will say her say through the bare schematic of a skull.

Rapt

Clutter 192

Written 21 April, 2016

———————— • ————————

When the moister, heavier atmospheres ally themselves
At night, and in the morning appear as misty rain, we
See that as the thicker horizons creep ever nearer,
It behooves us to retreat, retire, secret our drowsy
Perceptions to an inner room, and wait … wait. What are we
Waiting for? For the mirrors to tell us that our hair is bleached
By Time? For the face of the dragon sun to reappear?
For the recapitulation of regret that says "Believe,
Believe?" Spring has come, though joy now staggers in a foggy spell.

Everything green becomes grey haze, my body's solidity
Misting. All of the processes once used to process me,
All those defeated optimisms — disperse their energies.

Explosions, but inward ones, create grey versions of spring's
Blue paradises. The private, terrestrial movements of
The muscles now burn with these celestial inundations.
This is the ordinary sense of being lost, transformed
From noise to silence, from utter silence to poetry.
My life-long, invisible war reveals its violence in forms
Of social consternation: "Do this. Do that. Be free. Fit in.
Allow life's onslaught of destructions to be, and be enough,
And being still, though misty, be wound round by the folds of spring."

Oblivious
Clutter 193
Written 22 April, 2016

———————— • ————————

Looking at things with these tiny human eyes, which are smaller
Than the eyes of bees, fitted as they have been to the designs
Of commodity fashions, and not to skies — when we see
These miles-high billowings imploding-exploding overhead,
Closing to delving darknesses, opening into
Rippleless oceans of blue, it is as though their huge thunderheads,
Booming with colossal silences, is but the place where we
Are consumed by little titillations, where poets whine
In the language of advertisers, deaf to thunder.

The sexual appeal of specialty coffee drinks has killed
All the songbirds in Eden. The music is piped in now. You
Cannot help but hear it, wherever fine products are sold.

Formerly, there were well-attended lectures where erudite
Men could speak of the substratum of the psycho-physical
World as forever forming forms: clouds and the absence of clouds
As synonymous with the mind as dreams or bees. But we
Have culture now, and may put to rest the schizophrenic blues
And whites and darks and stars of heaven. We have these screens
We can carry in our pockets that shrink unwieldy rounds
To little squares. We have made progress. We need not care at all
If all the aliens on earth are crushed by falling skies.

Breathlessly Sinking
Clutter 194
Written 23 April, 2016

———— • ————

The boy in the man looked at the sky and dropped his eyes in
The clouds and not-clouds, as a boy might drop two stones in placid
Water: White. Blue. The two colors ply their way through the deeps,
Like warships tearing the waters into tatters. Maturity,
Or so it seems, has finally sunk to the bottom. Old
Men shuffle through the cold, dense fundament, pelted slowly
By slowly falling stones: Old. Men. But in the under-deep,
Beneath the fundament, the men in the mud lower their heads.
Maturity has no sky, it drowns in one dimension.

Having grown gills, and lidless eyes, insensitive to light,
But chemically receptive, the poet breathes in the cold
Flood, and senses blue-white sky as an inborn bliss: Bright. Night.

If you have listened, if you have read this far, I know you
Have a need for parable. Could it be that the sky is still
Real for you, still visible to something called an eye that
Follows gold light around a ceiling, so wonderfully
Different than the water's roof? Could it be that this gold
Of revolving fire still lights for you the fundament of speech,
And lets you revel in the unreal real? that the words that
Move the child inside the adult reveal the placid calm:
That not-surface, that you not-you, diving through bright white-blue.

In Bed with the Shutters Open
Clutter 195
Written 24 April, 2016

———— • ————

Of course it is not astronomically possible
For the moon to be full for three nights running, but tell that
To the psyche, which wakes the tortured body at three a.m.,
And races across the sky with the tattered clouds, journeying
Madly to anywhere but here. But here is where we are,
Moon-mad, but still, with an ocean of stillness that still goes churning
About in the midst of its depths, in a murderous blend
Of calm and wakefulness, intolerably glad. We feel that
We have reached an edge, beyond which we are free of trouble.

The tongue in our head says "It is not anatomically
Possible to be voiceless. At the very least, we might gesture,
Look up at the flying moon, lift up our hands and head, and weep."

But we will not do that. That would break the spell. We knew we
Had always needed this kind of stillness, where turbulence
Grows utterly, magically calm in the very throes
Of its pregnant lunacy, where the infant is still-born
In a cosmic, personless love, a god in the white stare
Of the moon, the here that is nowhere else but where we are,
The escape to bodiless bliss at last accomplished, the O
Of the mouth and the round of the moon now one, abundance
In the heart of poverty, and a silver fall through sleep.

On the Futility of Imitating Bird Calls

Clutter 196

Written 25 April, 2016

—————— • ——————

The eyes are not weapons, but they can cut, and on these mornings,
Dove-called into blue clarity, they cut through to the green realms
Of the Gardeners, whose wisdom guides my seeing. It is they
Who have instructed me in the points of these weapons, and shown
Me how to mix sight's steel with blood. They extract, from my visions
Of doves and morning skies, that elixir, which is the one known
Cure for a wasting death. A collective narcolepsy
Has put mankind to sleep, and most asleep when Mourning Doves call
Up the clarity of daylight, and conjure forth the spring.

The Gardeners whisper secrets too dark for the naive eyes:
"Art no longer conjures a truly transforming vision.
The sleepers will not allow it." My cutting points grow blind.

If, when the poet speaks, it is only to say "spring" and to
Trigger a deeper narcolepsy, should he care that
Only the Gardeners hear him? The loop flows smoothly from outer
To inner green, and the traffic of sleeping cities is
Destroyed. If only the visionary knows his vision,
He may sleep safely in the Gardeners' realm, singing what is
To those inhuman listeners, his critical daggers
Sheathed or blunted by the general narcotic. He knows that
The dead will not wake with only the magic of the dove's coo.

Imperious Understatement
Clutter 197
Written 26 April, 2016

———————— • ————————

The apologists for violence like to wave red flags
And shout things above corpses like: "They had an heroic
Disregard of Death!" But any child will tell you: "The leaf
Flags of trees, all piled in heaps in autumn, do not praise
Red in spring." "Any child …" that would be a euphemism
For the naive poet, who grows angry when saws make graves
Of living trees. And why? … his innocent regard for leaves.
To cry out from the forest wilderness of the self, to stick
To beliefs of floral kinship, is to gnaw a public gag.

The interior life of the dreamer is an alien
Hodge-podge, which the war's apologists call "surrealism" —
Though violence against green things murders imagination.

That every day dawns with saws and crying babies cannot deter
The poet's celebrations. He feels how sweetly the spring's
Soft breezes wield sunlight's knife to slice his heart to pieces.
His is an heroic disregard for death. He wears his shroud
Of leaves as a king wears coronation robes, his paroxysms
Of repressed delight kept secret. He whispers: "The world is loud.
Why should I shout to compete with violent saws. More pieces
Of my soul are killed each spring, and all these sonnetizing
Solipsisms seem selfish ways to make my anguish heard."

Enlightened Buzz
Clutter 198
Written 27 April, 2016

———————— • ————————

What is the purpose of all these words, dumping their great loads
Of gravel on the roof, breaking your sleep, rattling your torpid
Skull? Rain. You believe in the miracle of reading as a fly
Believes in the sky when the sun returns. It is something
That happens without your participation: a fable
Of blue crystals buzzing with other flies, crystals that ping
Off each other as they whiffle through space, your compound eyes
Seeing only segmentations, and never the fervid
Composite, never the verse that expands as it is told.

I know you could murder me with the word "entertainment,"
The entire miracle of god and Evolution disabled
By that crippled form of amused and fawning discontent.

The skeletons of songbirds, their flesh devoured by flies,
In mid-song, in mid-air, are fiercely granulated to
Petrified maggots, whose bodies, like gravel, pepper the brow
Of the skull, the heavy brow, thickened by buying a culture
Arranged for troglodytes. When the poet is mad, his babble
Becomes unfun. You believe in fun. You believe its manure
Can cure you, your brain the nesting site for flies, your beetle brow
Teaming with scatophagic desires. These words are for you,
Yet not for you. They come to startle you with insect light.

Feline Migration
Clutter 199
Written 28 April, 2016

Decoupled from exterior sensory stimuli,
The brain takes these repeated cross-continental journeys,
Each time stopping mid-way at a grey house to feed a grey
Cat. The skies are always grey. And each time the belly grips
In fear: Could the animal have been neglected for far
Too long? This terrible malaise, which keeps hinting that these trips
Have no symbolic value, and that the brain must simply fade
To grey, when the senses are turned off, awakes beyond sleep,
And haunts the day. When the symbols die, why bother to ask why?

Catnip (*Nepata cataria*) is a perennial
That cats seek solely to indulge in a chemical pleasure.
They chew the downy leaves, stare at space, perform "head over' rolls.

This rolling behavior is also seen in estrous females,
During so-called "normal" sexual displays. One reads, one hears.
The words spawn irresistible odors. One turns off the world.
But the Eros of attraction just grows stronger. One opens
The door to the house and prays, prays that the cat is still there,
That the cat is well, that the cat is rolling over on
The floor, that one might unite with the cat as its stare grows bold,
Even though nothing at all is there to see. Without that stare,
One knows that each trip is a meaningless, grey traversal.

Mundane Pain
Clutter 200
Written 29 April, 2016

———— • ————

My dad died this morning, a springtime surprise — late April.
Here, it's a beautiful, sunny day. But half a continent
Away, in the mountains, where his body is now only
An object for professional processing, winter coughs
Up its last gasps of snow. You can't really talk about grief.
It's just an ordinary day. You can't really say enough
About what is. My daughter has a daughter in her belly.
My brother's wife is having cancer surgery. The spent
Blooms of the roses are ousted by the new — late April.

In writing poetry, as in any path to Nowhere,
There are procedures that must be followed. We have only
To put one word after another, a dead march for deaf ears.

Late April. He was very old, my dad. It should not have come
As a shock. But Death makes the imperceptible explosive,
And in the wake of its percussion, a dirty silence
Rots. It's just an ordinary day — on the coast: bright sun,
In the mountains: snow. There are forms to sign, so the body
Can be disposed of. I must sign them. I am the eldest son.
But I am still so unaccustomed to this soiled silence
That will never be polished by his voice again, that will not live
On ordinary days, where new blooms bloom among spent ones.

Flotsam
Clutter 201
Written 30 April, 2016

As any obstetrician can tell you, the first twenty-four
Hours are critical for a premature infant, and the same
Is true for the son after the death of his father. Will
The fragile being habituate to this new, harsher
Environment? Will the underdeveloped lungs be able
To breathe? In this Bardo state, known as "the in-between," the seer
Without a body reads sentences of fire in the dark —all
The portentous words derived from dream-texts, whose fame
Is culled from obscurity. Just what are these burning words for?

Without light, or with only the light of their own cremation,
It is difficult to decode the phrases. It is a fall,
Seemingly endless and pointless, through breathless conflagration.

In the artificial paradise of the poem, one
Sees the spirit clearly, but the message does not translate
To the brilliant, but mundane light of day. The father flies
Like a spark into the night, and the son is left with only
The memory of flame, an immaturity that calls
For the son —so much himself like kindling — to see, to read,
To speak the messages differently. Beyond all daylight
Meaning, a film of ashes flows along the blood-stream, where spates
Of grief, from ordinary words, become illumination.

The Brightest Light of Genius
Clutter 202
Written 1 May, 2016

———————— • ————————

Old midwives know a baby chooses the time of its birth,
But by a mysterious process of volition that
Seems also to involve the intellect of stars. A reverse
De-volitional process occurs at the time of death, where
Time itself — with an intellect more acute than that of stars —
Chooses. My father kept being chosen and chosen, unaware
That his brain was choosing less and less. His forgetfulness
Became the intellect of Time, searching and searching for that
Perfect moment of departure, when his body could leave Earth.

Breathe through one nostril as if it were the other, the other
As if it were its twin. Where the breath crosses, there is a center,
A blue light in the head, where the choices of Time appear.

Here is the sleep that my father awakened to find stealing
The last of his memories away, the last of his body's
Breath. And now I see this brilliance in my head. It steals all
Sleep from me when I most crave it. If this is grief, then grief
Thinks like a person, a person who is absent, and yet stares
As a single, unblinking presence, whose one fierce light leaves
Its harrowed, sleepless victim wakeful in deepest night, yet evolves
As the ultimate fire of NO CHOICE. My father's body
Burns in this intellect, whose thoughts now think without thinking.

See, Saw
Clutter 203
Written 2 May, 2016

In these excruciatingly sleepless nights following
The death of my father, the eyes, staring with the boiled red
Rapaciousness of a wolf's, without any thought or pity,
Search the blank wilderness of space for words. This is natural,
Nature's reminder that grief is as much a part of life
As joy — which is what his smile taught me: Joy in the face of all
Catastrophe, a jumping, canine happiness just to be.
If you had seen him dance, or drive a nail, or play a hand
Of cards, or tease a child to laughter, you would have crowned him king.

You would have said that a boyhood of poverty, a war,
A long marriage, a fierce faith in the gifts of everyday life,
And the practice of ordinary decencies, deserved more.

But more of what … ? more forgetfulness? more helplessness in
The grip of extreme senescence? more of the breathless need
To speak the repeated, repeated words? The glad wilderness
Has taken back its own. This is natural. But so is sleep,
And so is this predator's staring into grief, this canine,
Joyous red in the boiled eyes, this wild rapacious leap
Into 4 a.m. blankness, this loss of faith in the mindless
Desert of silence, which swallows the words before they speak,
And leaves the heart adrift in this grand void that made, then took him.

Ashen Renewal
Clutter 204
Written 3 May, 2016

——————— • ———————

As a boy, when I would return to these storied Black Hills
To summer with grandparents, my pulse would quicken as the scent
Of pines infused my breath. The trees pressed near to the road, their
Closely packed trunks and boughs flowing by with the speed of the car,
And me always wanting to stop, and go *in* there, and be
Swallowed by the wild. Now, for miles and miles the hills are charred,
And the greens that my father's father inhaled and trusted, wear
The cindery vesture of fire. Yes, there are hurts that rend
The body and hurts that rend the soul. But what have these fires killed?

I return to inter my father's ashes. The acres
Of shadow skeletons that once were trees flow silently
By the car, scarring the hillsides with their crippled gestures.

My father was very, very old. And I am no longer
Young. The ashes, like winter snows, are growing deeper, wafting
About the May green of the mountains, but only with these
Metaphorical drifts that no one else can breathe, but me.
I once believed that grief would have more bite, its teeth,
Like those of a predator, sudden and tearing, not like these
Relics, which will stand for generations, bleak testimony
To another kind of feeling: silent, persistent, delving,
Full of wonder, as if its darker spring would bloom forever.

Trained and Untrained
Clutter 205
Written 4 May, 2016

———————— • ————————

Meek Speak and Mealy Talk, in a sudden, enormous
Acceleration, erotically seek each other
In the post-mortem Sargasso of oppositional
Flesh. Now, they can swim, spin, dive, in all directions through the
more
Than orgasmic element, and the old stodgy, bugaboos
Of senescence, forgetfulness, and feeble frustration, are,
In successive bursts of speed, defeated. All touches all,
As the mortal enemies of human nature, the other
To the One, cleave together, free in love at last.

This coital celebration of the ego and the spirit —
How inexhaustibly free it must be! And you, who
Grieve now, because the flesh is ashes, must bear witness to it.

You bear witness to it in the depths of a dream. You wake
From the spinning oval to a 2 a.m. dark, and look
At the numbers on the digital clock, and know, you just know,
That your long-dead mother and just-dead father have broken
Their headstones, and touch again in the passion that made you.
Still, at daylight, you will be compelled to repeat the old sin
Of weeping before strangers. At daylight, you will rise, and go
In the single direction that railroading Time allows, locked
To the track of convention, unable to say your say.

At Mount Rushmore
Clutter 206
Written 5 May, 2016

———————— • ————————

To speak of the arrangements of impersonal forces
That shape the all too personal human life is to leave
Unsaid the most crucial element. With dynamite, they
Blasted the rough portraits from the granite. Then workers by
The hundreds swarmed over the fractured mountain with jackhammers
To refine a human myth of greatness. The faces derived
From granite emerged, the awesome human agency engraved
For ages on impersonal Nature. Sunset. The greens
Of the pines bleed blue, a blue night's sable velvet staunches.

Time could not break my father with one blow, but with colossal,
Impersonal forces, it chiseled him to myth, these words formed
From once living flesh, making the trivial immortal.

To speak of the arrangements of impersonal forces
That shape our stories is to omit the crucial element:
Dream — the wished-for vapor of greatness, the broken breath of
Sentences, nearly incomprehensible, but subtly formed
Into a monument more adamant than granite. The unborn
Wait. A mistake has been made, years pass, and those worn
Accidents of Nature become an art blasted from love's
Hard labor. In the woods, at night, in ghostly, wooly garments,
A mountain goat lies bundled in slumber's deepest wilderness.

Pine Cones Made Fertile By Fire
Clutter 207
Written 6 May, 2016

———————————— • ————————————

The Ponderosa Pine in these mountains struggle to pull
Themselves out of granite hardship, their thin, straight columns seldom
Growing to any great bulk or stature, icy winters,
Short, hot, hail-battered summers, cyclonic rampages of wind,
Making them sparse and dwarfish. Yet as "forest," they are utterly
Magnificent. Then, when fire races through their stubborn clans, when
The bones of the steeps are strewn with their charred corpses, we are
No less impressed by the awful splendor of their deaths, their grim
Return to green ubiquity, and their love of the tranquil.

Amazing to think that my kin lie buried among them,
People as tough as they are, both in life and in death, the trees
With untiring calm quieting their histories of mayhem.

Amazing to sit in their ragged morning shadows, and see
The generality called "forest" become particular
Trees: women with warmth and passion, and men of violent temper,
And all with a lust for laughter. Amazing to see how death
Has blended their various, knobby eccentricities
Into one magnificent and enduring being — the breath
Of labored struggle become the breath of peace. Who they once were
Is what this place now is; a granite, wooded exemplar
Of life's weird knack for making forests great with stunted trees.

On Remembering the Sound of the Wind Through Mountain Valleys
Clutter 208
Written 7 May, 2016

•

The journey home does not have that same anticipatory
Glow as the journey out. Having traversed a continent,
And touched the farthest edge of adventure's elliptical —
Where we bury our dearest dead — to retrace the path that
Brought us such wonder and grief, seems dull. What can this reprise
Add to the first passage that could unfold deeper feelings? Yet,
There is, as in memory or dream, a strangeness as novel
As a zebra at tea with a rich widow in the distant
Mountains' stripes of late spring snow, which gleam through black
stands of pine trees.

We cannot call the journey of poetry a traversal
Of feeling by the crippled ghost of thought, though the beliefs
That feelings lend to thought do signal a weird reversal.

Both mountain and zebra strike one another, producing
A resonant chord. This is the first foray into that
"Tempest in a tea-cup" wherein the widow's symphony
Sounds. Sympathy/Symphony: as an illogical clashing
Of structure and emotion as sighs and insights, as earth breeze
And Death's great vacuum. First, ghosts startle us through journeying,
And then subdue us by returning. And when poetry
Speaks in this way, depth hollows the rich widow's cup. That
Is its wonder. This is its grief: That our dead must keep speaking.

A Goading Little Treatise on the Phenomenon of Continual Harassment

Clutter 209

Written 8 May, 2016

In the hours and hours it takes to cross these peopleless landscapes,
Where the sage-chaparral of the immense valley floors flee
With a sudden ruggedness to mountain austerities,
Snow-swept, even in late spring, one discovers isolation's
Deeper secrets. Even the misanthrope, fleeing the city,
Sick of the human disease, when he sees some road, its sanguine
Dust snaking the distance, he thinks of the hermit's daily
Activities: gathering sagebrush fuel, collecting honey,
Scooping drowned mice and geckos from the well, and he escapes …

He escapes into the heart of human loneliness, and he
Feels this symptom of his own disease, this noisy city,
Brooding in his pulse, as a distant chimera of peace.

And the hermit, alone, near a twittering desert wren,
As he sips sage-coffee, and recalls last night's huge stars,
Imagines that someone lonelier watches him, some noisier double,
Speeding away in the distance, and stealing the blue of his
Silence. And the smoke of this sadness rises from his coffee,
A sadness tinctured with anger and with grief. 'What is the cause,'
He thinks, 'of this disturbance? There is no one to trouble
My peace for miles and miles. There is no one around to care.
There is only this incessantly irritating wren.'

Internment

Clutter 210

Written 9 May, 2016

———— • ————

The grammars that admit us afresh into another's past
Are based upon elaborately structured arrangements
Of tastes and smells. The sour taste of gooseberries, and boys in
The woods, eating them from the bush, then, seeing who could whistle
First. One of these boys is my father, and like the gooseberry
Whistle, I do not yet exist. This poem does not exist. All
That exists is the structured arrangement — the ghosts hidden
In ghost olfactories, ghost mouths, awaiting inducements —
Like these words — to resurrect them from the non-existent past.

In those days a woman might birth a stillborn, and her husband
Would take the baby into the woods, and dispose of the body,
So that the coyotes could not get it: blood, pine, earth — a complex
scent.

Is it the stillborn's sleep that arranges the structure for this
Memory? My father, the child, hearing about this brother
Later, as the one who could not exist, as the remembered
Sadness or the missed joy, the sleeper's dream of apocalypse,
Awakening the son, in another time, this sour berry,
Puckering his breath and mouth with words? This is the most lost past,
Returning as the abortion's sad revenge. Last night, a weird
Dream shook my sleep awake, a cloud of roiling dust, that covered
The whole earth, and buried me, destroying all safe distance.

The Face in the Stone
Clutter 211
Written 10 May, 2016

———————— • ————————

The culture is swiftly evolving a type of Human
Being adapted only to noise and speed, the depth cue, known
As "movement parallax," wherein near objects rapidly
Zip by, and distant ones crawl backwards, has been murdered.
Near objects blur and distant ones disappear. There is no
Depth. Yet when a loved one dies, your life reverts. You are cured
Swiftly and irrevocably of the need for noise and speed.
The old movement parallax returns, only to be slowed,
And then, grindingly stopped. You are a mutant form of human.

Depth is your element, and you turn inward, where everything
Is suspended in total stillness. The one who has died grows
A form from shattered glass, clear, in an intimate glistening.

If any movement occurs, it is like the too slow or too
Fast rotation of multifaceted fragmentations, each
Like the distant stars, its own illumination. This — the face
Of the deceased — is simultaneously recalled through layers
Of crystallized Time: a boy on a pony, a half-grown
Youth in uniform, a young man in a wedding picture,
A father playing with his laughing children, an old man braced
Unsteadily by a nurse — each image a blended calm, each
Equally loved and lamented, each quiet as a statue.

After

Clutter 212

Written 11 May, 2016

The memories in my father's brain absconded long before
He died, but some of them found refuge in a scrapbook, where
I find this photo of his grandfather's dug-out cabin,
A geewhoppered squatage, capping a hole in the prairie.
A hand-written note by my great-aunt says that there were eight
Children in that hovel, a ninth in the tired, fertile belly
Of my great-great grandmother, a woman so lonely, that when
She heard a wagon a mile away, she would run to where
She might see its dust-trail rise … the dust settling as before.

Living as I do in a city a century of time
And a world of distance later, I know that far-away
Feeling of solitude, that child in the womb who cannot cry.

In that solitude, material manifestation
Disappears, and bliss ensues. But this bliss is temporary,
And when asked "How is it made abiding?," the sage, the unborn
Child, wrapped in silence, nevertheless is able to reply:
"By questioning each preconception." No woman with eight
Children, no squalid cabin, no passing wagon, no dust-grimed
Passage of Time through the lonely prairie, there is only the unborn
Witness of the page, the picture fading in its plastic sleeve,
The bliss in the wake of a sadness deprived of attention.

Fresh Air
Clutter 213
Written 12 May, 2016

——————— • ———————

The variety of leaf-shapes in a wall of untamed,
Unpruned, sun-dazzled foliage is exceeded only by
Its multitudes of light and shadow populations.
These cities of photosynthesizers cast saint-army
Swirlings of plant volatiles, which imbue our desperate lungs
With the shared elixir of life. Blood is saturated by
The breath of unseen saviors — my blood, your blood — while our children
Stare at pixilated screens. When the pharmaceutical lie
Negates the elixir, the abreaction kills the brain.

I have decided to become the Mohammed of flowers,
Specifically, on this bright morning, these geraniums,
Crimson, like the blood — your blood, my blood — with the Sun's one power.

I have decided to be the Elixir's Prophet, and to
Conquer the media acolytes with words that cannot be
Made into icons for the blind. Simple as blood — my blood, your
Blood, our blood — , I speak as A Host of Angels, my speaking
Inaudible to the infidels, and yet its tongue
Of crimson, tongue of flame, is a volatile blazing
Of invisible truth, a quiet truth in the great, white roar
Of deception. I am the scripture of the breeze-twirled leaves,
And of the simple blood-hued flower. I am truth's Word renewed.

Upon Becoming
Impervious To Persuasion
Clutter 214
Written 13 May, 2016

————————— • —————————

Certain days, said to be unlucky, or "inauspicious,"
To use another culture's terminology, seem to
Be as serenely blue as luck would have it, and the rants
Of politicians and advertisers, the first of whom
Dissipate and the second ignite all hope, slide as blandly
Through ears and head as they ever have. Yet something sharp caroms
Jaggedly around both brain and day, the calm, blue expanse
Torn raggedly by clouds. The surfaces are disturbed, cut through
To reveal a depth, an awful No-thing without a surface.

When I say awful, I mean "full of awe," or to refer
To another terminology, so explosively
Torn by "bliss" that things suddenly are not what they once were.

Last night, just after midnight, the moon set in the west. It
Had forged its shape into a yellow weapon, wielded by
That stark entity named Time. I dreamt, as I often do, of
The infinite sea, the water wounded again and again
By light, its surfaces disturbed. What terminology
Could adequately state my awe? When I awoke again,
There was this day, drifting about as blue serenity, love's
Surface sliding by my ragged sight, and with its sunlight
Saying: "You are blessed. No rant can wound your sinking spirit."

After Interring My Father's Ashes in the Veteran's Cemetery
Clutter 215
Written 14 May, 2016

———————— • ————————

In the north of this land, there is a small, bronze plaque engraved
With the image of a helmet in commemoration of
A past war, and further north, across the border, another
Plaque, with a different martial image, communes with it.
This pair's geophysical connection is sensed only
In dreams. Both plaques lie nearly buried in the earth, where it
Would be impossible to see them, were it not for their
Morbid emanations. Just those who have lately lost a loved
One have this dream. The objects are markers for psychic graves.

By harnessing the charge of expectancy or the E-wave
In the brain, it is possible to extend thought-energy,
And control flesh machines. This is called a cultural key change.

The tiny, waking volitional mind will move like a blind worm
Along Ley lines connecting the memories of war dead,
And, just as sensation still throbs through amputated limbs, we —
The temporary survivors of the violence — will feel
The presence of our dead as vibrations, which shake the fleshy
Body. Then, the purpose of these half-buried memorials
Will become clear: That we may share the sacrifice, that we
May bear the guilt and exultation of battles whose red
Letters still write their histories in dreams — that we may mourn.

How to Fill the Empty Day
with More Emptiness
Clutter 216

Written 15 May, 2016

———— • ————

To the lay seeker, that is, one not accursed by the drunkenness
Of flower empathy or dream infestation or by
Certain psychic debilitations caused by bird twitter
Or fly buzz or even by a neighbor's barking
Dog, Sunday morning sun is but a bubble of leisure
In which he may become the prey of another's hustling
Self-interest, instead of they of his. The trick is to fritter
Away one's time as if time had no more value than the cry
Of a crow fading in blue air: that trick called *poesis*.

Putting all vibrating issues aside, as say the play
Of air in the babbler's vocal chords, the idle career
Of the poet spreads a blue virulence through the blue day.

The sky's pervasiveness is his métier. The lay seeker,
However, knows the technology exists, wherein 'smart"
Devices may be programmed to repeat/repeat every
Conceivable form of poetry. The accursed voice is no
Longer a viable virus. The disease has been cured.
So now the diseased one's symptoms are only the blow
Of an algorithm's zephyr, performed more perfectly
By electronic winds. To the lay seeker, no beating heart
Need stir the tongue to make more blue this blur of Sunday air.

PHASE THREE

Another Man on the Dump
Clutter 612
Written 16 May, 2016

———————— • ————————

Multitudes of people crowd the skull in sleep, as if Time
Were the conflagration of a forest fire in which whole
Mountainsides of trees roared skyward in red tongues
Whose black words despoiled the blue morning with the billowing
Smoke of dreams. As one grows old, the techno-culture grows young,
And each day is like work in the factory of faux-green spring,
Its product the updated repeat of a delirium
Wherein complete strangers share a sexual arousal,
Not meant to elicit feelings, but to delete the mind.

Why should I care if poems are made by unconsecrated
Nano-machines, those ancient, secret rituals become
Impersonal hexes, far too publicly perpetrated?

My atavistic love-chants have grown mean, the once heroic
Music now un-wrapping the bling-bling of momentary
Titillations, which are enough … enough … provided they are
Incessantly repeated. I sit alone in the vast dump
Of old feelings, a Neolithic midden heap, whose noisome
Garbage uplifts its mountain as a giant toxic hump,
Inimical to progress. And yet there will be sorters
Of these discards, prognosticators of the past's worst follies,
Doomed bone collectors, condemned to pick through heaps of verbal
tics.

Another Angry Election Cycle
Clutter 512
Written 17 May, 2016

———————— • ————————

Among the exiles of the North, everyone allows their speech
To become degraded by the filth of personal anguish.
Whenever I have something immensely impersonal
To say, my speech grows tentative. The "I" thinks: 'What if I
Get it wrong? What if desire dishevels thought, and when I say
North, other exiles will think I mean geography, when I
Refer to those cold brain circuits containing hate's arsenal?'
In their prison of invisible rays, the exiles trudge through the mush
Of grey snow. They shout political slogans, while their brains freeze.

These weakling, volitionally blind ones grow loud with their
Recriminations. To hate, to blame others, this is their way
Of lauding freedom: Shoot to kill, when others cross our borders …

Build thick walls. For a long time now, I have been mixing blocks
Of cement out of the mush of words. One atop the other,
I stack them along my borders, and beyond these lines, I
Exile my desires. Yet I cannot control the weather.
Spring continues to intrude on winter. Green weeds invade
The cracks in my cement. The personal — piercing borders —
Breaks my exile, and recruits me once again in its blind
Army. I am the same as them. I too must hate The Other,
March in circles. I too must shout the slogan: "Death to thought!"

The Quiet Rant of
A Wounded, Sinking Spirit

Clutter 412

Written 18 May, 2016

——————— • ———————

On the mudflat of the estuary creek, the morning sun
Watches a lone cormorant grooming funereal feathers.
The bird's bright orange beak both an attribute of his body,
And of his reflection. An acacia tree, a few houses,
A green mountain, a morning sky look on. The surfaces
Rest, radiantly undisturbed. The purple mud rouses
Considerations of teeming micro-organisms, jittery
Generations of them, cycling as quick as a breath of air,
Fragment reflections, although the trembling cracklings gel as one.

Is it wrong to say that calm can be explosive, wrong to
Notice that the floating, flying fragments are also bright glass
Bits of imploded affect, the shards of a once-believed truth?

Is it wrong to see a little undertaker, his orange face
Tucked below the hump of his back, rubbing his black-gloved hands
Together in glee, all mourning, his inexhaustible
Commodity? Is it wrong to say that perceptions, because they
Vanish, can only reveal the surface of a process
That keeps on selling Death incessantly? Now, now I can say
That speech is a disturbance. It is Death's last breath that trembles
Its poetry, and leaves no resonance. Here, here the land
Is purple mud, where the dead slip swiftly through life's surface.

In Inquiry into the Anti-Identify of Post-Mortem Pre-Natal Existence

Clutter 312

Written 19 May, 2016

———————— • ————————

Life: a retrograde geriatrics' parade to the cradle
Of the grave, wherein the philosopher of the mundane
Makes lunar midnight from morning sun. In the future — which each
Hour grows more faint — jackhammers are breaking apart ancient
Cities to the knell of electronic church bells. Bird calls
Race through varieties of leaf-shapes, the dishevelment
Of avian music baffled through bafflements of leaves,
Some of which are heart-shaped, all of which are doused or enflamed
By drenching dark and light, none of which denote The Self …

"The Self" — an enigma, mostly defined by negatives,
Its fleshless flights and flashes blurred in the compound eyes of all
The flies of the Necropolis — a life that never lived.

Just how do the wombs of women become the tombs of men?
The philosopher of the fading flowers is obsessed by
Such mundane questions. He is who I am, but not the same,
Or else the same, but with a volatile difference. I seek
The truth in the leaf-twirled scriptures of bantering bird calls,
In that which is nebulous, and yet may still be named. He seeks
It in Time's burial processions. I seek the day in names.
He seeks the night in naming. In that terror of the I,
Which I call "me," He comforts with reverse annihilation.

A Nostalgia for Agitated Breath
Clutter 212
Written 20 May, 2016

———— • ————

In this once-definitive and now outdated book on
Imagery and healing, I read: "Our understanding of how
The brain functions has come from the study of damaged brains."
For seven years, I studied, with my own anguished limbic
Brain, my father's brain, as its empty spaces, like stretched dough, thinned,
And then tore into lesions with no remembrance, the wreck
That remained still warm with limbic affection. Now an insane
Calmness provokes me. He died three weeks ago. So? Why now
This relief? Because all that was piecemeal pain is completely gone.

The substrate is destroyed, the necrosis in the tissue
Has no host, and what remains is numbness. And yet when the wind
Shakes the trees, tearing new apertures for the sun to drop through …

I am reminded of how inextricably he remained
A part of Nature — not ever really being tamed. The boy in
The crude log hut with the hard dirt floor kept growing like the sod
Of the cabin's roof, a part of the living meadow reaching
Sunward, not quite content to be part of a house, and blend
Its wildness with domesticity. Perhaps he is growing
Still, though his brain is burned to ashes, and his son throws these odd
Words into the wind. Like wind, I thrash about as if — in
The throes of limbic violence — I might rouse a longed-for pain.

Dazzled Throwback
Clutter 112
Written 21 May, 2016

———————— • ————————

Certain times, certain places breed certain types of mutants.
In Nineteenth Century Europe, certain aberrations in
The genome produced an aboriginal return to sky
Obsession. Certain painters fetishized days like this one, when
Cloud gatherings and dispersals could not … could not … decide,
Which degree of light or half-light to impart. They fixed wind
On canvasses with pigment. They smeared on linen weave the cries
And silences of birds. They framed the freest exultations
Of water sprites. They trapped the frenzied human in light's trance.

I am not satisfied with the camera click that endeavors
To capture atmospheres in an instant, without the slow grind
Of a mastery that patiently spins seconds into hours.

I am not satisfied with temporal frenzy, with the quick
Cycloptic lens of No Man's eye, which seals eternity
In an instant's blink, destroying in that nick the leisure
Of a spirit fashioned of Time. I am not satisfied.
I long to stand enthralled before that Sybil, who defies
With motion, with stillness, all sudden capture, who makes Time
Pause or dance to feed an inexplicable need, whose stare
Slows hours to eras in mutant trance, all prods to hurry
Subsumed in clouds, my sight, no slave to clocks, the light's last addict.

Food For Thought
Clutter 012
Written 22 May, 2016

—————— • ——————

The ability to visualize is so crucial
To that ritual of rebirth known as "getting ready
For it." Billions of Human beings devouring billions of
Non-human beings, insect over insect — that is the vision.
Naturally it leads to a feeling of anonymity.
When this isolating sickness comes over me, I can
See my granddad in the woods burying a flour sack, his rough
Hands scraping a hole for his stillborn son. Now I am ready.
I know the grammatology of the past — its taste, its smell.

I obtain my potency from that anonymous relic's
Bones. The insects have stripped them so thoroughly that only
The memory remains — a taste, a smell, which can cure the sick.

The disposition to illness, or the rite by which demons
Conjure illness, has a name. It is called: "The Un-Ready,"
The premature or aborted stillborn, exposed too early
To the vision. One insect is as hungry as the next,
And as anonymous. If I imagine a baby
Buried in a flour sack, anonymously, why should that vex
The readers of this text or the ears that hear this poetry's
Stridulations? Fame cannot stick to the unborn baby's
Bones, nor words move humans consumed by inhuman demons.

The Phytotoxic Effects
of Swainsonine
Clutter 902
Written 23 May, 2016

———————— • ————————

Ambling hours, blue afternoons, breezes roaming without any
References to time, the circular, languid movements
Of shadows beneath the stunted vegetation of the
Chaparral, the mule deer and pronghorn venturing into
Open range to munch on locoweed, light in an animal
Stare, the vision shared with a distant poet, whose dreams roll through
This peopleless world like tumbleweed … in the city, the
Inauthentic, the unreal prevail, but here, words re-invent
A primal shamanic mask with timeless rituals of peace.

It may be that one's friend or spouse asks "Where have you been?"
And the pronghorn's or the mule deer's stare answers, the soul
Of the poet speechless, still grazing the desert inside him.

Perhaps you are puzzled. Why must I still wear the mask? Might
My invented spontaneity only disguise my
Citified compulsions, my words another form of
Cosmetic, designed to deceive the listener, hide the
Real? Like animals, I must camouflage myself with subtle
Movements and subtler colorations. I must confuse the
Predatory human, whose unreal, monster appetite loves
Time. It is the mask that guards my solitude, and lets the light
Conjure each blue afternoon into authentic dreams each night.

Tasseomancy
Clutter 802
Written 24 May, 2016

This most illuminated of sages tells us that the whole
Phenomenal world is entirely the product of that
Attribute of Mind which we call "waking." The Serengetis
Of this or that continent of thought teem with vast migrations
Of histories and landscapes, tea leaves from Ceylon, gathering
In the cracked cup of a moribund lord in his garden,
The Manor's upkeep paid by curious tourists, the heads of beasts'
Glass eyes, staring from paneled walls. Devotees marvel that
Wherever the sage walks, he is followed by animals.

Tame animals, wild animals, birds in the evening air,
Even fish in the green river, which winds near the walking
Path — they all follow, as though the sage's mind were their sole care.

If I tell you that there are silences hidden in these
Migratory distractions that are not produced by the waking
Mind, or by any phenomenon of the vanishing wild,
Or vision in a taxidermied eye, glassy with pain
Transfixed — you will ask, incredulous, "Why are you speaking
Words that cannot be heard, these useless vanities of the vain,
And throwing away your silence in wild sounds?" And here, I will
Answer, "I am not awake. Nor am I sleeping. My mouthings
Are in-volitionally produced, like Time read in tea leaves."

Passion
Clutter 702
Written 25 May, 2016

———— • ————

When I returned to the Black Hills after my father's passing,
I had to confront the question of the forest. Years of
Drought and the infestation of a certain beetle had turned
The pinegreen into dead-needle-russet, and fire had burned
Whole mountainsides to black. The miniature heaven that my
Mind maintained as nostalgia was killed by a vision that churned
In the gut, not the brain, a vision that I try to turn
Away from, but cannot. I have invested so much love
In the dying or the dead — my little heaven is burning.

Perhaps it has always been burning — this strange nostalgia for
Perishable fathers and forests. Perhaps these little mind
Forays are only ersatz models for something stranger.

I see it — Him — as a shadow behind this fire, a shadow
That *lights* this fire — a presence as featureless as a father's
Or a forest's ashes — this terrible arsonist, who
Has no face, no form, yet twists all faces in his own image.
He is the God of the sober poet, the masculine cry
That wakens the feminine muse, the words that hotly rampage
Through the gut to light the larger heaven of the heart. And you,
Who read this in your cool pine-shade, entranced by the fine weather,
You drowse, and cannot feel his breathing stirring the shadows.

A Granite Erratic Divides and Scrambles the Waters of a Stream
Clutter 602
Written 26 May, 2016

———————— • ————————

Let us consider hold-outs, a fitting meditation
For a shady spot bordering this creek — one of the last
Along the coast where Coho salmon and Steelhead trout still run.
No fish running today, but the stream does, sending light ripples,
Brighter than fish fins, down the valley's shaded snaking runnels.
So does the mind writhe, its dark streaming endearingly rippled
With flashes. Yet, on this calm afternoon, the thought of night comes,
A night of storms, of slashing tridents, a night where a flash
Might show an enduring face, as imposing as a mountain.

Grief — its stream of light-slashed turbulent tears grows hard, like
A last enamel round a sensitive root, a last white skull
With its last white tooth, a last hold-out from the stream of life.

Last night, I dreamed that a little door opened in one of those
Molars at the back of the mouth for some reason named "wisdom."
The tooth was a little house, empty, except for me, and some
Crude furniture, and this little photograph of family
On the wall — my grandmother seated with my father and uncles.
In the photo, she is still young, her eyes moist with the sheen
Of admiration, her smile bright with joy, and these four handsome
Men around her seem as enduring as mountains — her sons.
Like the passing stream, they flash, as I sit, in shade, growing old.

The Heart-Wrenching Conversion of Space and Speed to Noise and Silence
Clutter 502
Written 27 May, 2016

———————— • ————————

I stare out into space. Against an impenetrable
Green thicket, the white dot of a single gnat revolves. Heat
Begins telling the earth: "Burn this grass brown," and the squiggling
Mirage lines, which depict the lawn's unpitied agony,
Erode chemical rivulets through the physical brain.
These ask: "Does any of this matter?" There was a time when Meek
Speak and Mealy Talk raced off together, tightly entwining
Their vines of simultaneity around two griefs:
A mother's, a father's deaths. Now space goes white. A white gnat
twirls.

Explorers of these outer/inner regions know that any
One to one connection of sign to signified, wave to brain,
Is the speed of thought's betrayal of an unmoving grief.

From the thicket, suddenly, the stillness begins to swell
With the steady white noise of humming cicadas, the air
Growing ripe in its own quiet heat, as a fruit grows ripe
With its own plumping sweetness. The thin lines tangle, thicken,
And the spring day grows summery, the connection brain to pain
Blurring with an inexplicable ease. The vibrations
Of the cicadas grow swift in their self-abnegation, white
Life stirring white air, as here disperses into everywhere,
The departed voices languidly mating loud and still.

A Rough Ride to Nowhere
Clutter 402
Written 28 May, 2016

Among the few possessions that my father kept, while decades
And decades of possessions and memories utterly
Vanished, is this photograph of me on my grandfather's
Horse, Chief, a tan and white "paint," who has his head lowered in
The faded black and white snapshot, which captures his animal
Resentment, and my fear, although I am smiling. The grey sun
Has made everything grey, the background pines, my grandfather's
Tall, thin, overalled figure, my little U.S. Keds'-shod feet
Vainly reaching for the dangling stirrups — all in a fake gold frame.

Physicists talk of the "many instants interpretation"
Of time. Nothing moves, but dizzying numbers of pixel
Points fix their one-dimensional snapshots on the plenum.

What shifts is our perception of the stillness. That horse always
Did his best to rid himself of this pesky little greenhorn.
Chief bit me, stepped on me, kicked me, knocked me off with pine
limbs, scraped
Me off with tree trunks, bucked me into snowdrifts or into piles
Of pine needles, but my grandfather remained unruffled,
Just as he is in the picture, as if he knew that all
These action poses were only stills in a cosmos placed
In innumerable frames, but ready to be reborn
In any motionless moment that might be shuffled our way.

Before There Were Eyes to Gaze at Stars or Silence to Harbor the Word
Clutter 302
Written 29 May, 2016

These technological prostheses for memory remind
Us of those photos of loved ones where the retinas
Have caught the flash, and the gaze is turned a predatory
Red — the sweet people in our lives, especially the deceased,
Trading the charming or annoying eccentricities
Of their personalities for the generality
Of hunter and hunted: Nocturnal eyes in dreams, the wary
Green orbs of deer, and the fixed crimson ones of wolves, what was
Once pleasant reminiscence, now glaring from the depths of Time.

A revelation: Any attempt to re-assemble
The fragmented self by filming or framing is only
The camera's updated version of an age-old puzzle —

How to be the eat-or-be-eaten animal, yet slip free
Of the universal tragedy of death? A slippery
Problem indeed! O! even should these photographs be saved,
The faces in them will fade, unnamed. We will forget. We
Will be forgotten, and just this animal cycle of eat-
Be-eaten will wheel through a universal, primordial sleep —
Round eyes in a post-God space, where neither red nor green make
Any difference. In this interstice, rich with tragedy,
Those eyes that light the richest lights out-shine all memories.

Rounding Many Dark
Ciphers into One Bright One
Clutter 202
Written 30 May, 2016

You, or anyone, could, on a sunny holiday morning,
In late spring, half-try, and maybe half-succeed, in retreating
From this green realm of the senses, and this bee-buzz of thinking
That says "me," and by half-volitional, half-random gropings,
Discover a multiplicitous doubling and doubling,
Whereby the unborn and the dead — that strangest of coupling
Bodies without torsos — combine and recombine, amassing,
Almost as sound amasses in speech, or ease breeds ease in spring,
To give to no one the semblance of a form, to nothing, a being.

On a sunny holiday morning, the metal in mountains
Converses with the tiny iron boatmen who are sailing
In the blood. You, or anyone, might hear this conversation.

You, or anyone, might be defined by a process
Like electro-magnetism, the dead and the unborn,
Your very mortal parents and your immortal grandchildren,
With presences particular and loved, reduced to blood-born
Anguish or exultation. You might be anywhere doing,
Thinking nothing, when the late spring sun makes the morning warm
With ease. You might, with a little trying, or by even
Half-trying, discover the presence of a golden orb,
Where the me that is no one can find a luminous rest.

Vague Communion
Clutter 102
Written 31 May, 2016

Close up, the cliffs of this vast horseshoe bay are mottled gold, their
Crowns shagged with red and green vines. But as the gaze drifts further,
The blue-grey lavenders of the fog prevail, and only
The white churn of surf and the dark underlips of waves break
The ashen monotony. There and here so starkly vary,
But the precise point where they conflict is obscure. What remains
In this orphan solitude is the in-betweenness where sea
And beach choir a constant, wavering roar. Yet in this roar,
This whispering roar, the voices of our dead are weirdly snared.

A long dead, revered, and misinterpreted philosopher
Tells us that for art to exist, one thing is necessary:
Intoxication. An artificial heaven must occur —

A heaven of indefinable in-betweenness, where
Vivid color contrasts with nebulous blur, and the line
Between thin beach and vast sea, quick living and ashen dead,
Slips — wavering — through the body, and leaves us in breathless
Calm — though the sea still whispers its roar, and the dead still breathe
Into cavities of feeling vacated by the useless
Reason and the drunken senses. All that is calculated
And commodified is at last evaded, and from a fine,
Fine mist-interpretation comes something that is revered.

The Letter and
the Spirit of the Letter
Clutter 002
Written 1 June, 2016

———————— • ————————

Two juxtaposed, but un-synthesizable codes — code one,
The Real defies the image or the symbolic; code two, Syntax
Trumps vocabulary (though the reverse is commonly
Thought to be true). Today, I received a letter informing
Me that my mother's headstone has been destroyed, and replaced
By one where my father's name is shown on one side, and showing
On the other side, hers. When the weather is clear here, cloudy
Elsewhere, in space the two climates are juxtaposed. But the fact
Is, the two are one in Time — an obvious contradiction.

I am not the same person opening the letter as I
Am having viewed it. Some unreal boundary has been effaced,
And an imageless emotion is suddenly catalyzed.

This is a game of gold and silver, two distinct gratitudes
Refashioned by grief as a double torus whose inside
Feeling far exceeds its surface dimensions, a game the dead
Play with the living in the backwash of long-dissolved dreams.
The purpose of the game is revealed in a code, in the way
The landscape of the day is revealed by the sky. But it seems
No image in heaven, whether cloudy or clear overhead,
Could synthesize this massive weight inside, or tell me why
A little piece of paper could swell to such a magnitude.

Drunk Driver Weaving
Down the Road at Twilight
Clutter 991
Written 2 June, 2016

—————— • ——————

However bright the sun, its luminance pales when compared
To the grey memory of last night's dream, which I recall
With the same reluctance that a condemned man feels when he
Is dragged from his pre-dawn sleep to be hanged. I traveled
Through grey farm-country towns, my dead father driving a car
Without steering wheel, breaks, or accelerator. We rumble
By crumbling buildings set amidst fallow fields, and I see
Through the tall, Old-West-style windows, people at looms, where textiles
Of faded yellow are being mysteriously prepared.

The size of the buildings shows that these towns were once prosperous,
The wide fields green with bounty. Probably, too, some color
Other than grey graced the walls with some mood other than sadness.

One feels that one has seen all this before, but in a time when
The sky was full of noontide light, and happiness consumed
One with the most common intoxication, a youthful
Vitality, perhaps, so pervasive that it required no
Symbol to sustain it, a happiness like that ghost-car
With no human in control, a happiness that once rode
With the immortal living, and saw nothing in the passing tall
Windows, but the flash of colorful reflections. The looms
With their yellow shrouds were hidden, like the ghosts who wove them.

Return to Radio
Clutter 891
Written 3 June, 2016

———————— • ————————

We have tried, almost successfully, to kill all those people
Who, in their primitive savagery, have distributed
Mnemonic pegs through the landscape on which to string their stories.
Their words are the mythic sinews of a spirit-animal.
For them, time and space overlap and fuse. They accumulate
Flesh as surf and grass and rocks — the abstract made visible
For human contemplation. For us, landscapes have no stories.
Only people have stories: light people pixilated
And fleshless on flat screens, living on their YouTube channels.

My anger moves along the edge of these virtual realms,
Like an orphaned child running along a beach where great waves raise
White claws high into blue day, dislodging heaven's crystals.

Yes, these crystals sparkle all along the strand, but their jeweled
Brilliance is the least interesting thing about them, because
The child, even above the uncultured water roar, can hear
The crystals speaking. They are tuned into that spirit-channel,
Which broadcasts myths far deeper than those flashed by the light rays
On the flatland screens. Their stories tell of that Mother, who pulls
Her turquoise passion out of the green depths, her anger
Stealing the child's body, and drowning him, her diamond claws
Making wild sounds in his starved, baby ears, which soothe like star-
milk.

Airy Nothing

Clutter 791

Written 4 June, 2016

———————— • ————————

It is not as if we could ever find it again — silence —
As when a child, escaped from the metallic turbulence
Of parental expectations, and the poison of machine
Expectorations and intrusions — accidentally
Looks up, and sees in the slow, muggy overcast of day —
Which he is not the center of — the vast, calm ecstasy
Of a Person without a career. The constant low-grade spleen
Of suppressed adult tantrums sighs into atmospheres where chance
Is not mischance, but the beauty of subdued luminance.

To find such silence, we would have to know that we had lost
It, that something existed with its own center, that the day's
Career was not an ambition, but a fullness without cost.

There would perhaps be something — not found, because not looked
for — ,
Something as accidental as the weather, something more
Surreal than the neurotic imagination's metallic
Roar — a crystal container perhaps, like a champagne flute,
Wherein a golden newness bubbles through the quiet day,
Each bubble rising through an atmosphere made convolute
By a slow under and over rolling of vapor. The sick
Repetitive click of parental talk would cease to matter,
And spheres of air would dissolve that poisoned, metallic core.

Out to Pasture
Clutter 691
Written 5 June, 2016

———————— • ————————

You better not tell your spouse, boss or friend about your sickness,
Or let on that these tangled plant walls, like a skin of green
Sunlight, bellow orders at you as you sit in your garden.
Have you been near a large bovine? — the heaviness, the presence
Of a life that eats green, sleeps green, collects sunlight as you
Might collect memories? Strength lives in this beast, two-thousand
Pounds of it, coiled in a human, inhuman breath, the sun,
No longer an alien distance, but a food, a dream-
Body heavier than your meat body, a centering rest.

You look like everyone else. But inside, The Green is chanting:
"We are speaking. We are speaking. The Green Tribes call and call
you.
The Nations of animal density are lowly lowing …"

I want to speak directly to you now on the dangers
Of irony and direct speaking, the critical dangers
Of the general narcotic, the busy business sleep
That does not dream, and yet hallucinates. My animal
Has directed me to express this secret, and only you,
You, may hear it, not your spouse, boss, friend, not anyone at all,
Only the sick, the very happy sick, the sunlit beast,
Who feeds on sunlight. I want to tell you: "There is no danger.
There is only this milky density that breathes away your cares."

News Following the First Silver Thread
of Our Mother's Broken Wedding Ring
Clutter 591
Written 6 June, 2016

———————— • ————————

Meteor strike flattens forests in Siberia. The seas
Are choked to death by plastic bottles. War, famine, drought kill
Millions, make more millions refugees. National elections —
Become publicity stunts — stir mobs to violent furor.
World markets teeter towards disaster. Yet, the Self of selves
Remains serene in the turmoil, the poet's only care
Consumed by the subtle — that moon so close to the gross sun's
Light as to scarcely be visible, an edge of internal
Opal, waxing her curve towards what is revelatory.

But what is revelatory? … auroral arches rainbowed
Round the thin grin of a first phase moon? … the more than terrible
Discovery that the mask has used the spirit's face as food?

Even in the most exhaustive Encyclopedia of
Catastrophic Phenomena, this single obscure entry
Demands to be read. It is the poet's obsession, the pursuit
Of the ephemeral in the monstrous lair of the gross.
Every word born kills its mother in childbirth. Every child's
Orphaned cry becomes a paean of grief to that thin ghost
Of a premature moon. She rises at dawn, and is subdued
At sunset. She dies, and leaves no trace. Except that her tiny
Ray, by its very elliptical thinness, shows us love.

Growing Up
Clutter 491
Written 7 June, 2016

———————— • ————————

Once, as a boy, I was knocked out playing ball, and when I
Woke up, I was being stared at by an eye of sky, ringed by
A ring of playmates. I know that biography has no meaning,
Unless it vibrates with a metaphorical resonance,
But today, when I look at the sky, it is still looking
Back — down — on a boy who is just emerging from a trance.
A night fog is unraveling to reveal these deepening
Blues. Clarities ringed by ambiguities, my stunned I,
And that higher eye, roaming about the day's soft, breezy sighs.

There is a certain repulsion that a child feels towards people
Who are old, while the old find children so mesmerizing.
What insight was compacted in that punishing projectile?

Our ancestors are not the old and the dead, but the children
We once were, or the one child, struck on the head, and released
To the sky, where an ever-new, ever-changing Ancient
Watches events unfold. Biography does have a meaning,
But not that meaning matured in an old man's mind, the meaning
That says the personal I exists as a sigh's recounting
Of an ancient myth that hints that chance events are Heaven sent.
This is the Sender's breath within our breath, the insight's breeze
That stirs blurred whites around clear blues, and makes a boy a man.

Homeless at the Beach
Clutter 391
Written 8 June, 2016

People mincing around in the latest shoe fashions are
Doing what they can to trample the primal, oceanic
Mind, that mind with two voices, one for social interaction —
i.e. — piffle about shoes — and one an echo-locator
For submerged, ancestral emotions. In the commodity
World, all is surface, nothing is submerged. In the water
World of grief and tears and dreams, the need for navigation
Supersedes the need for ostentation, and the cry "Look! Look!"
Gives way to the whisper "Listen. Listen. Hear the poet's curse."

In the final stages of the soul's disease, everything can
Be reduced to causality, i.e., the causality
Of money — death by drowning in necessity's ocean.

To believe that we may walk in the shoes of The Elect,
That our need to buy is God's need to sell, and that this water
That we suck through gills is air, is to surrender our deeper
Destinies to the incidental: the prophet as huckster,
Stirring the fundament's muck into murky clouds. To believe
In the incidental is to drown. Still, what most matters
Is not our drowning, but our believing. On that final shore,
Where Tsunamis have ravaged the condominiums, poor
Barefoot bums rummage the wreckage for words. These are our poets.

In a Wooded Cemetery Where Time Has Erased the Names on the Headstones

Clutter 291

Written 9 June, 2016

———————— • ————————

A soft afternoon with a bird chattering in the distance —
What we would call his "instinct," the song that means nothing at all
To outsiders, but which genetically repeats in
Him, like the shape of his wing or the color of his feathers,
A song whose profundity comes as easy as this summer
Weather, a song that carries us into a dreamier,
Inhuman space, where we can forget, in its repetitions,
The anxiety of the outsider, the perpetual
Human need for some meaning to defend against happenstance.

The bird's voice fades, and the prodigal returns, his inner
Bird chirping in a dialect that carves out a greener
Summer, where there are no distances, and no outsiders.

The days are so long now that the epithet "late" graces
The afternoon for hours and hours, the bird's chirping or silence,
Shuffling — with equal indifference, equal ineptitude —
Through the rise and the fall of green branches and blue shadows.
All our defeated human need for meaning grows sleepier,
The outsider tucked inward as the shape of the day's glow
Folds round his body like wings of feathery solitude,
Wings of millennial colors, whose songs make silence silent,
And whose silence eases towards night, leaving no earthly traces.

Deep in the Red
of Uneconomic Growth
Clutter 191
Written 10 June, 2016

————————— • —————————

Any one of these vivid clusters of geranium
Blossoms could be obliterated from sight by the palm
Of an interceding hand. But, blown up to the proportion
Of a proscenium, even the dullest spectator will see
Soft continents of scarlet rivers, scarlet valleys, withered
Or plumping scarlet mountain ranges. Enormous striped bees
Collect golden powder from great orbicular stamen
Trees, and even the dullest spectator may find a vast realm
Whose profusions kill his natural habits of perception.

For more than a century, even the dullest spectators
Of movies have grown bored by such prodigies, habituated,
As they have been, to artifice. What could poor Nature offer?

Perhaps it is time to stop looking at flowers and begin
To look at looking. Inside is a continent of feeling
That — palm-sized or sky-sized — remains unaffected by any
Manipulation of scale. This is the commodity self,
Who continues growing his colorless desert of boredom, red
Drained to grey as his virtual treks become perpetual
Denaturings of what used to be felt as ecstasy.
He does not know how the artificial world kills seeing
By this relentless, predictable penchant for expansion.

The Stockbroker Invests in the Boredom Future's Market

Clutter 091

Written 11 June, 2016

———————— • ————————

How very difficult it is to grasp the acolyte's
Experience of the desert when the commodity
Arcade is pulsed directly through the brain with these clever
Wireless technologies, the wind sloping the sand into
Asymmetrically-shaped dunes — barchan, longitudinal,
Parabolic or transverse forms slithering snake-like through
The hermit's mind, and making slow inroads into senses bored
By the empty too-muchness of it all — Saint Anthony
In suburbia, hallucinating behind open eyes.

The hermit says: "To live the ascetic life of the soul
Among the shopping suburbanites is to be the lone fool
Amidst swarms of foolery. The desert provides for all."

Yes, there is a state in life uninterrupted even by
Death or by our present mania for buying-and-selling-
Euphoria. This is true, but only provisionally
True. In the desert, each moment, each sand grain, is the same,
But through prolonged treks of inattention, they start to reveal
Their simple historical forms: these poems of the insane
Suburban Anthony, who seeks the sacred aridity
Of a scripture devoid of any semblance of buying
Or selling, who seeks what is most impossible to find.

A Ghost Hemorrhaging Sanguine Emotions from the Mouth
Clutter 981
Written 12 June, 2016

———————— • ————————

The insides of eyelids, clown noses, roses, lips, cherries,
The heads of certain finches, the flaming door to hell,
The eyes of weasels glowing in a henhouse, poppies, soldier's
Wounds — the red things, and the words that scar like red, a father's
Words to his son: "Unless you are born with a silver
Spoon in your mouth, you've got to work every day of your
Life for someone else. You might hate it. But that doesn't matter.
You may as well get used to it." If words could have a smell,
Smell a color, color a sound, you know what these would be —

Red. And knowing this, one might wish one's fate to be that of
An animal — that weasel perhaps, who wants his hunger
Appeased by fat with feathers, who steals what he needs of love.

That the apotheosis of the tongue — the red tongue — might speak
In parables the color of chicken blood, that the words of
Cynical fathers might become the words of distraught poets,
That the insides of eyelids might flash red revelations
In letters fifty-years high ... Returned from the dead, my father
Appears in a vision. He is mouthing urgent instructions
That the bloodclots in his brain have muffled to scarlet silence,
The air in his throat making aspirated clicks. The love
He chokes on is so much like regret, it finally makes him bleed.

Epic Fragment
Clutter 881
Written 13 June, 2016

———————— • ————————

Already in the Epic of Gilgamesh, the City
Is depicted as a locus of corruption, and the wild
A place of untamed purity. Its incipit "He who
Saw deeper," tells in cuneiform logographs the story
Of how that corruption purifies itself. In order
To unearth the secret of Death's ubiquitous necessity,
We must transcend The Language of the City, and return to
The wild life inside poetic forms, where the addict is killed,
So that the King may be glorious in his humility.

When the City's King and the untamed one fight outside the bridal
Chamber, the untamed one wins. But later, his strength falters.
He sickens, dies, his voice that of a nightmare's animal.

He disappears at daylight, the paralysis of sleep
Supplanted by the frenzy of civilized debauchery.
But I tell you, I must tell you, I have seen that animal —
That almost human purity — almost speaking. I have been
Him in the wilder woods of words. I have entered the bridal
Chamber, not as groom, but as the uncouth, yet chaste champion
Of innocence. I know that you will feast upon your denials,
And praise them, as you praise sick ways of speaking. I know my pleas
Will only madden you, though I am He who sees the deep.

Bio-luminescent Birthday
Clutter 781
Written 14 June, 2016

—————— • ——————

At this hour sixty-seven years ago, a frightened young
Woman gave birth to a son too premature to breathe on
His own. The nascent consciousness of the non-breather delves
A sub-sea trench of dismal possibilities, a warm
Seepage of toxic chemicals invading his blood. This one
Somehow jumps mortality's timeline to escape harm,
And henceforth believes miracles alone, and not his own will,
Can save him. Often he re-visits this lightless canyon,
This place of pressure and depth, where he lives without lungs.

On the timeline, one travels a chronic, inescapable
Groove from infancy to senescence, digging a canyon
Of deeper darkness and frustration for the willful self.

But was the mother right to be afraid? The child was marked
From his first breathless instant for Death, and yet he somehow
Jumped the groove, and was gathered into timeless translucency.
If you squint through these aligned letters, you might glimpse this
Jellified creature, who has squiggled through a lesion
In Time to float in a bubble vivarium of bliss.
A globster, all tentacles, scuttling the depths of poetry,
When you read *his* words, you feel *your* soul, which speaks through the
hollow
Brilliance of a body that lights its own light through the dark.

Remorse

Clutter 681

Written 15 June, 2016

—————————— • ——————————

As a child, one of my ex-wives gathered round stones from the shores
Of Lake Michigan, and stored them in boxes under her
Bed. She painted cartoon faces on the stones. No child dare
Dangle foot or hand from the edge of the bed for fear that the
Terrible monster lurking there might cruelly snatch her life
Away. The dark is always grinding jagged teeth. No doubt, the
Calmness of stones, their impregnable, enduring nature,
Served as a defense against the monster, and the even worse
Fear of the monster, though the stones themselves have certainly
suffered.

The stones were hatched from soul-fire, grew into mountains, lost their
Footing, fell victims to the work of water, felt their sharp hides
Ground smooth by rounding forces, and emerged, immune from fear …

Or had they? For didn't those painted cartoon faces, for all
Their garish, toothy grins, say otherwise? That the monster's
Body had been divided, and worked by the imagination
Of a child, did not in any way curtail its potency,
Because the stony bites of a past of minutes, of ex-wives,
Of little nips of loss, of the grinding immediacy
Of the unknown, the unknowable, weighted the years with tons
Of malevolent gravel, each jagged shard of which could tear
The flesh of present happiness to feed a cannibal.

Pearly Moonlight
Brightens Black Backwater
Clutter 581
Written 16 June, 2016

———————— • ————————

A grunting bassoon chorus of angry frog-spirits tells
Us that this parking lot —for which their swamp was drained — is
haunted.
The chemical dead patches in their wetlands are
The same sick orange color as the demagogue's comb-over.
It stands to reason that if witches' curses have entered
The bodies of queers, then queers can never be made to suffer
Enough, and on those nights when even the advertisers
Sleep, the sound of gunfire mixes with the pastor's vaunted
Sermons, which exhort his flock to use their prayers to kill.

Nothing is queerer than believing that mere word-tissues might
Bridge the abyss of sorrow that leads to the soul. The weird
Concoctions of poets are taboos, synonymous with night.

We observe a moment of silence for the victims, so when
Enough victims accrue we might be able to sleep without
Narcotics. But now our sleep is haunted. When we close our eyes,
We dream. A centaur with orange hair and froggy face squats in
A chemical spill, and belches toxins. His grunts are wired
For sound, but not for sense. The charcoaled remains of queers blacken
His words, and more than blacken the souls of his acolytes.
Shame! Shame! This poem is taboo, its readers queers. Cast out
Those devils, and enter the fundamentalists' white heaven.

Clouded Vision

Clutter 481

Written 17 June, 2016

——————— • ———————

The hunger of the human eye, roaming the social sphere,
Remains trapped. It gnaws at surfaces until it dissolves
Foreground to background, and feels, in its defusing center,
The great, immense beast of this grey cloud, arising from the south
And moving east, with an almost imperceptible motion.
These shallowing effects of details on the mind, this mouth
Of the one rat gnawing the one, the final morsel, our fear
In the center of the maze, although believed volitional,
Is the quintessence of compulsion, the slave of the weather.

It is not raining, but there are little pricks of moisture
Touching the skin's surface, and causing the roaming human
Eye to squint a bit, unfixing its gnawing, rodent hunger.

Then, for a moment, the moments disappear, the maze's baffling
Patterns then unfold, becoming the flow of volumizing
Vapors, currents of background that collect all detail into
A final mesmerizing mass, Divine, because it is.
The rat-angel, gnawing the poison bait of its prison,
Forgets its ravenous need to scurry through mazes,
And flies like flocks of songbirds through those currents, which open
blue
Expanses in the grey, that which was nothing becoming
Palpable as something the sight can touch when it stops looking.

Naive Thoughts Upon Feeling the Pressures of Heaven's Touch

Clutter 381

Written 18 June, 2016

———————— • ————————

By making micro-thin slices of a corpse, digital
Photos can transform the whole body into a visual
Surface of changeable parts, the desire for programmable
Matter realized for reliable commodity
Reproduction. True, these phrases make quite poor jump-rope rhymes,
But children beneath such virtual heavens have no need
And no space to jump, no reason to find that rhythm which tells
Of joy for the sake of joy, and not for a product to sell.
For the New Child, people are dismembered-remembered at will.

I have spoken before of the alien being arising
From spring's exhalations, how scents, being too difficult to slice,
Too volatile to digitalize, still swirl in rosy rings.

Now, it is summer, and June's starker, hotter perfumes
Turn circles round the cycles of life's chaos. The children
Have fled into the past, their ancient bodies remembering
Pockets full of posies, and ashes, ashes, and final
Fallings. We are falling with them, as them, through untamed skies,
Undigitalized, and by turns, benign or vengeful,
With motions more capricious than a child's. All of the ringing
Rhymes are broken — unspoken, including the rhymes of children
Playing adult, as if such playing could avert their doom.

Lunacy Hemorrhaging
Clutter 281

Written 19 June, 2016

———————— • ————————

Consider the horrendous metaphorical intrusion
Of such statements as:: "I dream of my first wife, who is not my
Daughter's mother. She is coughing up blood in a white basin,
And the globule shapes form letters one can read." Words and dreams
Have weathers, and these weathers stir both inside and outside
The high wispy clouds of summer. The omens that idlers read,
The hooded figures of night, both make prognostications
That plunge the metaphors through mystery. In the sky: high,
White crisscrossed vapors; from the gut: crimson eructations.

In our idlest talks, we speak of the weather. "Nice day," we say,
Expecting agreement, not wanting to discuss those skies
Inside that churn through the words as memories of past pain.

So many decades ago, a woman leaves you, and you
Grow older in many kinds of weather. "Strange night," you say,
Expecting no agreement, as the placid pleasantries
Moonily wrap you round. Now, inside, the ulcer's ancient sore
Sloughs off its scab and once again you see her. The mourning sky,
With its crisscrossing vapors, drops down white wires which bore
Into your flesh, and like a puppet in the stricken, palsied
Grip of a love-lorn puppeteer, you tremble too, your pain,
The pain of heaven, as you stare up at the cloud-scared moon.

Open Heart Surgery
Clutter 181
Written 20 June, 2016

In a corner, in a small room, used for meditation
And sleep, there is a sepia-toned eight by ten picture
Of two children. They are dressed in their finest costumes as
Adults, in post-World War II fashions — my dad and mom on
Their wedding night. Mom has been gone for seven years, and Dad died
Six weeks ago. I salvaged the children's picture from among
His few effects. Time — mysterious time — has brought changes
From that night to this, and, though an infamous philosopher
Tells us that that which flows is immeasurable: Was he wrong?

My youth is torn from its moorings by Time's great flood, but like
These children's picture, my grief is fixed. Whoever I might
Be or might become, my years are measured by their unchanged eyes.

"The attention which is fixed, and time which is passing …" how
The philosopher discovered this nexus of convergence —
He claims — is by delving "deep into the realm of inner
Life," the domain less of philosophers, than of dreamers,
And less of dreamers, than of poets — the unborn inner life
Of this young pair, whose eyes fix on that ripple in the future,
Wherein their grieving son is drowned in words. In a corner,
In a room, for sleep and meditation, a sharp convergence
Delves into the heart, and nails the rushing pulse with sorrow.

Man and Totem Speak of Silence In Mutually Incomprehensible Vocalizations
Clutter 081
Written 21 June, 2016

———————— • ————————

You might think that I would fashion my gods after the hands
Of the doctor who caught me as I dropped too soon and unformed
From my mother's body, or from the nurse's hands, which placed
Me in the life-saving but touch-denying incubator.
No, my gods are not human hands, nor can yours be. Since you are
Caught now, as I was then, in this life and death brutish war
Of a bear's grip — your breath's animal — whose massive sleeping shape
Dreams the wondrous torpid dreams to which your human life
conforms,
Clutching you in words, and initiating you into her clan.

It is too much, too much to expect from the brightest day's
Day-facts that they erase the lights of winter's moons, which bore
Into your too thin human skin, with luminous yellow eyes …

Full on the solstice, and so bright that your hands cast shadow
Hands, black against gold, and as clearly etched in the physical
Sight as they are in the mythic, the bright human and the dark
Hibernator now locked impossibly together, the latter
Awakened by the rare celestial marriage of the round moist star
And the hemisphere's shortest, brightest night. The primal fear
And the primal savagery of being, myth and fact, embarked
Upon their uncertain trail of words, the fierce animal
And the scared human, emerged from long sleep to roar and bellow.

Even on the Hottest Days, At These Altitudes, Water Crystallizes

Clutter 971

Written 22 June, 2016

———————— • ————————

When I think of my father's last days, it is fitting that these
Days should be scrambled, wired for complex reversals, sequential
Calendar designations not quite jiving with the heat of
The high June sky, a hot blue, knotted and netted with white
Confusions. A computer model can show the thirty-five
Million links in one neocortical column. The I
Of who he was, and how I speak about him, is a product of
Windy diffusions, neuron breakages, the habitual balm
Of mental cohesion, buzzing about like dislodged bees.

The hive of my thinking has been harshly violated by
These protruding thrusts of words. I do not know why
Complexity stings me, he was as simple as the sky.

Unraveled vapors, the buzz of bee dispersals, the honeyed
Calm of a man who knew himself, not in the wandering mind,
But in the bones, the stone in the well that keeps the water
Pure at any depth. Life is complex. His death was simple.
He was old. He fell. He hit his head. He died. And that light,
Which fell to the stone in the depths of the well, was doused. But still
The water there runs clear and pure. I know that I will never
See those depths by looking up, but that is where the light is — in white
Ephemeral tangles of sultry skies, where hot tears freeze.

The Reminiscence
of a Seasoned Scholar
Clutter 871
Written 23 June, 2016

——————— • ———————

Even at the highest tip of high summer these severe
Limitations prompt us to retreat to that moment in spring
When the grey, bare branches of winter are annihilated
By green exultations, but not before a certain feeling
Of nostalgia has scarred the psyche with the memory
Of the last days of a dying father. Now, the fresh morning
Air bears the smell of straw, a burnt, antique odor, accepted
As a culmination, a point at the brightest tip, tipping
The year from its peak to the slow downslope of its dark nadir.

No houses, no trees for miles, flat, burnt fields, and a man
On a dirt road waiting alone for a bus that will carry
Him to a place of higher learning — and — a termination.

There is a smell in old books of spent wisdom. The bus has
Only a few riders: a soldier going home on leave,
An old woman knitting grey wool, the student you never
Became — the anonymous driver. The road is dusty,
And represents a psychic poverty. The horizon cleaves
To a narrow strip of distance, oppressed by a sky whose heat
Imparts a bleached-out destination, an uncertain future,
Perhaps, in the stone tower of an ancient library,
Where the book can be found and read — and understood at last.

The Genealogy of Morals
Clutter 771
Written 24 June, 2016

———————— • ————————

Not a cloud in the sky, but enough breeze to allow a lone
Buzzard to lock her wings and drift low over the rooftops
Of comfortable suburbia with her shadowy
Reminder. Earlier today, Mr. Byrd, lawyer, retired,
Was stung on his bald head by a bee, while drinking coffee
And bourbon in his garden. Resentful, with a swelling fire
Crowning his resentment, he watches a documentary
On Nazis, the darkness of his comfortable den fraught
With entertaining flickerings of newsreels grey as headstones.

A yellow finch sits on the grey flagstones of Mr. Byrd's garden,
His yellow darkened by the shadow of a yellow bee.
This momentary dusk, pea-sized, is swift — like intuition …

And Mr. Byrd — stinging — stung —, a little drunk in the early
Afternoon, ponders, briefly, the question of evil. The newsreels
Are black and white, which lends a moral comfort to this thinking.
He shouts at his wife to bring him another drink, but she
Has been dead for years. Now the TV is showing Nazis
Planning the death camps. Now it is showing the ovens. He
Sees a pleasant ad for suppositories, and nodding,
He falls asleep. From the grey garden, he hears an anguished call:
"Bird! Bird!" comes the cry — then the humming, triumphant song of
bees.

A Boy Plays a Joke On His Mother. He Squeezes Blackberry Juice on His Head, and Claims To Be Bleeding From A Merry-go-round Fall

Clutter 671

Written 25 June, 2016

———————— • ————————

In the unpruned areas, the naked minimalist speaks
Less. He sits among blackberry thorns, scratched on the surface,
Hoping to minimize his exposure, hoping against hope
That the heat of the afternoon will not stir breezes, will
Not rouse the thorns to act. A sycamore sprouts Rococo
Crows, one for every twig in its immense fan, each breathes in calm,
Each expels exultation. The net result? Loud silence. No
Minimalism in those crows' voices. They show that the best
Ornamentalists scratch Rocco-caws among chattering leaves.

The poet's throat coughs a sphere of fire, summarizing
The day star's complex messages. The hot wind blows and blows,
And the thorns touch naked flesh with circular surface dazzlings.

The minimalist tastes fear. The juice of the blackberries
Makes intermixing jubilations through surface flowings,
Hemorrhaging excess. Irony expands distance, relieves
Intensity. Irony extracts thorns. The crows eat berries
As black as crows' feathers. They step out of character, and the Post
Modern intellect breaks its own taboos. Now, you must hear me.
I will speak directly of the red emotions. I will bleed
On the scholar's white paper. I will shout through the chattering
Matrix, thorny words. I will wallow in superfluities.

What Is the Sound of One Voice Shouting from a Crowd of Shouting Voices?
Clutter 571
Written 26 June, 2016

———— • ————

Amplify the sound of the tiniest gnat's wings, and you hear
First a bee's hum, then a Humming Bird's whirr, and then, by ramping
The rate by many orders of magnitude, a booming
Succession of mid-summer thunderstorms. Black clouds march down
From the mountains and pound the valley towns with fists of hail.
Now, from the ruins, the paranoid asks himself: "Was the town
Destroyed by Nature or by Imagination? Little wings
Fan in rapid succession — the monstrous lies of the ranting
Politicians, the paranoid watching gnats spin in hot air.

Once there were newspapers, which would print closely-packed columns
Of facts of the gnat's anatomy. When paranoids read the small,
Black print, the sound of thunder was shrunk to a gnat's proportions.

The tiniest whining was almost … almost heard. "Please, please,"
Said the tiny wings, "Do not read the poet's pain as mere
Allegory. He does not prattle on about prattling
Politicians, or the abysmal groans of the run-amok
Imagination, or even of the angry thunder's hail.
He winds his little whine in his little jail, reading the book
Of events in cloistered air, where he feels a cyclone shaking
His frail wings, and making little into bigger terrors.
The image of a spec, he flails inside the cosmos of a pea."

A Utilitarian Explanation
for Vaporware
Clutter 471
Written 27 June, 2016

————————— • —————————

Specificity is the poet's métier. The gold
Caps in your father's smile, the pride of army dentistry,
Recalling that war, which ended with the first nuclear
Annihilations, and also that time he gloated after
Beating you again in a game of cribbage. A golden gleam
Rushes out of the grey background of history, the far
Growing near in a flash that cuts through the foggy blurs
Of a dead but revived depression, so near to ecstasy
Now, because it shows someone young, who died, enfeebled and old.

Last night's moon, today at dusk, is a half-erased grey stone,
Which slides its tear down the west's blue slope — the vagaries
Of the past rolled through an ashen smudge of cremated bones.

See how the summer leaves flit wildly through the various breeze-
Altered irregularities of treetops, all reaching to
Touch that sinking lunar ash. Into this turbulent mass
Fly birds, and from it, birds emerge. Some of the birds are finches
Whose flights streak gold. If these analogies
Seem foggy, so be it. Depression climbs out of its ditches
On nebulous rungs, where every step ascending in loose ash
Finds, in its desperate need, a rung that holds. When the half-moon
Sinks, the heart leaps, revived by the shine of sunset's golden teeth.

Bergsonian Meditations
Above Phoenix Lake
Clutter 371
Written 28 June, 2016

———————— • ————————

A sky-blue dragonfly skims green-gold lake reflections
Until she finds a color that matches her. She hovers,
Quivering over quivering sky-mirrors. What we see
Is framed, segmented from what we must intuit — the real,
The ever-changing flow, just out of sight. This is the lure
Of ignorance, those speculations which somehow are called
"Faith," and make gods from the dark unknowable. Tall cattail reeds
Border the quivering speculations, but when the water
Is backcombed by the wind, we suddenly see down — and in …

Another world below the surface skin, of cloudier green
Foliage, which blooms in forest fogs, presenting a fuzzier
Version of ignorance, suggestive of other-worldly scenes.

They say that truth is solid. In the frame: shame, the primal
Shame of ego-ghosts amidst a world of images. They say
That ghosts, like memories, haunt the edges, and when I track
An image to its edge, emotions rise, emotions more
Real than the forms which conjured them. It is not the water,
But the trembling of the water, the quivering mother,
Who drowns and begets us anew in her dark womb, the look
Of things, of even beautiful things, no more than framed
Delusions, the flits in the sky-filled eye where insects tremble.

Sleep Walking on
Less Than Solid Ground

Clutter 271

Written 29 June, 2016

————————— • —————————

A dream built this garish casino on an immense glacier,
The wedding guests having to scale jagged walls of dirty
Black ice in evening clothes to find their tables, cynical
Commentary portraying such incongruousness as normal,
The chill of collective madness condensed to images
That can neither be ignored nor understood. Yet social
Niceties continue to be observed. Always the normal
Leaks paradox, this, the revenge of smothered anxiety.
One feels blue ice seizing each breath of air.

The implication "wedding" was perhaps premature.
One might be witnessing in this disingenuousness
A fund raiser for the politics of avarice and fear.

Clowns in tuxedos, clownettes in silk and pearls, their ant hordes
Swarming ice for prestigious display, the camera
Replacing the wheel as futility's symbol. If crying
Is heard in the distance, it has no meaning. It is only
One voice from the pile of unheard voices. And this stillness
That lurks in the body of the glacier? — it is only
The premature breathlessness of that thunder, whose booming
Will silence all when the ice throne splits, and the cold coma
In this dream of chance wakens the sleepers with the primal word.

To My Granddaughter on Her Birthday
Clutter 171
Written 30 June, 2016

————————— • —————————

A finger of lavender fog intercedes between green
Mountain and cerulean morning sky, a shifting wind
Chasing away a week of oppressive heat with marine
Layer freshness, the cool miracle coming with relief
And joy. The sky excites, and exuberance cleanses the mind.
My Son-in-Law calls — my daughter has birthed a daughter. The sea
Has borne its fecundity through a night of sleepless dreams,
Wondering: "When will her labor end, and the child come? When?
When?"
Pressure, pain, contractions — and then a squall of ecstasy.

The tides flow in with new vigor, as do the nucleotides
Of heredity, your small, red, sleeping face — as yet blind
To the wild forces that made you — subdues with peace fierce Time.

Child, when you are as old as I am now, you may have cause to
Wonder: "Am I loved?" You may rise from a rumpled sleep, your
dreams
Still scrambled, and on their way to foggy disappearance,
And question if the breeze that cools your skin has any care at all
For who you are. The years will have passed by then, and done Time's
Work, shaping your life with unforeseen events, and taking all
You gave, while giving more. And in that grapple, the distance
Between sleep and fatigue will close. The wind will stream
This covenant of words, and you will feel how much I loved you.

Lighter than Air
Clutter 071
Written 1 July, 2016

———————— • ————————

The breeze blows freshness through this day-afterness emotion,
Its tremoring hand a blind man's rummaging for something in
A cluttered drawer. By conflating feeling, hand, weather,
One can say that the drawer holds the wedding band of one's
Dead mother, one's daughter's baby pictures, one's failure
To grasp some molecule of happiness — like that sudden
Joy which comes at the birth of one's grandchild, the day after
The event, when that burst of life fades to nostalgia. The wind —
This day-after wind — carries the uterine scent of ocean.

When one breathes, not the after-age, but this present atmosphere,
The entire past is reified in the Now. One encounters
The multiplicitous self, who sums up all encounters.

With the extraordinary fury of a genius
Possessed with a continuous flow of inspiration, one
Senses a sure hand making climactic markings on
The impregnable sky, a clutter of lines cross-hatching
The psyche with molecules of ocean, nostalgia's murmers
Drowning in an ordinary moment of paternal feeling,
The everyday world of weather, as the day before one
Dies, the day after one is born, brings that flux which seethes where one
Feels one's immortality as a breeze that swiftly passes.

Lieder Lied

Clutter 961

Written 2 July, 2016

My friend's body is as big as ambition can make it. He
Flies to the edge of outer space, a thin blue arc atop
A fat white one, while, above both, flutters an infinite
Blanket of stars. He has three mansions: one in the mountains, one
In a forest, one near the sea. He runs a successful
Business, and plays piano with that genius-spark which comes,
Like grace, to sensitive amateurs. My enemy sits
In a hollow in the desert, inert with grief. His lot
Is that of the dust which flies through sandstorms. My enemy weeps.

If only my friend and my enemy might reach that peak
Of emotional congruence, wherein congenital
Languor and incessant movement might magically meet.

If only the spinning dust motes and the fluttering panoply
Of stars could collect their hostile motilities in stillness …
But those "if onlies" are only fantasies. My enemy
Wastes back to skeleton, my friend grows fat on hermit's meat.
And in between my cycles wane and wax, the insubstantial
Pivot of this pair, the tick whose axle turns eternity,
And makes forever roll around, enthralled. Who might I be
If not this "V" that splits white key from black? The two notes crest
Around a third, which crown a chord. Then silence inundates me.

Someone, A Stranger, Remembers His Deceased Parents
Clutter 861
Written 3 July, 2016

———————— • ————————

Late afternoon sunstrobes in these long summer nappings are
Depositing details in the lengthening shadows, so
That the houses, grass blades, red petunias, the fragrant snow
Of blossoms from flowering ligustrum, collect like memories
In the trembling ellipses of the apertures of trees.
From this deep inland peace, a shoreline of consciousness is reached,
The shallow waves rolling and rounding pebbles along long rows
Of cream-white lace, each stone glistening, but opaque, each a low
Gluttering of surf, each a solemn musing of green choirs.

Suppose you rest on this shore, and news arrives as the breeze
On the crests of the waves, the news of a distant tragedy —
The death of one who loved you unconditionally.

The sky is a pale pearlescence, the sea the same, and you
Think of the lost details of that continent, where summer
Days are stretching their last gold lights into harrowing opals
That flash with love's last joys. The one, the ones, who cherished you as
You, have cast their bodies into sinking Time, their voices weak
As persons, strong as Nature, their radiant breath, your breath, as
Night comes on, catching you napping beyond the edge of calm,
At the final edge where consciousness dissolves, but where
The you as you is soaked in love, as though by bliss entombed.

Resurrection through Drowning
Clutter 761
Written 4 July, 2016

On this dream beach, there must be, just off-shore, submerged fissures
And peaks, because the surf rushes in irregularly,
Shooting long pseudopods over lateral dunes, retreating
Waves colliding with advancing ones, and trapping the seeker
On a pocket beach between them. Even the logic of dreams —
That dream-geo-logic — says "The power in these waters
Is the power of extinction, the power of return." Wings
And arms fold back to fins, then sleek through the uterine sea —
All science is the cryptozoology of weird dream creatures.

Because today is today, and no other, this science
Is deeper than any mere surface one. It is the study
Of the odd — not the species — of the seeker in his trance.

All this tells us that poetry, although extinct, defies
Extinction. It tells us that these surface skimmers by the hordes
Remain oblivious to that unique globster lurking
In the deeps, and battening on verbal superfluities
As the snow of its detritus comes to him. If mystery's
Music dies in public, it will surely live on privately.
You will be strolling down a public beach, crowded with preening
Creatures all of one species, and you will feel the horror
Of being the one stranger who hears the ocean's beckoning cries.

Following a Convolutedly Technical Digestive Process, Three Dimensions are Happily Reduced to Two

Clutter 661

Written 5 July, 2016

———————— • ————————

A scrub jay sits atop a pear tree in the garden's corner,
A pear tree so fortressed by other vines and shrubberies
That its fruits are safe from our predations. For decades we
Have let these trivial outer emotions grow wildly,
The harvest of what matters blocked by a conspiracy
That hides the fruits of ordinary living behind the screens
Of social diversions. Now the jay squawks harshly, harshly
Sounding the trumpet of redemption, an ordinary
Assault on ears deaf to that scripture, which leaks from green corners.

The wind whispers in the leaves, and the conspirators blend green
Treacheries into common sounds at the peripheries
Of awareness, swift miracles cloaked in blurs of common speed.

After being shat by the Media Monster, this feces looks
Just as our children once did, but something smells funny.
The ordinary is no longer miraculous, the jay
In the pear tree is not sensational, and the odd old man
Who spouts words like: "Green summer pulp becomes autumnal cream,"
Is only a boring eccentric. The strange emotion
He claims to feel in stillness is but a killing yawn that preys
On these new children's programmed thrills, his three-dimensional wheeze
No match for their flat-screen tree, or their flat bird's synthetic squawk.

Adamic Artistry
Clutter 561
Written 6 July, 2016

———————— • ————————

Among the greatest of the last Century's painters was one
Who day after day covered immense canvasses with what some
Called "objectless color fields," but which he obliquely referred
To as "precise composite portraits of the sum of human
Emotion." Day after day, I write about birds and leaves,
My redundant vision as innocent as a baby's, an
Intoxicating babbling, my aesthetic product, my weird
Obsession with making the commonplace weird, the entire sum
Of my mud-pie creations, the clod-talk of a dirt person.

A poetic or pictorial world wherein matter
Dissolves back to its potent fundamentals, a baby
With an adult's proportions, and bite — is what we are after.

Our word, paint, or musical compositions are wallowing
In primal mud, mud from which the dead and the unborn
Derive their nascent forms. A mad bird breaks through glass, and a
child
Buries the body in a shoebox, and covers the dirt with leaves —
Or linen with paint, or silence with music or poetry,
These first crazy acts of contrition are a crime the baby
Attributes to his own neglect. It is this first act of self-
Negation, this first random foray into self-formed scorn,
That fixes his fixations, and fills his wounds with woundings.

Godly Greeting
Clutter 461
Written 7 July, 2016

———————— • ————————

You could go to the ends of the cosmos and not find one sight
More interesting or boring than this wall of foliage,
Whose impenetrable intricacies undulate across
The back of this suburban property. Anchored on one end
By a spindly Chinese Privet, and on the other by
An impossibly dense pear tree, this body is a blend
Of different species of green, its inextricable mass
More prevalent than its individuals, its hushed verbiage
A babble of sun flashes and shade deeps, which baffle — and blind.

The pointillism of living plants, the almost inaudible
Gurgle of sap manufactured from honeyed sun, the sky
Mirrors, which collect, reflect, and refract the floral self …

That which entrances your merely animal presence, and fades
Into background rustlings — its heart, lungs, and organs of perception
Spread out in conscious ubiquity, fifty yards long,
A life-span thick, and thirty feet high. A sanctuary
For insects, a temple for contemplatives, an untamed blight
For fastidious topiary pruners, a mazy,
Undiscovered country for children, where bubbles of birdsong
Burst as the twittering voices of the newly dead, the one
Who throngs, the intense Green Lord, who kisses without a face.

An Undiscovered Country Drive
Clutter 361
Written 8 July, 2016

——————— • ———————

I can see by the way your eyes reflect this late afternoon
Summer sky that you are perfectly purposeless, one of those
Aimless wanderers who follow the unmarked backroads. These wind
Through giant melon-round hills, which in spring dazzled the traveler
With bright viridians, but which now have ripened to flaxen
Fineness, their ripplings reminding you of those ideal toddlers
In Victorian portraiture, whose hair symbolized a kind
Fragile innocence. But you, you are not innocent. You chose
This naive rambling because night, night, for you, will fall too soon.

The moon, unlike you, seems almost to be born in the west,
Chased down post-midnight darkness by resolute stars, the thin
Announcement of its rebirth tincturing a golden crescent.

But the globe which supports the crescent is black, and that is what
Your eyes reveal, even in broad daylight, their pupils hollowed
By an anxiety that you hoped would be cured by
Aimless wandering. By fall, the child's hair will be burnt brown, in
Some places even scuffed back to dirt, but perhaps a goblin
Moon, full, and blazing in infrared splendor, will rise in
The east, and make the ghost hills seem to breathe new life. The abyss
Of the question your wandering lost sight of will be a road,
A black road to that terminus your childish heart always sought.

Depth Charges
Clutter 261
Written 9 July, 2016

—————— • ——————

Three days ago I hiked up the steep, wooded embankment
Of a dam, until I came to a vast, lonely lake, where
I perched on a bleached tree stump, and allowed the wind-stirred waves
To kill my sense of self with mutating colors. Then I
Walked around and studied the eccentric shapes of driftwood,
The corpses of trees being more beautiful than those of men. I
Thought of a small church, whose floor crowned ten thousand graves.
On hot days,
The cracked paving oozed long, black flies, which would make children
quiver
At what they called "body bugs." The tree shapes are tortured and bent.

Three months back my cousin and father died a few days apart.
The one I always disliked, the other I loved. You would
Think that each death would twist its own shape through the tortured
heart.

You would think that the pale ghosts of driftwood would be less lovely
Than the water's transient mesmerizing wavelets. You
Would think that the twisted eccentricities of once living
Trees would be too sad to place near the rippling ecstasies
Of these hypnotic lights, and that the skeletal driftwood
Would conjure up the body bugs of grotesque memories,
Their relics as horrifying as the grief seen mocking
The living waters. But no. It all blends perfectly, the hues
Of the quivering waves, the white bones — both blood-kin in the deeps.

A Composition from
the Center for Nude Music

Clutter 161

Written 10 July, 2016

———————— • ————————

Midday summer heat, drooping leaves, one jay squawking, squawking
His dissolution of the poet's mythic memory —
No nightingale, no moon, no absent or lost love. In this long
Decayed and incestuous lineage, he is the youngest
Princeling brother, never to ascend to the moribund throne,
And yet the bloodline, the bloodflow, still pushes its red crest
Into his dream, in which cardboard kingdoms, still fragilely throng
In tiny, segmented squares, rising and falling in a sleep
That resists interpretation — like the jay's harsh squawking.

Any visual mapping of the segmented multitudes
Of decentralized social clans would show, no line, but a foam
Of leaderless mobs — the princeling poet's post-boredom brood.

Think, learn to think, dream, learn to dream of the flow that underlies
The segmentations. These bubbles of isolation — we call
Perception — long to be more than heat and memory. They
Long to recover their ancient royalty, and sail on
The wriggling stream of Time. Each princeling, in his squalor, knows
That those tiny cardboard kingdoms are but games, the songs
Of a poetry too long bereft of the nightingale's refrains,
The song of an inept bird on his drooping twig, who balls
A ragged tune through the hot air of kingdoms in decline.

Imaginary Keepsake
Clutter 061
Written 11 July, 2016

—————— • ——————

Orphan feelings — these tremendous, but seldom poeticized
Experiences at the soft boundaries where logic
Is liquefied, like food in a gut racked with illness. You may
As well seek a gate in the summer heat — there, where your lover
Waits, as forlorn as you are, cloud shapes voiding her body
As she picks at threads from her embroidered gown. This is the lore
Of poetry in an age where fine feeling is effaced
Because loud excitement is preferred to silken lace, tricks
Of the intellect to this heart, which breaks among broken lines.

Whether her gown is embroidered with flowers or with songbirds,
It makes no difference, these tangled, pulled threads are the same. She
Has grown sad waiting, unable to pronounce the saving word.

Do you know how blessed you would be to be like her? She feels
What she is missing, and although the river she walks is
A silken serpent reflecting eons of summer skies, she
Has found the gate, the place to wait, and she knows what to do
While waiting. Her eyes gleam with a star of ecstasy,
Like a tear that has vitrified, a delicate thing, so true
To her orphan feeling. Do you know how blessed you would be
To possess this tear, and keep it in a little Chinese vase?
Do you know how blessed you would be if this relic were real?

The Triple Goddess Returns in Another of Her Ordinary Theomorphs

Clutter 951

Written 12 July, 2016

———————— • ————————

Scrub Jays have been raising their fledglings around here since before
This suburban neighborhood was built. So when three squawking
Juveniles sit and de-louse in the dust of the drought-killed
Lawn, we only wonder: "Do they know about cats?" A syllogistic
Progression of logical linkages is the best art
To soothe an ornithologist — but what of the blue, quick
Ruffling of feathers, the hyperventilating breath, the bill,
Cracked and black, that seeks a way to make music that has nothing
Beautiful or poetic about it, and only wounds the ear?

Blues logically categorized as "cool" colors can be
Made "hot", but the material eye knows nothing of this art,
Which defies vision, and sees the flame in the bird's screams.

Sometimes that which is vertiginously divine comes slashing
Through, when the linkages of Time are broken. The wounded ear
Hears, and the daylight-blinded eye sees — and these three spirits —
From another, broader reality — confront the dizzy
Suburbanite. He becomes the voice of an extinct art,
The thrashing, hyperventilating juvenile, lousy
With bird-clan prophesies. He becomes the symptomatic
Expression of Dame Nature's Virgin-Mother-Crone, the mad seer,
Groveling in dust, and stabbing the air with hot, blue squawkings.

Sap

Clutter 851

Written 13 July, 2016

Torture could not compel me to say this. But the green spirits
Will press one to talk. An invasive species of ivy
Has worked sorcery with its volatiles. "Fresh air!" you say,
"Fresh air! And yellow umbrels, so rich in nectar, and black-purple
Berries, each with its five seeds, food for stinging bees, for falling
Sparrows, but poison to us human fretings — these most cruel
Openers of the eyes of dream!" The electrified vine-snakes
Call the dark blue demons from earth. They fight in breeze-torn leaves,
While these wild words break the rational mind's tame ambits …

Or so you say, or so you say — wild and tame are riven in
Two by a knife of flame that splits the heart and brain, and putting
Your face into this battle-smoke, you breathe life's conflagration.

The earthy, airy scent! The mucilaginous cure! The vein
Stems, the heart-shaped leaves, the running for miles, for centuries
Without the need for human lungs to breathe! Torture could not
Compel me to say this. But these intense pathological
Prolongations of stillness, these green invasive mergings
Of common-animal/common-vegetable-sense crawl
Through the interstices of my bones, like air-roots fixed to rock,
Like the lines of a poetry fumbling through dazzling dreams,
Like a madcap rebirth in the tribe of the primally sane.

A Blinding Allegorical Displacement with a Twist

Clutter 751

Written 14 July, 2016

———————— • ————————

What is that incessant pounding? It distracts me. But first: "My
Story." How did I lose the eye? Some raid or other. Years flow
By and blur the hard edges of all that past rapaciousness.
I now see only the black leather patch, and your face — flat —
As all things are flat — , asking all your rapacious questions.
On one side: unending night, on the other: fantasy. That
Answer disappoints you. You crave the pirate's villainous
Booty. But without risk. Without trial. Without the hangman's rope.
You crave the neurologist's answer: "How brain cells make eyes lie."

What is that incessant pounding? But I digress. I believe
My eye was lost — just as all vision is — by those explosions
Of light — by spangled gems on waves, by star-bursts on night seas.

What is that incessant pounding? I am admittedly
A villain, and this whole talk of neuroplasticity
Is beyond me. I saw things I wanted to see. I stole,
And hoarded light. Look: this is evasion, this is memory,
This is clinging to spars when the black ship has gone down. The spin
That the vortex left by its swift sinking is the way the sea
Takes vengeance. This is "My Story" — as true as any told,
As false as any. What is that pounding? It distracts me.
Ah yes, the carpenter's scaffold, the just end to all stories.

Chlorophylled
Clutter 651
Written 15 July, 2016

———————— • ————————

Every day I see the "They," the great, green organismics
Who grow as grass, shrubs, trees, around my house — the They speaking
To themselves, to me, signaling their multiple poetries,
The They's words taking solid, liquid, gaseous forms. The They
Are highly emotional, exquisitely aware. The They
Enter my skull through my meager sensory portals. The They
Assess me for mutual sentience. Perhaps in my empty
Interiors, an image of trees is found. "This proves nothing,"
They say, "a reflex of sunlight, no more. It does no magic."

"It does not choose the optimum variant. It cannot
Manage its energy resources. It hoards territory,
But only to render it sterile. It kills feeling with thought."

Oh, I remember a time when I was a child, a time
When I saw for the sake of seeing, and now I have broken
Through my mere remembrance, to be and see the kingdom of
The They. And you, you who have not been kidnapped by their tribes,
You see only the changeling that you think is me. Your speech
Is bereft of the haunting crystal music, and you describe
The scalpel of your mind as knowledge, disdaining my green love.
Oh, I am this greater They whose poems are only spoken
When the eerie song of the breeze-harped leaves breathes inhuman sighs.

Heavy Reading
Clutter 551
Written 16 July, 2016

———————— • ————————

Late afternoon, and the whole summer seems condensed to that
Moment when a child stretches forth a finger, touches the screen's
Breeze-riffled surface, and instigates the blossoming of a
Rainbow — surface tittilation — all surface — the Master
Deceiver's answer to the child philosopher's first idle
Question. These primal forays into the green mystery whirr
By like explosion debris, the shrapnel pollen cutting a
Thin swathe of light across a vegetable screen of trees
And sky, and leaving the surface almost — almost intact.

Insight in-breathed as a smell shows that we must be inside
The deceiver. Henceforth, the scholar of the surface-whirl
Becomes the reader of an opaque weight with three false sides.

The books of lead have wings, but cannot fly, each page a nearly
Toxic density embedded with rubble, and the pages
Number in the thousands, the books as big as temples, the shelves
Arranged in massive boulevards, wide and empty — except
For that curious child with his probing finger. The lethal
Question for the healthful answer — that is his lonely quest.
He is the tiniest morsel in the Moloch, the self
Digested by the self, the leaden meaning in those pages
Riffled with summary conclusions, yet fixed by destiny.

Once, A Soap Bubble
Popped in a Dark Room
Clutter 451
Written 17 July, 2016

———————— • ————————

Just beyond the delicate surface tension of the planet's
Blue, atmospheric bubble, a constant storm rages. This storm
Is lethal — it is the background of the deceased father, once
The son's, the planet's, protector, but now dispersed as that black
Radiation of the ultimate outer space. The bubble's fate
Is that of sudden bursting — so irresistible a fact
That every child seeks its nothingness — although he knows, once
Broken, the illusion of protection can never re-form.
My father died. The grief that he left finds no one to protect.

As my body ages, my skin grows as thin as a bubble's.
Its surface tension reflective, and prismatic, a spate
Of radiation that kills the outer with the inner self.

Or are these archetypes reversible, inner and outer,
Son and father, these crackling radiations in deep space,
Not quite so empty or benign as surface meditation
Might pretend? The child's safety, extracted from black danger,
Rests on the tip of a curious prod. And the bubble's fate,
Though pre-ordained, might have a rainbow life, which, as it shimmers,
Shimmers a spectrum of every emotion's light, its end
A sudden exultation, its delicate condensate
Of surface tensions, burst in a rainbow mist of happy tears.

Night Watchman

Clutter 351

Written 18 July, 2016

———— • ————

Perspective matters. From space, the planet spins, the atmosphere
Is alive, and with fluid hands is seen to be slowly molding
The oceans and even the continents to her will. No
Human being exists, no would-be mother whose baby
Has miscarried. These things are explained simply. When someone
dies,
The body is no good, and would spoil if kept near. The way we
Solve this dilemma is 1) through fire, returning flesh to smoke
And air, or 2) through burial, returning flesh to earth — things
That exist without pain, things that require neither thought nor care.

Now it is summer, bucolic summer, sweet, full summer,
A time for being, as winter is for waiting, spring a time
For hope, and autumn for recollection. Now it is summer.

I think of my mother with a dead child in her womb, and I
Think of this brother or sister who did not come before me,
My mind in space and watching this tiny planet, a world
Once near to someone, but now shrinking, like the globe of a tree
In summer that shrinks back to seed, or, in retreating time,
Blinks like a star, a dot of lost potential in a sea
Of hollow ebony. Perspective matters. What has been spoiled
Is still redeemable, the lost life, the potential me
That keeps on shrinking as darkness grows, still shows this baby's eye.

Hovering

Clutter 251

Written 19 July, 2016

—————— • ——————

What could be flying up there so tiny that marauding
Dragonflies weave predatory dances in order to
Feast upon it? The dragonflies are orange, and the sky
Is blue. Note the contrast. This is your point of departure.
Whenever you leave the present moment, the colossal forms
Appear — the rock city in the desert, where orange and blue stir
Bigger configurations. That tiny fissure — the I —
Splits instant-last from instant-next, and grows a mountain, while you,
You stand, tiny, in awe, in the Petra of forgotten things.

Those who visit this city long to forgo the dreary
Life of waking, and enter its permanent dream. What is born
Here must endure, collecting the silences of centuries.

Its columned facades open into enormous chambers,
Where the echoes of women in childbirth condense into
The statues of those Gods most worthy to enthrone themselves
In the womb of Earth. And here They wait for you, the emotions
You have suppressed, red giants in black gloom, all of pain's storms,
Stilled. All of those predatory moments, weaving around in
Vacant space in search of tiny things, stilled. The pulse-dance, stilled,
And the feast, finished. And you, with all your insect longings, you,
In the heart's fissure, are fixed in flight upon hot, summer air.

The News Now Trending Through the Land of Ricket-Ridden Urchins
Clutter 151
Written 20 July, 2016

———————— • ————————

In the face of your outrageousness, reviving the long
Discredited doctrine of humourism seems justified.
How else explain your party's cannibalism? This black
Acrimonious bile squeezed from your ventricle linings,
And slithering through your insane speeches, has no doubt produced
Yours and your followers addiction to human flesh. Nothing
In the scientific literature accounts for it. Reason lacks
The capacity to grasp what metaphor invokes, a lie
Purging a lie, as like cures like, in the medicine of wrongs.

Extreme poverty of spirit — Extreme isolation —
A Mississippian atavism, which spews through gapped-toothed
Rage its cultish need to devour its own crook-backed children —

Fear's brown river sludging slowly under a July sky
White with summer's torpor — A shack of corrugated tin,
Tarpaper, castoff thoughts, all cobbled together from spavined
Laziness, and climatological necessity —
The Bible that your father's father read, which, in lieu
Of literacy, serves rote perversion — a dupe — the easy
Mark for a demagogue's cons — a crude aboriginal blend
Of history's bigotries, with shards of shattered mirrors in
Your gut —a hunger to eat before being eaten — a child's cry.

Sub-Human
Clutter 051
Written 21 July, 2016

The interviewer is the heavenly picture of haute
Couture and expensive coiffure, and she has come to this
Ragged edge of what she views as civilization to
Present to her audience a denizen of Hell. In the vulgar
Depths of virulent kudzu growth and ignorance, in the heart
Of the Bible belt, he comes out of his tarpaper
Shack, almost toothless, and bearing those stains of compression you
Find as the gruel crushed under garbage piles. Hell smells, and the whiff
She gets of this is a stench she — and we — could never condone.

Is the whole point of the great glass towers of her city
An attempt to reify the freedom of the sky? … their arts
Of deception, a way to denigrate his poverty … ?

A way to push the irrational background of his ugly,
Bigoted, and odiferous life into that grubbiest
Cube of the grid labeled "marginal?" That heaven might need,
As its foundation, the thoughts of a cruel simpleton is news
That her audience may not want to hear. His talk is that wart
Tucked in the sophisticate's armpit, which one night starts to ooze
Malignant pus. As a journalist, her objectivity
Is the stain of her professionalism. She must resist
Her contempt, and let the camera record her noble deed.

Hazel

Clutter 941

Written 22 July, 2016

———————— • ————————

Something as all-pervasive as the weather invites you
To sit in the catalepsy of meditation until,
In the temple of nine-hundred and ninety-nine columns,
You are column one-thousand. Rats, ants feast upon the flesh
That was once your body, without disturbing your quiescence.
The respirator is removed from your mother's lips, and a rush
Of white force makes the temple-mountain stronger, and turns the
bones
In your body to jagged bolts of lightning. Electrical
Strobes freeze the mind's rotating machine. You stop, and ask: "Who?"

You stop, and ask "Who?" because segmentations twirl, or grow
Still, in accordance with a law of mysterious sentience,
A law that weaves mother-weather from skeins of tear-drop rainbows.

Oily chemical archways now roof the temple, and raise
The columns under their glad sky. The idiosyncrasies
Of your minute life are dazzled by her death, and if you sit,
Or move, or thrash through grief's rapidities, this catalepsy
Of radiating hues consumes you. The bubble-self is lanced,
And "poof!" the pronouns vanish. You and she are but surface sheen,
Without a surface, in a cataclysm of spirit
Derived from the intensely ordinary. The breeze shuffles leaves,
Or the tongue speaks, but every sound that sounds is her sweet name.

Elemental Activity
Clutter 841
Written 23 July, 2016

———— • ————

Low tide odors, and a wind sweeping in from the inland
Deserts announce together that today will be hot. The in/
Out movements of the tide bring an intense fecundity
Right into the house, along with another in/out motion:
The tide of sexual inundation, man/woman always
Swimming in the effluvia of one another's ocean.
You, simply gliding round the house, watering orchids, the sea
A part of your gestures, leaning, stooping, moving out and in
Of eddies of affection, me, feeling you close at hand.

As institutions, seclusion and the veil are very old.
No congress of mere mortal genitalia can convey
What passes invisibly between two loving people.

The body hides these things. The sense of a separate I,
The curtain of aging skin, both block our view of what is
Always oceanic. How extraordinary these latent
Energies! One senses fountains of light spraying blank space
With forests, cities, clouds, seas! — and it's all done without the weight
Of physical molecules, it's all done as runoff's waste,
It's all done through the strength of that hydraulics of breath sent
From and through angels — the odors of low tide, of orchids,
The spirit's bliss in the in and out of two orgasmic sighs.

Willing Prey
Clutter 741
Written 24 July, 2016

———————— • ————————

Amidst the jumbled clutter of my desk — books, wires, pencils,
Lamps, papers, eyeglasses, my computer, a little yellow
Bag from a casino that I don't know what to do with,
And which contains my dead parents' wedding rings, there stands a small
Cast-iron statuette of an owl, an object a great deal
Heavier than it looks, preternaturally heavy — with all
This density with its weight, and all this intensity with
Its stare. The twin goddesses of its eyes, like twin breasts, follow
My movements. They feed and castigate, their gaze a cosmic milk.

Because the taboo of thinking of one's parents' sex veils
One's view of eternity, Death and Time steal the so called "real"
Mother, and substitute symbolic effigies of word-milk.

Sentimentalists speak rapturously of the "white light"
That calls from that constrictive end of the uterine tunnel
We re-enter at the time of death. But, in that moment —
Which is all our cluttered moments condensed to one — in that
Moment, the owl re-seizes us, as, once more vulnerable,
We run through the night of the symbolic. The word's thin milk, that
Is our only source of satisfaction and destruction, rent
From the moonlight, and feeding us the terrifying Real.
Amidst the jumbled clutter of my desk, her talons strike.

The Last Shaman Stepping to the Beat of a Planetary Rhythm

Clutter 641

Written 25 July, 2016

———————— • ————————

It is far too late in the day to begin lecturing
Accountants on the dead zones in the ocean. Winter storms,
Drenching rains, the green hysterics of spring, these remain
Only as the brown crater of summer drought. The sole human
Being among countless replicas cannot get out of this hole,
Nor does he want to. He stomps around kicking up dust. Who can
Read these signs, but the man who makes them? Who can explain
How their little clouds rise and fall or how their instant forms
An everlasting myth on the death of the everlasting?

The accountants are lost souls doomed to count everything forever.
They can count molecules of air flowing through the finest holes
Of a sieve, but they can never count all of the Earth's poor.

Below my ocean dead zone, a trench of unfathomable
Pressure and cold gives rise to white smokers and black smokers.
It is as if the feet of a shuffling ogre were stirring
The muck with volcanic ire. This is my scripture of origin,
Which the human being discovers roiling round in his soul
As the ogre kicks dreams through sleep. This is my summer prison,
Where, without effort, his feet tell how his heart speaks, counting
What the doomed accountants missed. He can number all the poor
Sparrows as they fall. He can dance forever in a hole.

After a Lifetime of Intense Exploration, the Oceanographer Discovers the Planet's Most Abundant Life Form

Clutter 541

Written 26 July, 2016

—————— • ——————

As one ages, those violent March upheavals which ripped
Up the mucky floor of the estuary creek to make
Of violent emotion that nutrient we called 'love," grow
Calm. The tide retreats, its slack waters winnowing slowly
Back to ocean. The mudflats shine with the blank heat of blank skies,
Summer languor sapping the storms of spring, love's memories
Vanishing in blank reflections. Where did the violence go?
And where do the years collect their raging tears? The raked-
Up muck, now exposed, shows not the slightest remnant of those fits.

Forget the sky, forget this summer heat, evolved from former
Passionate turbulence, now you must study these subsea climes
At the verge of the sunlit zones, these homes for micro-scars.

One micro-liter of feeling at these depths is teeming
With the tiniest details — self-luminating creatures:
Her smell as she left her bath, the light in her eyes as she looked
Through rain-streaked glass, the parting of her lips when she felt lost,
Her curled hands twitching as she slept, the thick book of her sighs.
As one ages, these minute details emerge. No longer tossed
By crude emotion, the ocean grows more subtle, and what shook
The heart with violence, now calms it with little wonders —
Little wounders — as through dark deeps one sees these glimmer-beings.

The Mayor Issues
a Statement to the Press
Clutter 441

Written 27 July, 2016

———————— • ————————

I know from a lifetime of listening to this city
That there are side streets that forget, that are forgotten. At
The dead-end of one of these streets, under seething mattresses
Of crushing vegetation, is my house, its architecture
Deformed by green intrusions, its glass eyes cracked, its roof caved-in
By draperies of ivy. The castings of worms have inured
Its foundation to sagging, and impious sparrows nest
In its skeletal rafters. Here, amidst the droppings of rats,
And the bunching of shadows, I wallow in reverie.

For years and years and years, my father's Alzheimer's quietly
Broke the structures of his mind. He forgot. He was forgotten,
As oblivion's vegetation encroached, confounded, seethed.

According to modernity's apostate, "Apostasy
Is permissible when desire is pure," and what is purer
Than neglect? to simply surrender, and at last allow
The energy of self, self-alienated, to break
The city's dialectic hold. The decay outside comes in,
As Nature's too-fertile tangles of revelation, the fake
Constructions undone by the true. The live worms in the hollows
Of my thought, the chirrup-chirrup of lascivious birds,
These are the poetries I use to silence the loud city.

Everything Becomes More Vivid Following the Marvelous Event
Clutter 341
Written 28 July, 2016

———————— • ————————

Stop reading right now before you start, otherwise I will
Compel you to traverse mists and mists of Time, in a journey
Wherein your micro-listening must grow as minute as those
Molecules of perception able to pierce the close-packed grain
Of museum-piece marbles: fame and pain, for you, becoming
Fused. I refer you to the knell of renaissance church bells, sane
Sounds denoting underlying martyrdoms. The arrows
Of Saint Sebastian, your depth perception on the journey,
The birth of your first child, thick foliage obscuring a squirrel.

I refer you to the obsessed artist who first paints molecules,
Then organs, then bones, then — with a one-haired squirrel brush tracing
Each single hair — the whole cloud-russet tail of the squirrel.

The revelatory details of the foliage continue
To descend cell by cell, church bell by bell, minutely
Through the corridors of space, while expanding in the spell
Of temporal sound. The child — your child — your first-born child —
crying
The cry of all evolution, while at the window, tapping
At the glass: the nursery of foliage hides its rodent. Things
That are ordinary are most miraculous things. The knell
Of expanding tones, expanding vision, not stopped by leaves
Or squirrels or by any kind of mystified, marble you.

Re-Union

Clutter 241

Written 29 July, 2016

———— • ————

The summer heat has wiped out all the rose blossoms as surely
As if it were winter frost. The sun we were friends with in
The spring is far too pitiless now — an X-ray sun, a sun
That exposes, not only the withered exterior
Of the leaf, but the dry river channels of leaf veins, the sum
Of the leaf's losses, and of some woman's garden of gestures
Which were once our heart's sweet roses. A photo from my cousin
Comes today, it is one of our grandmother. She is still young.
She is still smiling. She is still that fountain thwarting summer's heat.

In the book of lies, at the vaporous edge of love's intense
Explosion, the old cliché of a hooded figure waits, come
In the heat of our last breath to take our withered spirit hence.

In the book of the heart, it is this face, this smile, this sweetness
That has gathered every rose, which pulls us through death's hot
Catastrophe. That crystal frost of fire's last kiss of decay
Alive again in her love's spring. Of all our many losses, this one
Was first, the first rose fallen, the first revived, the one
Whose power was a dearer sun, the terrestrial human
Sun, more giving than that pitiless light in heaven. Today
I received this picture of my Honey, and all the fisted knots
Of my lost joys, opened their hands and filled my pulse with roses.

The Whining and Barking Ceremony of the "Dog Dance"
Clutter 141
Written 30 July, 2016

————————— • —————————

Even in these most gentrified enclaves of the city,
Some element of savagery persists. People keep dogs,
And on these hot summer afternoons, though the dogs are silent,
We can feel the echoes of their confinement as amputees
Still feel the agony of their lost limbs. These animals
Are each the last survivors of a pack, and their lonely
Speech will start again in the cool of evening, the calm air rent
By their desultory needs. These canine sounds in the fogs
Of human sound pierce the courteous masks of the gentry.

The creator god is veiled. He is anxious to see his
Human creation, but he remembers that time when the veil
Fell, and he saw. One eye dissolved, and the human died of bliss.

And that is why, to this day, all the citified gentry
Must wear masks, and worship a masked god. That the dogs, for all
The disintegration of their clans, still see, not eye to eye,
But snout to snout. Their god sniffs out all doubt. Their loyalty
Proves that. But for us, divinity is metaphorical.
The whole of the city exists to express this senseless plea:
"Death must not be." And yet death lives, and these pets are our polite
Burials of savagery. They form our routine denials —
The dogs are silenced by the heat, and the snarl is the city's.

Meditation on a Parched Lawn
Clutter 041
Written 31 July, 2016

———— • ————

As a child on summer days, often I lay on the ground,
And looked at the sky, and listened to the grass growing. Can
You imagine a finger sliding across wrinkled foil, with an
Underlying channeling of honey? The growing grass made
Music much like that, with the sky as silent audience.
There was a feline quality to my devotion. Cats may
Sleep on a welcome mat, supremely assured that they can,
And that no one would ever dare step on them, their dreams purring
Along, like mine, both harmonized with the growing grass sounds.

Are the systems of spirits — as has been written — arranged
Along paired axes, grass/sky, cat/dream — their quiet radiance
An imperceptibly swift spin, that, when slowed, emits "The Strange ..."

"The Strange," the miraculous communion that the childish
Poet still entices, though in these mean summer days, the grass
Is silenced by drought — or nearly so. The word that made the sky
Take note is now enfeebled and innocuous. What grows
Is not grass, but despair. Can you imagine the emergence
Of this new music, growing like cracks in glass, like cracks in bones?
We have made the strangely miraculous strangely dull, and why
We have done so remains a mystery. Under the brown grass,
Lies the body of a child. Perhaps you can hear his anguish.

How Silence Spins
Distance at Sunset
Clutter 931
Written 1 August, 2016

———————— • ————————

This was one of those Monday summer afternoons when the sun
Hoarded all its gold, exuding only miserly white
Heat. So, now, when the evening breeze releases these riches —
Coins dazzling through jittery shadow apertures — we feel
Gratitude, gratitude as something ceremonious,
And ever so quaintly exotic, something slightly formal,
As if an official, called to court, sends condolences
To his wife in the form of a poem, and she, the wife,
Responds in kind. Neither poem will fulfill its aspiration.

These words of parting convey ten-thousand regrets. What could they
Say to convey their loss, and express what the sun expresses,
Dispersing its lavishness? The day's gold is passing away.

The official in his golden carriage pulls velvet curtains
To block his view of the mountains. The wheels creak as they roll
Over treacherous cobbles. The road is crowded by dizzy
Steeps, and the breath of the laboring horses smells just like
Sorrow. A sharp sleet starts to blow. Meanwhile, the wife expresses
Herself with embroidered lines, silk songbird-words that try and try
To fly, and close the distance. She writes: "My sadness mutes me.
It seems I am not destined to share my heart." Imperial
Sunset gilds the cold, white paper, and stills her swan-quill pen.

Hole Maker
Clutter 831
Written 2 August, 2016

———— • ————

The same brisk breeze that swept low clouds across the pre-dawn sky
Has, as the morning hours fled, swept the grey away. The sky grew
White, then blue, with nobody watching. The sky has summarized
Equivalencies inside the brain, where mosaics of cell
Types cling together in layered skeins of bunched and folded sheets,
These tangled maps and maplets, extracting meaning as each cell
Is awash in heavenly sights. This is the enterprise
Of making the layers One Heavenly Personhood. He stews
On the morals of His underlings, and speaks His one word: "I."

The sailors', the farmers', the lovers' most daring adventure
Is to see in the sky a mind with their desires, is to see
In each fluttering sheet of breeze-stirred lights, a moral order.

No clouds now, just blank blue. And the many layers of maps
And maplets depict a Giant's mind, much like our own — an
Unknown country: the unborn body or the body in
The grave. I am no farmer, perhaps no sailor, and if
A lover, a most inept one. I am a poet, whose speech
Evokes an audience of one — a solitary in the mist
That was, before the wind erased me. I am that alien,
Earthy personage, more empty than the Giant's infant
Mind. Among promiscuous tangles, I am the moral gap.

Knowing My Body to Be Devoid of Intelligence, I Compassionately Remember My Humbler Relations

Clutter 731

Written 3 August, 2016

———————— • ————————

Only the most mythomaniac of brooding idlers
Can appreciate this fact: On our continent, rodents,
Not primates, occupy the arboreal niche. The brooder
Thinks: It is absurd to imagine a squirrel Hanuman
As desireless devotee. A varmint-allegory
Of courage cannot inhabit our local trees. Fat cushions
Of intellectual sloth bury hoards of the brooder's
Insights, squirreled away like nuts in a thousand-thousand
Niches — in those proper nouns, which propagate like cancers.

In addition to birds, John James Audubon also painted
Squirrels — exquisitely detailed squirrels. You could say he
Painted the finest of furs as desire consummated.

Snipers in the Civil War apprenticed with squirrel guns. They
Could hit the eye of a squirrel a league away. The brooder
Thinks about the eyes of men. For all their detail, Audubon's
Squirrels look odd. He shot his models first, then painted them. They
Read like the myths of gods which never existed, like complete
Fabrications born from obsessive brooding — and — like the way
Images breed when stripped of every semblance of devotion.
They look like metastasized facts that grew into tumors.
They look like the labored science of a primate gone insane.

Entangled
Clutter 631
Written 4 August, 2016

——————— • ———————

You could do worse than choosing the common English ivy
As your psychopomp into the soul realm of ubiquitous
Space and time. First, go to your garden wall, and like a painter
Determined to map every vein of every leaf, let your eye
Begin to meticulously trace this green, embracing
Creature. Like a lover tracing the face of your beloved, sigh
Or swoon, if you must, but do allow your sight to abjure
Mere physical light, and collect itself beyond the brain-nest
At the assemblage point above your head. Here, start your journey.

We have attached all our sympathies to human bodies.
This must change. We know but one central spine, while the winding
Stems of The Green Lords transcend many centers with their armies.

Our mundane forms of speaking break the trance, while poetic forms
Deepen it. You have long ago departed the body
Affixing its bony armature in the garden. You
Are no longer you. You have dispersed your center, and entwined
The sun's love round his gift of green. You are No One embracing
Everything. You look left and see right. You are divine.
You have common-ivy-insight into lines, wherein the you
That is, is now a poem. What is the true shape of your story?
Absence — absence of privileged centers, presence of growing forms.

Life Boat

Clutter 531

Written 5 August, 2016

———————— • ————————

"Poets are the unacknowledged legislators of the world,"
Or so wrote Percy Bysshe Shelley, who drowned, in what many
Believe to have been a suicide, but which I prefer to
Interpret as a mystical act of merging with the sea.
Politicians, their heads just above a sea of rage, stand
Tip-toe on the hearts of poets. Thus we know that sea
Levels are rising. We listen to politicians, not to
Poets. We drown in what Blake called "the sea of time and space,"
which he
Showed as Newton with calipers, trying to square the circle.

The gravitas of denial: a sub-aqueous throne
Encrusted with barnacles and lichens, where a naked man,
Enthralled by his own figures, obliviously broods alone.

In the post-continental world, whose people, if any,
Will breathe with gills, and live in a truthless realm, immune to
Drowning, no one will know names. "Newton," "Blake," "Shelley" will
be
But a spittle of rage in the current of political
Cross-talk. Names will be meaningless mountains of sub-surface sand,
And darkness and pressure will be our lonely lot, denials
As superfluous as fact. While up here, a new poetry,
One without legislation, will drift about on the blue
Of an endless surface, like light on the face of the sea.

L'art Japonaise: Crow Gliding with Beak Closed; Sparrows Copulating in Dust

Clutter 431

Written 6 August, 2016

———— • ————

On this early August afternoon, the fine weather
Smiles with fresh sea breezes. These have sailed across many leagues
Of open ocean with news of an anniversary. Do
You know that moment when lovers eyes' — having traversed the most
Beautiful of landscapes — forests, mountains, meadows, blue views
Of sky and sea — suddenly darken with disturbing hosts
Of premonitions? — the wing-shadow of a crow set loose
For a crucial instant of remorse, a radiation leak
X-raying through the decades to recrudesce past terrors.

When "Little Boy" fell on Hiroshima, how many crows were
Counted among the dead? How many sparrows fell? And whose
Was this black rain washing down to Hell — without a God to care?

No matter how bucolic the landscape, how beautiful
The weather, there remains the dark chance of an accidental
Detonation of fissionable material. Little
Boy has loved and lost before. The landscape has gone dark. The black
Rain has often fallen through those eyes, which said "I love you,"
But now say "I am gone." We cannot, can never redact
The cloud of the past, which always tells of shadows in free-fall.
The flight of the crow, the dying sparrows' lascivious call,
Expose those sentimentalists, who cannot love at all.

Alchemical Cathartic for Untouchables

Clutter 331

Written 7 August, 2016

---•---

The ancient forms of poetry recitation, like certain
Types of weather — sunny, not too warm — resulted in an effect
Technically referred to as "cardiorespiratory
Synchronization." *That* disease has been almost completely
Eradicated. But symptoms, following exposure, can
Lie dormant for decades. Then, something as small as one leaf
Tonguing sky-reflections trigger a reaction — uncanny
Leprous granulomas of the eyes, reparatory acts,
Nerves, skin attack the body with ecstatic lexicons.

"Shall I compare thee to a summer's day?" No. I think I shall
Not. The sun is destroyed by a single gesture. One hand-span
Veils his hyperbole. The culture's health is health's betrayal.

The flowers of evil are artificial flowers,
And the body that reads the first infectious book lives henceforth
Impervious to weather: a leper, now exiled in
A colony of one, all shunning his asynchronous
Lack of style. It is said that a malady's first cause can
Also be its last cure. *That* is poetry's ancient curse —
To cure its audience through these ghastly symptoms, wherein
The poet suffered inspiration. The outcast learns to speak of war
As love, his verses the homeopathy of Sulphur.

Sir Phillip Sydney Reincarnates as an Old Codger Feeding Pigeons in the Park

Clutter 231

Written 8 August, 2016

———————— • ————————

Blog tag: "Sad seeker seeks soothing from urban bird's cooing,"
Which in tradition's well-tread vernacular reads: "A dove
Calls the sleeper from the depths of dream." Headline: WE ARE
PERPETRATING THE SIXTH MASS SPECIES CRISIS. Dreams echo
Disturbing images of the S.M.S.C. Flies swarm
The bodies of dead doves. Death drones supplant love's cooing woes
With grotesque ecological sorrows. The seeker
Knows that "living death, dear wounds, fair storms, and freezing fires" show love's
Most current "hellish pains" with lacey words unfit for wooing.

The Queen's most noble courtiers no longer lavish sonnets
Of quaint praises to lovers all named "Star." The planet warms
More quietly than a soldier, pierced by love's dart, turns poet.

Unlike Elizabethan sonneteers, their flight is bullet
Straight. Quick-eyed, slender-tailed, when they ascend, their wings make
Whistling or whinnying sounds, and their calls, drawn-out and soft,
Remind the lonely of laments, their name synonymous
With Mourning. Their subtle grey-brown feathers, viewed close up, will charm
The sight with shimmering iridescence. From conspicuous
Perches, unmated males, plaintively, softly cast aloft
One round note followed by two rounder echoes. Their thin breasts make
A gamey meat, and they are hunted, and skewered on mental spits.

The Making of Art-Glass
Begins with Blowing Bubbles
Clutter 131
Written 9 August, 2016

—————————— • ——————————

I am suspicious of those who assert that one might describe
One's own person solely through photographs or anecdotes,
Vital statistics or quotes. We live in an ocean of crushing
Pressure, a glassworks of evolution, and these pressures,
Through eons, develop soul-creatures, Medusae, of whom
We have no conscious perception. These primitive adaptors
Of the first oceans are our translucent organ-mass, rowing
Or pulsing bell-shaped morphologies through time. We cannot go
Diving in mirrors unless our human shapes morph through these tribes.

In the new field of "Object Studies," objectologists
Have focused their research on jellyfish made of glass. In dark rooms
Their models of *Aequorea* fixate the exquisite.

And yet, like love, it is all so delicate. One word too
Harsh, or only slightly false, and those relentless pressures
Do their work. The glass is shattered, and the fragments scatter,
Like glistening bubbles fizzing to tinier bubbles,
And the whole question of the soul goes effervescing through
The mysterium's eddies. I cannot ever "know" myself,
Since what I call the self, has no existence. So — who you are,
Or who I am, or how or if we try to love each other,
Seem matters that most matter when fragility lets light through.

An Intimate Photograph
of an Unmade Bed
Clutter 031
Written 10 August, 2016

————— • —————

The acquisition of emotion cannot be equated
With the acquisition of objects, and yet objects absorb
Our emotions, and become records of our psychic states.
Imagine these objects — these words — cavorting on one side
Of a sheet of paper. We shall label this "Self-Portrait One."
On the verso of this sheet, we will place your object-I's,
As say, the various shapes of your pillow when you wake —
A shape for every morning of your life. Do you hear that roar?
These are waves erasing your face with feelings evaded.

The paper ages from white to sepia-toned, the lines
That formed a signature grow faint, but wrinkle lines, like those on
Pillow cases, evolve more cryptic glyphs — fine and ultra-fine —

Meta and ultra-meta-fine, the cotton so subtly
Embossed with ever subtler weavings of emotion. First rays
Of sunlight rake across this form, wherein your dreams were born,
Wherein they found their grave. The color of the light is faded
Rose. The light falls through a tree. The rays turn faded green. No one
Has seen the beauty of these changes. No one was fated
To see them. And yet they are felt. They turn force to form.
They write in the shifting sands new tracks of emotion. They
Make of your feelings acquisitions as timeless as the sea.

In the Beginning Was Her Word
Clutter 921
Written 11 August, 2016

————————— • —————————

On the wall of a room I use for sleep and meditation
Is a photo of my mother on her wedding day. She
Is just out of her teens, and has already lived through one
Worldwide depression, and one World War, and her eyes, which are
Magnified in the glass of round wire spectacles (the which I
Always thought were as much a part of her features as her
Mouth or skin), are vivacious with fear. The legendary sum
Of all her hauntings still live in those eyes. They follow me
Always — fear — but not just fear — life in the spirit's dimensions.

You will read these words, and with a spectacular transference
Of meaning, will think of your own mother, and how her eyes
Follow you, and you will miss the point of this utterance.

No. No. These eyes, and the ghosts of their vivacious fear, in need
Of their fragile prostheses to see her duty, can only
Be meant for the son who reads their love. This mystery
Is only pierced when one transcends the realm of identity,
The phrases "Your mother," "My mother," the blinding pronoun "I,"
Are first and finally the hauntings of the spirit, that SHE
Of living terror, who protects, and who tames life's calamities
Through simple domestic acts. SHE feeds. SHE heals the sick. SHE cleans
The dirty. And the sum of her scolding is Creation's speech.

After Many Trials,
The Experiment Came to Nothing
Clutter 821
Written 12 August, 2016

———————— • ————————

After a month of fasting, participants in the study
Reported bizarre dissolutions of identity —
The feelings of the sidewalk as the foot traversed it, the taste
Of moss as it greened a shaded wall, the movement of a word
Inside the mouth — "There is a flicking sensation, as if light
Stiffened for an instant and clicks against the teeth, or the word
Is felt rumbling across the ridges of the palate, dripping taste,
Like stalactites in a cave, an experience equally
Profound for listener as for speaker — a shared ecstasy."

How these notes intrigue! "The whole world became my bed. I felt
I could float anywhere without sinking. An absence of light
Or sound enveloped me, yet this was deeply sensual."

How should we read ? — "It seemed molecules of water or of air
Had infused each pore of my body, even those of organs
Deep in the enclaves of the self, bone, muscle, nerves, any least
Semblance of solidity becoming jellies of neon
Atremble as blissful translucence, a sweetly mothering light
That I could trust. I felt protected, yet shook with emotion."
Or this? — "I was always so hungry, but not in the least
For food. It was the void I craved. Oh!, to live as I am
Is ghastly! I must be air! — as light as air! — the Word in air!"

What the Poet, Thrown Out
of Plato's *Republic*, Had to Say
Clutter 721
Written 13 August, 2016

The trendy thing would be to talk about bats, a.k.a.,
Chiroptera, just in the hematophagous sense, vampires
Now being all the rage, not as evil manifestations,
But as symbols of desire — the languid taste for blood being
Evidently the new aphrodisiac for young people
Bored even with the drug of Eros. But I am not going
To do that. The drinks of flying mammals do not concern
Me. I care for their biosonar skills, and never tire
Of imagining myself threading the baffles of a cave.

"What cave is that?" you ask, and I, with my convoluted face
That catches every sound, every word in its grotesque baffles,
Answer, "Why, the cave of the night-poem, the cave of caves."

We have talked about boredom ad nauseam, that languor
Of spirit inverted in church belfries, waiting for nightfall
To go batty, to flutter about in the baffles of a dream,
To multiply our un-personhoods through the points-of-view
Of cultural Draculas — Vlad-the-Impaler as the self
Of selves, on the prowl for minor titillations. "I hate you,
My love," the squeaky mantra of youth's mad affairs. It would seem
That there is no way through such darkness. It would seem that all
This flitting about needs a more poetic form of sonar.

What I Found in the Depths of a Distant Gaze
Clutter 621
Written 14 August, 2016

—————— • ——————

Somewhere on the face of the earth, there is a person, whose
Features represent the composite of all of your many
Experiences. She may not be an Aphrodite,
And when you see her fragile body in a dream — bent, beaten
Down by hard labor and bitterness, your own bitterness
Becomes real to you, embodied, wise in pain, a woman
Whose eyes tell stories you do not want to hear. One story
Involves the disappearance of a child after a journey
Of many lifetimes. It is unclear if the child is you.

East of the Black Hills is a treeless, rolling prairie, where
My mother was reared. At the end of her life, we went there, and
Here, she showed me the unmarked graves of two of her brothers.

Just these two indentations in the earth. One for a boy who
Died from a tonsillectomy performed on the kitchen
Table, and the other of an unnamed infant, who died
An hour after birth. My mother always wore glasses, but I
Recall her eyes, green, and compacted from looking at land
Whose horizons had collapsed to these faint cavities. I
Recall their willingness to work, to perform endless duties —
Cleaning, cooking, caring — but seeing no hope of freedom,
Except for that freedom that comes from doing what one must do.

Communion

Clutter 521

Written 15 August, 2016

In spite of the warnings of many fairy tales, often
I go into the deep woods because I need to break free
From the Once-Upon-a-Time into No-Time, into
A wandering state of being that dissolves the boundaries that
Separate me from not-me, and leave only forest. What
Arises then is an harmonious complexity that
Blends tiny, brief milkmaid blossoms with redwoods which brood
For millennia on fog and sun. What does the witch eat
But those who are lost in the depths of this meditation?

The children orphaned by their parents' poverty, and sent
Into the heart of abandonment, into the depths of the Green World, fat
With fairy tale fears, are trapped in her house of astonishment.

These No-Time seeds produce the fruit of delirium, so sweet
To the adult who needs to recover his dreams, who needs
To hear the forest whispering words of fire in all her
Witchy cacklings: "Oneness is Oneness." That is the lure
That draws me into danger, that is the candy house, that
Is the oven cracking with old bones. Tiny petals, four,
White, tinged with pale rose or lavender, the milkmaid flower,
Is the candy I hunger for. This spirit at my feet,
Is the child she has caged, and fattened for her feast.

Blob

Clutter 421

Written 16 August, 2016

Mirror rumors — the returned reflection — a self devolved
From any sexual gender to an IT with eyes, all
The other senses but thin, ribbony tentacles fluttering
Backwards in the irresistible Tsunami of
Advertising. IT sees images devoid of any smell
Or volume, and an ocean of desire spreads vilely above
What used to be depths of emotion to make brief, jangling
Slogans. The IT's eyes look for things to buy. The tentacles
Are starving for something to cling to as ITS gaze revolves.

Squids jetting ink propel themselves through submerged asylum
Halls where Ezra Pound — preserved in formaldehyde — still calls
For a sanity of multilingual stratagems.

But IT refuses to hear what IT cannot see. IT has
Lost the capacity to volumize lexicons. IT cannot
Detect those funny smells with ITS sanitized olfactories:
The poetry of the satirist whose rumors deepen
Mirrors. Meanwhile, Ezra Pound, in his formaldehyde vial
Keeps belching words into the yellow fluid, his phlegm
A kind of acid which softens the glass chamber. When he
Speaks, a voluminous odor intrudes. He cannot
Live nor die, yet keeps expanding his gelatinous mass.

At Sunset, the Doddering Old Professor Recites Romantic Verses on the Beach
Clutter 321
Written 17 August, 2016

————————— • —————————

Something prevents us from ever thinking about that day
When a lifetime of looking will have degenerated
Into habit, and even those dearest things — our own face,
Our own body — will depart, like a passionate love whom we
Have tired of, the very door, the very moment of parting
Become a blur of bland indifference made watery
By senescence, not by tears. "I love you" becomes a phrase
Retreating like a wan echo in a macerated
Ear. The lover tells the lover, "I am bored," and the sun turns grey.

The tragedy will unfold so gradually that you will
Not even see the color drain from the leaves, or the flickering,
Which made you so anxious, become eternally settled.

At this point, you are most vulnerable to predatory
Dreams, the cities of your past, the great masses of people
You said you loved, but lost, your fears, your shame, your body, all
Will slide down as streams slide to the ocean, and now you see,
Beyond looking, the lurid tiger stripes of waves, waves rolling
Relentlessly towards the curious dreamer. And who is he,
This prey in the tiger's eye, alone on the beach, this small
And inattentive victim of ennui? He is the final
Distraction, the stranger reading love poems by the sea.

Amateur Private Eye
Clutter 221
Written 18 August, 2016

———————— • ————————

There are diagnoses collected in the teeth from all those
Conversations unwillingly overheard. These mysteries
Require detectives of the spirit, those almost slovenly
Sleuths, whose clues are derived from edges — the odd word
Among odd-word-droppings, which like an old bull out to pasture,
You chew as the cud of other people's dreams. You have heard
Of the great proliferation of detective stories.
The culture cannot get enough of murder and mystery.
It is as if mayhem must precede our chance to be whole.

The hard things in the body, the teeth, the bones, can even
Survive the decay which follows death. They are the clues, the cures
For the soul's demise, and they grind at the edge of perception.

We lie in the dark, in a rubble of broken teeth, broken
Images, our metaphors eluding comprehension,
And yet there is this person, slovenly, probing, searching
The rubble for answers. He is always the outsider,
A bit unscrupulous, a bit daft, but able to endure
Disgrace for justice. The indefatigable questioner,
He hears the facts in what he overhears,. He reads a thing's
Essential quality from weapons and from wounds. He comes
To the edge, goes past the edge, and finds the crime inside him.

Programming Emotion
Clutter 121
Written 19 August, 2016

———————— • ————————

Hasn't your study of computer simulations convinced
You that simple behaviors, the feelings derived from the scent
Of the lily, perhaps, can result from enormously
Complicated substrates of computation? In performing
Schumann's *Dicterliebe*, for example, the fifth song, *"Ich will*
Meine Seele Tauchen," has the pianist repeating
A simple motif in the treble clef, while a jubilee
Of running figurations in the bass create a ferment
Of sound that replicates the perfume of the lily's chalice.

Heine and Schumann, the singer and the pianist, must shape
From alien elements the lily's simple kiss, the seal
Of her mute mouth unlocked from depths which churn a simple surface.

You, you however, too schooled and damaged by summaries
Of love, you live in the twilight of ignorance, your past
Romances, unlike the song's poet, obliterated
By the cruelest bludgeoning of years, until, until
Those sounds, like the flower's actual scent, bring back a thrill
Enriched by artistry. It is not that the artist's pill
Is bitterer than yours, but its losses are compounded
From other elements, from a discipline of hands, of lacks,
Of voice that stir more complex scents from creamier lilies.

Abortive Conception
Clutter 021
Written 20 August, 2016

———————— • ————————

At the salon, the brilliant composer made it perfectly
Clear that a lifetime city dweller need not concern himself
In the least with Nature. True, the sparrows warbled
Up the sun between the buildings, but they were still so dirty,
And their lice carried disease. No, his works would have relevance,
Relevance on the contemporary intellectual scene,
As in the hubbub of strangers ascending in the steel
Box of an elevator, their breathing synched by the cable's
Subtle clicks, their thoughts controlled by the city's machinery.

My mother miscarried a baby before I was born.
She lugged the fetus for a month, knowing that the Absence
Called "Death" had already claimed it, and had despoiled its form.

The brilliant composer at the salon despoils forms. He
Has made it clear that relevance — in the intellectual
Sense — must be synchronized with Absence, that the whispering
Strangers in the elevator are not ascending, and that,
As they plummet to a predestined stop, it is only chance
That will end the composition, and not silence. We seek that
Art which the city-brain concocts without the warbling
Of dirty sparrows. We seek that mother, staring at a wall,
Who listens for some stir inside her, whose song could ease her grief.

Like Hot Summer Water
Through a Sieve of Winter Frost
Clutter 911

Written 21 August, 2016

———————— • ————————

I am told that the tiny swimmers that I see when I gaze
Into the afternoon summer sky are white corpuscles.
In mid-ocean, a man in a very small, bright yellow
Boat floats on the clearest calms of turquoise waters. He peers
Down — deep down — at the pallid body of an animal,
Whose motions beckon him. There are souls towards which the mind
veers,
Though the risks of solitude and drowning are great. The yellow
Boat casts sharp, knife-shaped reflections on the water's gentle
Undulations, as our thoughts go winding through their maze.

I am going to sleep now, and will dream about the broken
Shards of Grecian vases, the fragments where the potter's skill
Shows the sleekest of human forms cavorting with dolphins.

Thomas Steans Eliot, the pinched-nosed banker, spoke of "sea-
Wood," "which burned green and orange" "in which sad light a carvèd
Dolphin swam," but when I awaken from his synthetic
Perfumes, I am still enthralled by the clarity of my
Own blood's swimmers, and still pondering the tentacles
Of these mysterious fragments, so busy in this sky
Inside my eye, so difficult to describe with their frenetic
Drifting, jumping movements against immense pellucid
Heights — a man, a boat, and yellow knives that carve a turquoise sea.

Summing Up the Unknowable
in a Lightless Realm
Clutter 811

Written 22 August, 2016

———————— • ————————

The author of the Apocalyptic Cyclopedia
Of Advanced Magic(k)al Arts has emphatically declared
"Magic does not tolerate belief." The spell: Summer. Monday.
Languor. Afternoon. Breeze-leaf-talk. Hazy white sky. Solitude.
Out of a half sleep comes a future that is incomplete,
Always failing in some crucial detail, just as the lassitude
Of the past fails, always erasing details. It is the way
Of the non-ordinary to hide itself, the most weird
Things masked by that which declares the common its simulacra.

The twin Creator Gods stand back to back, each thinking himself
All powerful, each believing himself complete
In every detail. Each is trying to wake himself. Each fails.

Each duelist walks the baffles of his cave, each counting
The bats that hang upside-down from the ceiling. 'The bats,' each
Thinks, 'are the sleeping hours, reversing sight in dream.' The bats are
No such thing. They are the blank before the start, the stop before
The end. They are the sonar masters, the magic's poetry.
The afternoon grows weary of Time's logic, and languor
Subdues the hazy distillation. Each you, each me are
One, one bat that hangs in solitude, wrapped in black dreams.
Each tolls a bell of darkness, filled with summary echoings.

Antique Conversation
with a Xenophobe
Clutter 711
Written 23 August, 2016

———————— • ————————

Certain flat-earther millenarian sects of England
In the seventeenth and eighteenth centuries began to
Practice inverted burial, the corpse perpendicular,
And head down. Why? Because the world would be up-side-down after
The apocalypse, and the dead would be on their feet once more,
Praising a new sun, following resurrection. Interred,
In the interim, I suppose, they will have to endure
The indignity of death's reversal, reversed, and get used
To their hair getting tangled with grass roots, as best they can.

I can imagine talking to one of them after my last
Descent, and listening to wisdom derived from dirt, this Lord
Of our underground sleep, astonished by his broken rest.

I do not think Hell will shock me so much as the New Earth will
Shock him — he who was dreaming with pale roots underground will
Be surprised that the bloodless worms of the Word will have changed
To green exuberance, and the whole disaster of the End
Days will be passé. Then, I shall be living with the poor
That Jesus said would always be among us. We could be friends,
Perhaps, but friends in passing. I wonder, will a new rage
Consume him again, mad with nostalgia for his dreadful
Past, which can no longer feast on fear, or send me down to Hell.

Bittersweet

Clutter 611

Written 24 August, 2016

———— • ————

I seem to have developed a painter's addiction to
The way this afternoon's light wraps the last, rotting blobs of fruit
Still clinging to our spindly, neglected orange tree. The spheres
Are collapsing from within, and warping into grotesque
Shapes, the dimpled rinds dehydrated in some places, while
In others still showing moist, plump health. My visual cortex
Can make nothing of most of these adjectives, the eyes look where
The light's hooks hook their attention, not caring that the fruit
Is inedible, aware only of their luminous truth.

What terrible ordeals we endure for words like "rotting,"
And "grotesque," ordeals that help us acquire the dubious skill
Of judgement, and the ability to corrupt our seeing.

I seem to have developed a poet's addiction to
The way words — charged as they are with emotion — can defeat
Our Day Star's power to foment pure physical beauty.
The blob of my head, my desiccated skin, unplucked by
Fame or Fortune, rots in a litter of words, inedible
As to meaning, but still ripe fruit as sound. Sound — the last good-bye
To judgement — the hooked heart hooked with invisible beauty —
The sun of a breeze that shakes the poor, spindly tree, and treats
The ear with fruits, which, rotting, still grow sweet with grotesque
truths.

Post-Modern Variation
on a Romantic Theme
Clutter 511
Written 25 August, 2016

———— • ————

You might ask why we allow these birdfeeders to hang empty
In our back yard, when delight might be ours for cheap birdseeds.
Well, they attracted rats too, which hosted a parasite
That fed also on human blood, an infestation too gross
To endure, and too terrible to eradicate. Bitten,
We threw ourselves into a frenzy of cleansing, the most
Murderous of traps and chemicals employed to set things right.
Things were set right. But the yard is quiet now. And though freed
Of mites, an aridness pervades the air — *la belle dame sans merci.*

In his watercolor called "The Dead Knight," Robert Bateman
Depicted a landscape of shimmering greenery wherein
A white face, small as a sprig of Queen Anne's Lace, lay hidden.

It is irrelevant to extract morals from these clottings
Of events — the backyard feeders, rats, itchy skin eruptions,
The palely loitering presence of Keatsean Death, all
Of this astonishing detail of watercolor grasses,
Needles, leaves, wax-white faces, and wisps of lacy blossoms,
They all add up to this: The weight of boredom, the masses
Of illegible associations where miracle
Lies dead, and stands no chance, no chance at all, of resurrection.
Here, in late summer, no breeze stirs in the leaves, and no bird sings.

The Quiet Theater of the Absurd
Clutter 411
Written 26 August, 2016

—————————— • ——————————

On this coast, typically in summer, when inland heat
Collides with cool air masses, arising from the ocean,
Advection fog occurs. Often it takes the whole morning
For the accompanying winds to sweep the density clear,
And allow the sunlight access to the hysterical trees.
On the ground, no shadows suddenly birth shadows, which tear
Golden mouths in themselves, as, opening and closing,
They whisper-mime a message. How strange these gesticulations!
The sun is out, but the fog still blurs the weather's windy speech.

Undoubtedly, mime predates articulate speech, and by
The earliest days of Greek theater, it was already
An art silently expressive of moral lapses and lies.

Gestures are so direct, and the trembling shadows of the trees,
Turn comically Chaplinesque, or in another flick, seem
As tragic as the mute death of a child or an animal —
The Harlequin sun juxtaposed with this specter of darkness,
In rapid changes of costume and character. But speech
Too has its gestures, bright sounds and dark ones, words that caress,
And words that steal the breath, as the child or the animal,
Resurrected in a line of verse, plunges us through black sleep,
Or like the windy fog, drives us through rainbow obscurities.

Scavenged Again and Again
Clutter 311
Written 27 August, 2016

———————— • ————————

After an afternoon nap, I awaken from one dream
Into another, the two species differing only
Slightly, the tiny birds in *this* one's blue cavity,
Crossing the sky's mosaics with wind-tossed trees beneath their
Finest featherings, while the earth in *that* one's stomach heaps itself
Into an anthracitic mound, only, after some fanfare
Of smoke and thunder, to cleanly split into a perfectly
Cut Christian cross. These two animals keep fighting over me,
As hyenas do a kill. Are these things what they seem to seem?

What I seem to seem is awake, but if that were so, why
Is it that I can never return to the start? Why will
This or that doubled one keep doubling the lines of my sight?

Sometimes it seems I seem to be a god, creating my
Fluidly rubbery creations from images dripped
From the teeth of hyena hungers. But the species of my
Planet do not obey me. The birds will not sing my praises
From their trees, and the coal cross below keeps blazing the child
I buried. What is it about these wayward images
That hold their Lord and Master in their thrall, so that what I
Seem to seem to have to be is nothing much at all. It
Hurts to be this flummoxed Why, this offspring of a double lie.

Bird Watching
Clutter 211
Written 28 August, 2016

———————— • ————————

Having become cancerous as a consequence of extreme
Self-aggrandizement, these cells of the body devoted
To vision cloud to a dull opacity. Today's facets
Of crystal transparencies obliterated by this
Lazy-eyed trick have become mechanical — no distances,
No depth, just shrunken screens of blue or green, of which we say: "This
Is a tree, this a sky. Nothing to see here, a meaningless
Churning of Chance, devoid of artistry, the parroted
Phrases of bird-brain evolution, no hint of poetry."

Yet, when fibrous masses of light connect to other
Fibrous lines, the perception of each inch of these distances,
These depths, takes on a crystalline quality, blazing and pure.

The masses becoming the sparks of leaves, the sparkings of bright air,
The concords and relations of details, sublime in their
Breezy interactions, and this, and this, we say, has meaning,
Chance has meaning, and the artistry, though parroted, is
Poetic. This is the sight, whose flashing iridescences —
Emerald or sapphire or ruby — spin gem elixirs. This
Is the voice whose squawking has a shape — of ivy fluttering,
Of common words, of anything connected to the weather—
Masses of layered, lacey glass shining in spreading feathers.

Dozing in Class
Clutter 111
Written 29 August, 2016

———————— • ————————

In the test room, we are given a nineteenth century
Novel ostensibly about the devout protagonist's
Infatuation with identical twins, one his sister,
The other his fiancé. This miscellany comprised
Of convoluted syntax and lexiconic fetishes
Is soon reveled to be an allegory where "I"
Stands for one and "you" stands for another kind of lover —
Both morally diseased, as when the latest poem shifts
The meaning of a former, compounding ambiguities.

Those being tested, embroiled in these academic questions,
Are like crustaceans a-scuttle on deserted beaches,
The next tongue of the surf expunging the last words written.

Be that as it may, I would refer the befuddled reader
To the ocean. Not the ocean of mundane shores, but the pool
Of dreams. What have you or I to do with these allegories?
How can anyone outside them save us, and safely break in-
To this tumult of swiftly swirling chaos, which crashes
Its violent surf into our pulse? You and I, caught in
These strangling currents, desire a life-saving poetry.
We desire an imageless sleep — a swirling opaline pool
Of darkening, swirling silence, immune to heart-break's thunders.

Beyond Good and Evil
Clutter 011
Written 30 August, 2016

———— • ————

On his Death Certificate, the cause of my father's death
Is listed as "accidental," which shocked me because I
Was led to believe that he died in his sleep. He was very,
Very old, unable to walk without assistance, or bathe,
Or "toilet" himself. But that did not stop him. He needed to
Move, to fall, because these two destinies are always the fate
Of fathers. We cannot protect ourselves from accidents. We
Cannot protect our fathers from themselves — although we must try,
And in our grief, we speed to that inertia that ends in death.

His fall was months ago, and I am still sorting through his old
Photographs and letters. I will always be sorting through
Them. I will sort and sort until I myself have grown old.

All of these words are words on the Certificate, opaque
To the indoctrinated self, whose fragile transparency
Is incapable of hiding evil. The father's laws
Are contradictory. They stem from the arbitrary truths
Of his authority, not from light. We are not privy to
The sources of their power. We are their victims, willing to
Bow to these fierce contradictions, because we always saw
His strength behind his laws. His Nature is immensity —
The inexhaustible love that only accidents can make.

PHASE FOUR

An Unexpected Respite of Dead Calm
Clutter 901
Written 31August, 2016

———————— • ————————

I would call it "a brilliant excursion of experience
Into artifice," but the artist who dubs herself "Sister
Nature" calls it "performance art for materials." In
Her piece named "Rain Room," she has dangled various
Lengths of monofilament plumb-lines, shining klieg lights through
them,
So that the rays split into dazzling prisms. As spectators pass
Though, the plumb-lines revolve and sway, as a solo violin
Plays a sea-sick-see-saw phrase. The spectators enjoy weird
Feelings of vertigo, as their bodies toy with dissonance.

I remember looking through last winter's rippling sheets of rain,
Each anonymous comet leaving a trail of prisms
In lonely winter veils, and I felt an oceanic pain.

My mother had died, and my father, now dead, was dying.
So, Sister Nature was a spate of tears. But winter died,
And summer's drought ensued, and spring's green lives all withered
Down to brown. The late, hot afternoon shuffles sea breezes through
The drooping foliage. I hear those rustling sounds, and merge with
them.
Their sea-bright-sea-born whispering bears me up, as I sail through
Their light-fused harmonies. The Rain Room's rocking has disappeared,
And only this expanse of day remains. Someone has died,
And someone is crying about it. But no one feels a thing.

The Medium is the Membrane's Mutilation
Clutter 801
Written 1 September, 2016

Reproducible mediums like photography or
Videos can never record post Tsunami or Cyclone
Devastation, although the eyes marvel at the images,
Adding them to those of couples strolling down Club Med
White-sand, segregated beaches beside clear turquoise waters.
These techno-distancing tricks can beautify any blend
Of property damage and death. To look at them pleases us.
Not so these devastating works by George Grosz. They show the blown
Apart entrails of souls, strewn through the craters between world wars.

His ink sketch, "*Mord*," is drawn with child sticks. Outside a tenement,
Two dead lie stiff in dirt: one man, one pregnant dog. The sun shares
The face of a whore. Both stare at the scene in scared astonishment.

Our presidential candidate is a bloated arrogance
Derived from accumulated devastations. We love his
Face, though it's depraved, because it radiates our terrors
And our meanness. We love his voice because our victims hate it.
We neither know nor care to know gross art. We only love our
Fear. Our fear sustains us, our fear and our images of it —
Reproducible, immortal, beautiful. We cherish our
Recordings of Tsunamis, of cyclones, of these ravages
Of mindless, natural force. They show the strength of ignorance.

This Limp Sack Drowning In Cold Seas May Only Be Saved by Oddities
Clutter 701
Written 2 September, 2016

———————— • ————————

In the dream I was in the hold of some kind of freighter,
Toiling in mid-ocean. The space has white, portal-less walls,
And is void of furniture or machinery. Our beloved
Ex-president is there. He points to something not noticed
Before. It looks like a giant, pasteboard egg carton, each
Compartment holding — what? I lean closer. Closer. The head
Of a great nutria-sized rat darts out, and our beloved
Ex-president laughs, and says "Look, there are a dozen. We call
Them 'horses for elephants," each one a different color.

Scratch one on the head — scratch — scratch — his dense fur is a silken
Red, his eyes black pin-heads, shiny as fish eggs. What is he
Supposed to symbolize? And should I be afraid of him?

In India, Ganesh is he who transcends obstacles —
An elephant who rides a rat. The images cannot be
Reduced to abstract qualities — greed, wealth, the belief that
The rat can squeeze into any corner and that his rider
Can crush all lack — no — the images preside over each
Organ of the body. They can make the heart go a-flutter,
Or the pulse goes flat. And the elephant, no matter how fat,
No matter how silly as symbol, can squeeze into a dream.
He can restore the president's long abdicated will.

On the Dangerous
Reticence of the Rationalist
Clutter 601
Written 3 September, 2016

———————— • ————————

We are always talking about that one thing without knowing
That we are talking about it, the lover on the other
Side of the world, decades of barren fields, the earth broken
By drought even to the depths of our buried dead, the chants
For miracle which unleash miracle, the suicides
Revived among hungry jackals, whose throats no longer rant
Of politics, but grow as mellifluous as woven
Winds freshened with birdsong — men and women praying together
In saffron robes round great layered mounds of satin blossoming.

We are always talking about that one thing, that thing destroyed by
Talk and distance, our cynical thought forever on the side
Of the mirror that is black, where the gods are heartlessly blind.

We are always talking, but only with the cracked talk of drought,
And only with thoughts that think they might walk by reason from cold
To warm without traversing the desert or the ice-bound poles.
We are always talking, talking, and talking, but never
Praying, and never wearing the saffron sun like music, like
Dawn togetherness in passion's blossoming. We are never
Unleashed as the miracle of rain, nor ever drowned in shoals
Of poetry. We are always talking, like old men, old
Women, lying alone in bed, whose talk coughs blood-clot doubts.

The Strength of One Straw
in a Whirling Gale
Clutter 501
Written 4 September, 2016

In the new utopia, all the neighborhoods are upscale,
And are deserted, even on Sundays, because the happy
Families have all entered the commodity arcade
Where the products have transcended usefulness, ascending
To the heaven of celebrity. Everyone has a name,
And all names have floating commodity valuations. Things
Like persons are superfluous, it is the glamour that claims
The enclaves of existence, the glamour of a happy
Substitute-self in a surrogate world — the point-of-sale.

My alien — deposited, strangely unhurt, by the odd
Caprices of a virtual hurricane beyond the bonds of fame —
Is a dummy of straw with a tongue like an iron rod.

The rod pierces everything. It breaks appliances, wrecks cars,
Disrupts simplistic propaganda slogans, disputes the claims
Of the advertisers, and covets a body, useful,
But obsolete, and never an object of celebrity.
In its attic is the hoarded junk of childhood's first shames.
In its kitchen are the boiled bones of orphans. In its pantry
Are the condiments of witches. In its toilet is the soul.
Like dead air on a broadcast, the rod pierces every name
With silence. Like silence, the rod praises things as they are.

Divination of the
Dumb to the Deaf
Clutter 401
Written 5 September, 2016

———— • ————

The darker practitioners of the art, termiting daily
Into the dry-rot of this era's techno-inanities,
Make absolute denials of absolutisms. Any
Particular hour of any particular day is Time's
Maquette for an anonymous poetry's pathetic cries
That blubber only in irrelevant sighs. The termite's
Appetite devours sounds, sights, smells, feelings — little things that leave
Odd shaped castings in the burrow as the wastings of beauty,
A toxic scat, but it's all the techno-ninnies want to eat.

In late summer, a leaf falls from a worried sycamore,
Its yellow anguish prophesizing autumn. As it writes
Its crumpled lines, it scrapes on barren dirt a song that withers.

The darker practitioners of the art, drifting through summer
Ease, can feel this prophet's intensity, this poetry
That sticks in the brain's irrelevant visions of peace,
This model of Time's busy insect secrets, secreting
The remnants of health in the midst of disease. If they must sigh,
Because one leaf must fall, they sigh from an anguished deepening.
And why this must be so, has no techno-inanity
Solution. The absolutism of this poetry
Is that its most potent prophecies shout silence to clogged ears.

Emergency Life–Saving Operation
Clutter 301
Written 6 September, 2016

———— • ————

To be schooled in the concentration required to hear, let
Alone, to recite a poem, one must be able to follow
Ordinary daylight like a knife dissecting the brain:
Optic nerve, optic chiasm, thalamus, the optic
Radiations — rainbow after rainbow, until the rain
Of photons bursts through to insight, and that splendid magic
Of the visual cortex transforms mud to jewels. The stained
Glass of the mind's cathedral illumines all that sorrow
Of the heart's cloister, and someone becomes a poet.

Someone — not you, never you — the listener, the reciter,
Wallows in synesthesias of sight and sound. To explain
This, daylight gives analogies — great trees rustling in blue air …

Great surgical vivisections of the most ordinary
Bodies, doing the most ordinary things — a man sitting
In a chair, sipping his coffee, a pregnant woman growing
A son or a daughter, a widow by a window, knitting —
The poem speaks of these things with singing lights. It is the same
For the schooled and the unschooled, but the schooled are feeling something
Bright — like spirit — the schooled can concentrate their minds, tracing
The scalpel of words, and with this extreme focus — following
That read cut — they extract diamonds from the ordinary.

Before The Word, God Cried, Lamenting the Sparrows that Would Fall
Clutter 201
Written 7 September, 2016

————— • —————

Intolerable afternoon heat has driven even
The poorest of sparrows into the thicket-deep shade of
Of a youth hostel's shrubberies. They puff out their feathers, sleep,
And dream. The doors are left open. A bird flies into a room.
It starts to chirp where young lovers, asleep in each other's
Arms, perspire, and dream. They have just met — traveling — too soon
To wake, to part, to resume their parents' flightless lives, where sleep
Is never foreign, never post-coital, never the drug of
A Gypsy road, with only poor sparrows for companions.

These are common terrors, the body's heat exploding, the cat
Creeping nearer, the bird's wings turned to human arms, the power
Of flight negated — the sun — stuck in the sky — parental — fat.

Often on hot days when my blood sugar falls, I somehow fail
To maintain a personal or even human coherence.
The common idioms, flashing from the depths, no longer
Belong to my poor history. They are the sparrow's fears
Articulated in the sweat of lovers. Like great waters
Falling, they make a leonine roar.   In the corner,
The cat lurks, more terrible than poetry in the hearer's
Ear. We are all one. — one — in love and in fear. And the nonsense
Of a personal, human self, collects in inhuman wails.

A Whisper From Under the Ruins
Clutter 101
Written 8 September, 2016

———— • ————

In every prelude to disaster, you will always find
The balloon-man demagogue, puffed up by the misplaced fears
Of his virulent followers. Think old black and white films
Of London during the Blitz, the fat barrage balloons cabled
Ineffectually to the burning city, the poem
A rubble of metaphors, the poet under the rubble,
Crushed by broken brick and splintered timbers. In the mad realms
Of history, fantasy prevails, the rampage of Hell's gears
Grinding flesh in the Bosch-like machine of distempered Time.

The image of evil is that of a buffoon. The buffoon
Has to be cruel, or he will be laughed into oblivion.
The prelude is a party, complete with festive balloons.

The clean-up at Sandy Hook and the clean-up at Auschwitz are
Not seen as the blood pulsing through one's own nightmare, but are felt
Instead as hot air filling the body politic — the signs
And portents of Hell shrunk to a Smart Phone's scale. An extreme
Caricature is the leader of the damned, a clown with comb-
Over hair posturing before cretins. The video screens
Are festive with fame and with premonitions of flame. Eyes,
Bright with rage and dull with ignorance, renew the Druid cult
Of the Wicker Man, and the poet's anguish fuels the fire.

Birth Trauma
Clutter 001
Written 9 September, 2016

———————— • ————————

Like imported vermin, certain thoughts overrun the mind,
Profusely proliferating, and devouring any
Healthful flora and fauna, so that a monoculture
Dominates a wasteland that only multiplies wastage.
For women, like my mother, who have lost babies, either through
Miscarriage or infant mortality, the body's spoilage,
Following the event, stays with them, its tragic nature,
Destroying their good nature, and adding the taint of worry
To all their motherly cares. Who was I in my mother's mind?

Question: Can the collapse of whole civilizations just be
The sad result of one idea gone bad, one profuse
Solution derived from the crazed affect from one lost baby?

One thinks of the Grecian "paradox of the heap." Subtract
One sand grain, then another; subtract one fret, then another.
When does the mind grow free of its heap of troubles? And what
Becomes of the final grain of sand? There is no point in
That adding and subtracting, when the grief you long to lose
Is something less, or the child you yearn to love is not some version
Of that verminous feeling, which has overwhelmed you. What
You have is the ghost of what you grieve for — the stranger
You never loved, the child of tears who brings your laughter back.

Moonlight on Swirling Water
Clutter 99
Written 10 September, 2016

Saturday afternoon, and the pellucid calm of the sky,
Immaculate as silence, shines in sharp contrast to the
Maniacal screaming of the stadium. That violence
Ships noise rudely through suburban trees, the ship breaking slowly
Apart as it rolls against a mountain, whose heights hold so
Few people. So few people can live without that noise, the peace
They say they want, subverted by a gibberish that fans
Out through the city like engulfing tides. What is it that the
People need that they cannot find in this hushed September sky?

The boys who play the game all sustain not so subtle head
Injuries. You can tell by the way they talk, like men whose throats
Are growing money tumors, like men who are already dead.

The body of Jesus walks across water, dragging this pole,
Which is half of the cross that will kill him. The pole is made
Of contradictory thoughts, the violence of people
Who say they are fighting for peace. The stadium echoes
Their faith, as their sons rain blows on each other, and the load
Of the pole grows heavier for their Lord, as the water road
Grows ever more turbulent. The moon has risen — its frail
Boat drifts above the crowd. Jesus has climbed aboard. He has raised
His shroud on the pole. That sail puffs out with noise, and ports
bruised souls.

Drowning Separately Together
Clutter 89
Written 11 September, 2016

———————— • ————————

Although the weather is still warm, the days are getting shorter,
And the middle-aged cousin whom you have never met, sends
You her sentimental verses, gooey with generalized
Emotion. How could she know that the word "pain" no longer means
Pain. An infant wraps her tiny fist around her father's
Finger. That was then. Now his hand is palsied, and trees grow lean,
And begin to drop their leaves. The wind shakes the veins of the tribe's
Elders, and they know they must prepare the ritual victim.
The blood of lost children leaks red on leaves, and nights grow longer.

Fathers have no time for their daughters, no time for themselves,
And all the minutes' little white coffins stretch across water
As treacherous, broken bridges for emotional cripples …

For the king must always be ritualistically cut,
Or else his devotion means nothing. And the customs demand
That the infant daughter be buried under aromatic
Heaps of crimson leaves. The words exchanged or the silences
Exchanged between mother and son or father and daughter
Will not make a bridge, even of coffins. The verses
Sent to cousins who are strangers, though they are oceanic
In intention, will only mask the pain, not show it. The hand
Of the infant grips her father's finger — then — slips free of it.

Prayer for Forgiveness, or the Divorced Father's Distant Lament
Clutter 79
Written 12 September, 2016

——————— • ———————

(Note: Telesphores was a "demiurge" whose stone figures were placed
beside the statues of the Greek healing god, Asklepios. His myth and
meaning was expounded by the great 20th century mythographer, Carl
Kerényi. Telesphores is the divine, stunted child that we become again
when we parent our children.)

Why do I always talk of trees as if they were people,
As if they were scholars of the sky, great sages imbued
With knowledge of the seasons, a million moods of moonlight
And of morning, the morning your child was born, the night your
Mother or your father died? The scholar-mythographer,
Carl Kerényi walked through cypress groves, where figures,
Like Telesphores, the dwarfish child, still hold the priestly knife,
And lurk beside the statue of the god. Those trees reveal truths
About our nightmare lineage, which haunt us when the nights grow still.

Moon-shadows of the flame-shaped cypress trees, devouring white
Marble orchards, are scholars teaching us about the terrors
Of ancient, childish hurts, the feelings that we kill to thrive.

We can never know our children; our parents can never know
Us. Telesphores has a blunt, stone body, his big head,
Squarish and hooded. Along with his knife, he holds a scroll,
A message from or to the healing god. His name means "finisher."

My daughter is hundreds of miles from here, and the years
That separate us are filled with voids, awaiting some cure
The god withholds. Why do I talk of trees? They are not people,
And yet they show us beauty when we mourn. Among the dead,
Lie seeds, seeds that are touched by moonlight, like our old parents'
bones.

Babe In the Woods
Clutter 69
Written 13 September, 2016

———————— • ————————

Yesterday I explored a grove of redwoods, which, oddly,
Bore my given name. The forms I saw there were extremely
Complicated — an intricate chaos of trees and light —
And emotions. I must confess, I have always had trouble
With authority. There were fallen trunks, which a century
Had carved and hollowed, the root balls twisted, gnarled, their old
First probes exposed. I must confess I am a child. Old as I
Am, I cannot squeeze into some puzzle-box "adult" Me —
That entity swelled by self-fret, I could never quite be.

The police often wear black uniforms, but their black is
Oppressive, not like the misshapen blacks of the hollow trees,
Whose blacks defy order, and foment jumbles of happiness.

The trees are colossal, wonderful, but their stumps too are
Grand. Why? Because they invite us to look at the beauty
Of the negative, the black shadows of tubes hollowed
By insect appetite, polished by weather. I think the child
Harbors a secret affection for Death, whose authority,
Black as it is, defies parents, taunts police, and looms with all
The innocent wealth of chaos. These trees are not set in rows,
Like desks at school. They call this grove *Roy's Redwoods* — but me, me,
I prefer to call it "my work," the work of a childish idler.

The Gene Pool is an Ocean
Clutter 59
Written 14 September, 2016

———————— • ————————

We can smell the perfume of spring's green beginnings and summer's
Fulfillments in aromatic cloud-tides of red. Leaves
Of a mid-September mid-morning exude essences
Of our past, our dead remembered as living entities
In an odor that has a color, that has a presence.
If the past is now living in the Now, our living must be
Living in the future, our bodies the reminiscences
Of dreamers under autumnal trees. Whose skeletons are these
On sunset's shores, where the old ones spent their childhood's lost
summers?

This exercise is called "Wading in the Shallows." If you
Would go deeper, you must follow this ribbon of word-sense
To the ocean trenches, where pressure shapes a different you.

Cloud mutant, tiny, spinning, self-illuminating, you form
A diatomic mandala as delicate as glass,
And as vulnerable as sand to shallow feelings. You see
On the wall of the just awakened dreamer, the photographs
Of family — mother, father, grandparents, great-grandparents,
Reduced to grey-toned flatness, their faces the epitaph
Of that future you, who is no longer human, but a leaf,
A color, an odor, a wind-bent autumn tree. Red masses
Of leaves, in crashing waves of scent, bear you to shore, death-born.

An Epilogue to a Famous Fairy Tale
Clutter 49
Written 15 September, 2016

———— • ————

Impossible as it seems, the colossal forms of summer
Have, in a few days, shrunk down to this crepuscular corner
Of autumn. In this corner, redolent, even in cities,
With harvest burnt-umber perfumes, lovers await the smaller
Alcoves of winter. The fat, summery trees, flourishing in
Green elephantine splendor, and shouldering out the sky, are
Growing gold and crimson, intensifying, yet shedding their sheathes
Of hope, for a romance that grows more rich, yet ever leaner,
To be finally exposed as eccentric bones in winter.

My words move tenderly over these effigies. Perhaps you
Too can remember how eyes, once flashing fire, withdraw in
Cleansing ashes — the Cinderella smoke chased up the flue.

The hearth is cold. The prince, who was king, is dead. No warm kiss
Wakens him. But must the widow grieve? The rheum, red in
Her eyes, has bourn a harvest, and though the winter rats filch
Nips of grain, enough and more, remains. The widow drowses, her
Fine and frost-white head alive with dreams. She need not imagine
What she hopes, she has lived it. She has loved beneath the summer
Trees. She has taken chances. She has made thin spring's potential
Actual. The ashes that she stirs bead pearls of tears — in
A few days, her green turned grey, but love still burns in the ashes.

Torsos Without Heads,
Heads Without Torsos

Clutter 39

Written 16 September, 2016

—————— • ——————

The tame foliage presses against the window. An hour
Before dawn, and leaf faces — smeared with the house glare of what
Some sleepless genius calls "the iconography of the mad" —
Return the insomniac to the jungle. Upon digging
Through the midden of ideas, the archeologist makes
A shocking discovery — human skulls, exhibiting
Jagged holes in their foreheads — oculi for stringing — the sad
Evidence of human sacrifice. What intrudes upon thought,
As the leaves twist into the glass, is an image of horror.

Primitives that we are — that I am — in our tongue, the word "leaf"
Also refers to the pages of a book, an untamed place,
Where savage acts may calm us, but only through savage beliefs.

A fantastic assemblage of brilliant feathers comprise
The poet's cape, his mask an iridescence of polished
Abalone, his insomniac dance a ritual
Self-decapitation. "HAY YAH YAH! HAY YAH YAH!" he chants
As the green electrified knives flense his tame flesh, those blades
The thirsty mouths that drink his blood. He reads. And his quiet rant
At five a.m., while all the household lies asleep, enthralls
No human. No matter. It was not meant for them. No, his sash
Of skulls placates a God, whose dark word still awaits its sunrise.

A Political Prisoner Comforts a Mother Whose Son Will Die in War
Clutter 29
Written 17 September, 2016

—————— • ——————

An ornamental plum tree whose copper leaves grow scarlet
As the summer days succumb to autumn — An election year,
And the disease of politics infects even people
Of good will, and makes them eager to kill each other. Look
Closely, the cells of the desiccated leaves, seen by the bee
God, with ultra-violet vision, will be deep blue, though locked
In the death grip of warm, yet shrinking days. And the seer will
See, as if from a great height, those cells as prisons. It is fear
That drives us mad, that microbe in the candidate's rabid spit.

In ancient China, the poets, sad in bee-hum, got drunk in
Autumn on the ripe plum's wine. Their poems rose up through leaves
As red as the blood of battle, words soaked with conflict's crimson.

Violence is so simple, we need only let emotion
Sweep us away, and the metamorphosis of death will grip
The peaceful plum, and squeeze out blood. The poets who survive will
Be imprisoned, having, as usual, backed the losing side.
Here, they will bleed out complicated lines, poems replete
With esoteric, erudite allusions. These lines will hide
Their fleeting visions. But close your eyes. Let your thoughts go still,
And a mountain, golden as honey, will rise in bee-hum. Slip
Down through dream light. Be saved by complex, rainbow
constellations.

Delivering Letters
Clutter 19

Written 18 September, 2016

———————— • ————————

This morning I have immersed myself in the words of a man
Thought mad because he said that people stripped of history,
Poetry, and myth were as casques of locusts, emptied
Even of insect life and stridulations, the hollow
Rattlings only of hollowness. I think of my grandfather,
With none of that pulp inside him, delivering the post
On horseback, a two day route, crossing the Belle Fourche*, icy
In winter, filled only with heart and guts, eyebrows, lashes bristly
With frost spikes, white, vaporous breath, enveloping horse and man.

The river was crossed nine* times at fords shallow enough for
The horse to wade or swim, white to the croup and the withers,
While his rider — the unpoetic myth — kept forcing the fords.

"Com'io divenni allor gelato e fioco …"*
If I call him a powerful poem, a force of Nature,
His toughness and endurance, stronger than rivers, more austere
Than winter, the chitinous hollow of my of heart up-wells.
My talk then freezes this warm, autumn morning, and pours
His blood into my fragile vessel. I feel his force. It muscles
Through my veins, a coiling genetic river, which I must ford
Again. Again, again, I feel the flow of Time, in the twists and turns
Of words. Again, again, I hatch my larval fire from blank snow.

* The Bell Fourche River traverses Wyoming and South Dakota, and, via the Cheyenne and Missouri rivers, is part of the Mississippi watershed.

* In Dante's Inferno, the 9th circle is a lake of ice, where those who have betrayed their relatives, stand frozen to their necks.

*Com'io divenni allor gelato e fioco (How I became then, ice and infirmity)

Bank

Clutter 09

Written 19 September, 2016

———————— • ————————

Corte Madera Creek still has its assertive moments, in
Winter spate, rising as something more than decoration,
Forcing the owners of upscale boutiques and antique stores
To sandbag their foundations for fear of that erotic
Incursion. This presence is more than its dank estuary
Odors in dry, late summer, its spreading banks making muck-slick
Colors — yellow-blue or purple-pewter, as dawn or dusk pours
Slants of light across them. Its flow goes a seaward direction,
Its tides another, its sex like last year's dreams — forgotten.

We separate them, smell on one side, sight on the other,
But they mix, salt water and fresh, in tidal iniquities,
Cleft of stream, sun lingam, forever coming together.

That repetitive shout of ecstasy, that hatchery
For bird and fish and mammal, now mostly ghosts, the water reduced
To a trickle, the teeming sexual thrusts cut down by
Drought, and culverted flood control, and our need to be small
And safe, our desire, stronger than sex, to expunge our dreams.
That shout is choked to death by the city's perpetual growl.
Except that the poet still hears it. For him the wind's soft sigh,
The stream's slow flow, and the mix of light and odor, accrued
In poems, still flood the spirit's deep repositories.

Thumbnail Self-Portrait Sketch
Clutter 98
Written 20 September, 2016

———————— • ————————

Making giant, but lightning-quick contour drawings of the eye,
Front view, side view, the big, big hole in the skull from which the slick
Orb protrudes, the delicate upper lid, the calmer lower,
The first the forehead's shape, the other the cheek bones' — this open
Vulnerability, this first avenue of risk, wary
When open, ready to blink, but still more wary when closed, when
Vision turns only on the fire of the mind. The mad career
That light takes, raining from the skies to make great magic
In the brain, where seeing involves the I, and not the eye.

When are we most vulnerable to risk? Pursuing our abject
Courage. What do we have the fortitude to see? The one leaf?
Or a mountain range of trees? Eons? Or one timid clock tick?

The drawings I make are very tiny — dots really, or
A bevy of dots, a pointillist landscape of the eye
In an aging face, wherein the mountain ranges of brow
Ridges, cheekbones, forehead surround the fearful ocular
Crater, as the Rushmore of an alien, the body,
However gigantic, still buried in the mountain, and stored
As the mystic spore that aspires to be a mountain. What grows
Beyond my vision — my tiny art — is what is feared: the eye
Too small to ever illustrate the I in that red crater.

At the Verge of a Marge
Clutter 88
Written 21 September, 2016

--- • ---

You enter solitude's stagnation, and though unmoving,
Seeing no one, eyes closed, sometimes sleeping, though forever
Awake, you feel the rush of oceans pushing through you. These are
Not dreams, but visions inside of dreams, not accumulations
Of memory only, but also of aspiration,
And of imagination, sea coasts, colored with intense blends
Of green hills, turquoise waters, purple rock, cobalt skies, the roars
Of sea-silence booming in no one's ears, a freedom that pours
Through the grid and breaks and forms the grid as a God who sings.

This God is no simpering antiquity skulking under
The cloak of a Grecian name, no professor's Poseidon,
Poking the thought with wordy tritons of a scholar's blunders.

It is the sudden, artless intoxication of a feast,
A buzzard's feast or a crow's to suddenly find the roadkill
Of history, newly crushed by the grid of Time and by
Implacable Death — it is life in a sudden burst of
Living, the immediacy of speeding revelation
That comes when the velocity suddenly stops, and enough
And more than enough, for the first time ever, satisfies
Your scavenging hunger. Artifice dies in art, and your stilled
Emotion drowns emotion in a song sung by the sea.

Oh, Hoarder, Hoarder,
How Does Your Garden Grow
Clutter 78
Written 22 September, 2016

———————— • ————————

Go into any older person's house, and you will find
The kitsch of forty years ago squirreled away in dusty
Corners, the dust itself revered as the golden detritus
Of memories that were already cheap when they were made,
And have had to be deified to give them value. We
Long ago read the fairy tales where the treasure only stays
Treasure when it remains buried, and what we thought precious
When we look at it with fresh eyes — our children's children's after we
Are dead — will seem but trash, the trinkets of a trinket mind.

These are not galleries at Versailles of art that was purchased
At the cost of noble sacrifice, and whose makers' chief
Belief was that it should be magnificent, and made to last.

But what now is magnificent? What now is noble? Go
Into any older person's mind, and wade through attics
And basements full of keepsakes, the trinketry of trinket lives,
And sort and dig, yet you will find no art. Even their dreams will
Be kitsch, even the death of their loved ones. And it will seem
As if life itself was a cheat, that the past — your past — was filled
Only with inconsequential material things. Now that lie
Has accumulated relics: bent keys, broken dolls, fuzzy dice.
Which all lie in the fragile skull, sprouting their fuzzy, old molds.

On the Benefits of Recycling
Clutter 68
Written 23 September, 2016

———————— • ————————

Signs by the highway declare that these miles and miles of dead
Orchards were "created by congress," because cities sucked dry
The irrigation canals. Elsewhere, floods drown cities, killing
Farms and futures — levees break, and decades of engineering
Are swept aside in an instant's fury. When an old man
Reads about "the ceremony of innocence," he finds things
Spinning out of control. He knows old age itself, re-living
Years of drought or spate, is the unlucky fate of bodies
Attacked by Time. He feels the collective's pain in his own dread.

But something cracks the mask of catastrophe, a child's smile
Perhaps, an intimate brightness, a body recalled, which ran
For running's sake, a greening, restoring the blight — for a while.

I see these photos of my grandson, and these of my father
And grandfather, and see in the mirror an ecology
On the brink of sudden, cataclysmic collapse. Somewhere,
Someplace, someone is making decisions with the ease of official
Sanction, with stolen authority, which say that Saturn's sons can
Rule our lives again, and Zeus, Time's slayer, lies dead in the fields.
His big death has made our small ones, and vice versa. The war
Of gods is generational war. But my grandson's baby
Face knows nothing of this. His innocence kills Time once more.

Paper Patriotism
Clutter 58
Written 24 September, 2016

———— • ————

This week I received Presidential Certificate number
Four-one-B-three in honor of my "belovèd deceased
Veteran." The stiff, mottled paper, with the golden eagle
Seal, honors, in florid calligraphy, the memory
Of my father, who died an old, old man, and is now buried,
As are millions more, in a national cemetery.
On his Death Certificate, the cause shown is "accidental,"
Because he fell out of bed on his feeble way to relieve
His bladder. He fell right through Time en route to another war.

Was he asleep when he fell, and did he awaken, surprised,
In the crematorium, that his old flesh was flame, emptied
Of everything but honor, and writhing through livid skies?

I was surprised. He had survived everything — poverty,
War, the loss of my mother, and the loss of his memory.
I thought he would outlive Time, and even anonymity.
But he did not. He fell, as everyone does and must, the
Accidental eventually, and most certainly,
Delivering its cruel certificate. Still, I admired the
Way the lines flowed across the page, how the calligraphy
Made much of the words "devoted" and "selfless" and "country,"
And how the eagle's stern visage looked immortal and deadly.

A Fool Sees Not the Same
Sky as a Wise Man Sees
Clutter 48
Written 25 September, 2016

————————— • —————————

The green lusts of spring, the russet loneliness of autumn,
The primal lovers surrounded by their children, exuberant
Summer and austere winter, the two, less than innocent
Fodder for custody battles in the interregnum —
As you or I or someone in the weather grow absent
With a different form of love. The ego's incessant drum,
Thumping good/bad/bad good, dissolves in the aberrant
Contemplation of Death's insolvency, the permanent
Divorce of lust from loneliness — our wedding in the sun.

You will forget the pit-of-the-stomach feeling, whose text wrote
"Ice" last winter, and you will forget summer's ravishments
Of heat. You will forget forgetting — those readings got by rote.

Those strange legalities, which bound your shards together into
That chaos, which cuts your flesh from others — glass tumbling in
You gut. The laws of reason and even of the heart's affairs
Will seem to be nothing but legal fictions, since only
These golden, swirling swarms exist, these lights in Israel's tents
In desert waste, terrestrial stars beneath the heavenly
Pips, fore-bits of dawn that kiss the night awake. This is the air,
The ordinary air, you breathe with no perceived divisions,
As, stripped of judgment, you, the sum, color these grey skies blue.

The Hobbyists
Clutter 38
Written 26 September, 2016

————— • —————

You, in later times, if you are safely connected to
The Earth, as we are not, you will not believe me when I tell
You that these relics are elaborate coloring books made
For adults — Mandalas, exotic birds, Bargello patterns,
The following and filling of whose winding blanks were meant to
Calm. They were used mostly by our older women, since men
Preferred drugs, and had long since denied connection. The women played
With them for hours in pregnant meditation, a long, long fall
Back to the Mother, like that sparrow the male god threw.

The male god numbered the feathers of that brown bird, as he
Cast him down to the irrational ground, and you, you, if you
Read this maternal Bible, will find him there among dead leaves.

And you, you in your re-connected life, will see the leaves
Turn color in the autumn in rainbow Mandalas, whose lights
Spell "Death." You, you will hear the sparrows chirping in dawn's dazzle,
And you will see the notes flit through the heavens, as flame-shaped
Stitcheries of flight. And you will wonder why these calmer truths
Could not appease those mothers of lost children, whose lives became
The flatness of flat screens. Why, why was the sparrow made to fall,
If only to be numbered with the dead? And you will trace light,
As through stained glass, where widows sit and color winding sheets.

Typical Topos: Couple on a Beach.
The East a Citrus Strip
Clutter 28
Written 27 September, 2016

———————— • ————————

The birthing of poetry requires something more than making
Those swooning vocalizations known as "love lyrics." Every
Articulation will be but fuzzy second-handedness
Until the body itself is transformed. The novice must stand,
Barefoot, and stare at the sun each dawn, working up from moments
To hours as the days stroll through the seasons. It is then, then
Only, that the tongue's animal cells will sprout chloroplasts,
Which, like the leaves of plants, can refine the raw energy
Of sun into legible sugars — food free for the taking.

Oh, My Love, My Love, it is only to feed Thee this sweetness
That I stand, discalced, in poverty's pitiless torment,
Lit up to the gills with the dawning, and mesmerized by bliss.

How strange it is to feel in the human body the ancient
Tree fossils, which form the base of the sea cliff. A couple,
Hand in hand, strolls on the strand. The waves come in, engulf the
strand,
And drown them. But the great stone trunks remain. The birthing of
Poetry requires stillness, ocean depth, and the violent
Rhythms of waves. It requires a special kind of love,
A love like light on leaves, a transformation of sun, a man,
A woman, who feast on each other's photons, and grow still.
The birthing of poetry is this green pair's ascendance.

Fever and Frost
Clutter 18
Written 28 September, 2016

———— • ————

Not a cloud in the sky, yet the heat continues weaving
Its squiggling mirages through the immaculate azure.
It stirs in us an unspecified longing. Corridors
Of air, unseen, whiffle with the chirr of wings. Butterflies,
Birds, departed speech — slight, absent things — now drive the current.
You cannot forget the loves you knew, because those many flights
Direct your weightless feelings through what was, but is no more.
This, the disease of the year's last heat, has burned the lover
Invisibly, the ice of many winters vaporizing.

The painting is medieval. It shows the kneeling magi,
Robed in butterfly-brilliant vestments, and looking aslant
At something beyond the frame. That something is tearing their eyes.

We take our cues for emotion, in this false summer, from
That winter that is coming, yet has left us. I will not say
The words that you expect, the words that shape the air, and coax
The tears. I will only depict these shadows on the ground
Of something fluttering aloft. I will only staunch the rants
Of indelicate talk, and hint at the delicate sounds
That shape the silence. Not a cloud in the sky, not the float
Of one bright cloud, not a wisp of those high ice crystals that play
In heaven, even when dying days are far, Oh far, too warm.

Indigenous Encounter
Clutter 08
Written 29 September, 2016

———————— • ————————

After first contact, the starved remnants of shattered tribes emerge
From isolation in the Amazon, first wanting clothing
And food, and then they latch on to the anthropologists'
Cameras — strong medicine for those exterminated
Like vermin — to be shot, yet be impervious to pain,
And immortal. What we can see, we need not touch. A shrunken head
Is easily procured, and its manna preserved without risk.
After first contact, no flesh contact is needed, since filching
Life's light-bodies frees the remnants to virtually emerge.

Space and framed space allow for different degrees of freedom.
Framed space spares us from movement, spares us the sadness of decay.
While space mandates dangerous contact and the need for weapons.

First contact: holding my newborn daughter in my arms, and now,
Thirty years later, collecting all the agony of
Separation into a photographic heaven, which feels
Like hell. My dear, dear lost one, how are we going to fill
Those gaps of isolation with these two-dimensional planes
That have no odor, no taste of sweetness, no touch that thrills?
There are deadly animals in the jungle, beasts that kill
Remnants — jaguars, other humans, history, hate and love.
There are deadly thoughts too, and rivers swollen with old sorrows.

Something that Happens
at Night this Time of Year
Clutter 97
Written 30 September, 2016

———————— • ————————

The revelation will not be seen at arm's length on a screen
That you can hold in your hand, and in spite of the word "reveal,"
It will not be seen at all. A monster without form moves through
The air, and in one hour, the heat of summer becomes the cool
Of autumn. All the gawkers throw down their prosthetic eyes,
And with prosthetic feet go to the edge of edges. The role
Of speech will cease to be promotional. The words will break through
The screen, and, sewn like dragon's teeth, they will begin the final
Telling. You will feel the chlorophyll draining from your leaves.

I have spoken before of the choir that sings "Begin!" spat
Out teeth in predatory tirades, and told how the lies
Of past and future become the prey of Now — the first, the last.

I have tunneled beyond the primate, whose eyes face front, to see
The victim of its appetites, who, from tall Savannah grass,
Lifts over frightened earth its heartless binocular stick.
I have bored with my tooth a hole to guide the root for that
Tree whose winter branches fruit with stars. When I speak, the blind
Gawkers suddenly feel. They touch the child in the monster's lap,
The need in the jumbles of emotion. They cure the sick
Separation. When I speak, my phrases will finally cast
That child of sorrow into the ocean's midnight ecstasies.

A Walk Through Harrowed Fields at Death of Day
Clutter 87
Written 1 October, 2016

———————— • ————————

"Whether it lies over or under the dirt, the body
Will always rot." Plotinus, who equated being with beauty,
Said that. The country rube in the crystal palace of noble
Deliberations will see only an old man on a cot
Of horse-hair ticking. He does not strive to give back that great Self,
Which is Divine, to the Divine in all, but, dying, his cough
Startles a hovering fly, while a snake beneath the cot crawls
Out through a hole in the wall at the flash of death. The rube sees
No light here. His ignorance is the rot that rots all bodies.

Withdraw into your Self, and look. Look. There they are: the mansions
Of the philosophers, the architects of the Self,
Reflecting the architecture of waves in just proportion.

Glass tombstones by the sea at sunset, where the indigo snakes,
Which fled through the hovel's hole, flash orange while falling, curling
Into black, as the mirror burns with sunset's golden deeds.
The rube in the country strolls through harvested fields, uneven
Ground breaking his stride and his thoughts. The crows cull
Through dry stalks for kernels, the left-over corn of wisdom.
A flock of starlings swirls around a silo, where mice glean
What they can, while the many sinuous words, lurking, coiling
In the mind, hiss news of worlds that mystics germinate.

On the Difficulty of Following the Destiny of a Single Rain Drop

Clutter 77

Written 2 October, 2016

———————— • ————————

Not enough rain to fill a thimble, but the first in months, plus
Low white massings of clouds bunched at their bases with grays
That promise more. NOW is the IS that is, but the jump-
Cut montages of perception persuade us that yesterday's
Winds presaged that which tomorrow will bring to fruition.
We watch continuously to see this vivisection, flayed
Red viscera making visceral associations, lumps
Of meat seen through large, moist bovine eyes, the flickering play
Of candlelight, dinner for two, and magpies under pie crust.

It is impossible to tell a tale that is not at its
Heart a lie about these bundles of stitched-up dissections.
The rain is falling harder, but the sun still shines a bit.

The sun still shines a bit, and the wind arranges for patches
Of blue sky, for a Now that seems to be in motion.
The mind forgets its fragmentary nature, and wholly
Drifts with the holy drift of things. We feel what the eyes
Can never show us — the unity of light's commotion,
The shapes in the shotgun spray of particles, like fish eyes
In the curl of ocean waves, making the fragmentary
Rise as a single momentary narrative. We swim in
Insight, not in vision. This fluid netting has enmeshed us.

A Red Fluid on White Porcelain
Clutter 67
Written 3 October, 2016

———— • ————

The insomniac rises at 4 a.m., his throat aflame
With the acid blood of the lamb — the crisis of words, devolved
From the crisis of the aging body, the atheist
Poet expounding on stigmata, the bandaged hands of
Padre Pia bleeding the Cantos of Ezra Pound. Oh man
Of many jagged associations, each jagged shard of
Which cuts its incongruous path through the grist
Of your body, your soul this blood you spit of hope dissolved,
How is it that your inspiration must always come from pain?

Is it the music of traffic that you hear, or the squeak
Of night's elliptically spinning fires? Everyone hears the bland
Tunes of the first, and thinks these grinding gears are heaven-speak.

At 4 a.m., in the silence of silence, the pitiful
Insomniac confronts the eccentric nature of the Self.
He spits out shards of glass, the jewels of sharp discovery
Glistening in the sink. They murdered Jesus and locked
Up Ezra Pound, and no one sermonizes at 4 a.m.
On the contradictions of faith and mortal flesh, the shock
Of the collision is just too great, the discovery
Of the atheistic saint too eccentrically laughable,
And the night, the dying night, just too interminable.

For These Ghosts Up
is Down, Down Up

For Joe Bloom

Clutter 57

Written 4 October, 2016

———————— • ————————

Diurnal convection currents are the morning's unseen
Sculptors of these rising mounds and towers of cumulus
Clouds, their crowns so brilliant white against the upper reaches
Of cerulean that they involve their scholar-poets in
A kind of purity of drunkenness, detached from land.
I send my friend a Chinese poem in English translation
As an example of discreet innuendo, its phrases
Never coarsened by direct statement, clouds drifting between us
On autumn breezes, which ruffle songs through voluminous sleeves.

According to Wang Fu-chih, emotion and scene, though named
Differently, unite without trace of boundary. But who can
Rise in such convections, without a heavy, earthly stain?

Our aging bodies move heavily towards death, uniting
With a subterranean crowd in the oblivion
Of anonymity. From this war, no one returns. Long ago
I took a stone and smashed my foot. I cannot march with the mass.
I stand, unfit, and watch the trials of clouds. They form and
Reform, appear and disappear. No shape they make can last.
And yet they drift so painlessly through space, their crowns all snow,
Their feet gray ashes. On a dead tree branch, prayer flags hum in
A chill wind. Under the earth our dead are silently marching.

White Water
Clutter 47
Written 5 October, 2016

———————— • ————————

The voices of children passing by the house strike the ear
Of a grandfather as sun strikes frost. The high-pitched chatter
Releases a prismatic plume of vapor — memory
Essences, relived for a moment as vibrant emotion.
A rubber-wheeled pony cart in which an older brother
Drives two younger sisters over prairie trails, hard frozen —
The girls under quilts, complaining at each jolt, the high-pitched glee
Of the brother, enjoying their torment, the air, cold and clear,
Curling in crisps of breath, breath's plumes of ice-starred, sunlit, vapors.

The prairie in winter is a sea of white, where a horse
And rider find their way from the tops of fence posts, the clatter
Of Time's hooves on concrete snow, ringing life back to a corpse.

What we remember, like the turbulence of the sea, revels
In randomness. My mother in that cart, my father on
That horse, are lifted from wintry death by warm autumn breezes.
They ghost through the house as the voices of children. That high-
pitched
Chatter is the whistling of icy winds and the clatter
Of those symbolical pale-horse hooves. What are these sounds by which
The house is shattered, as by a wave whose chance force reaches
Through calm, and drowns the present moment in the past? And what
comes
After this Tsunamic crash, which drags me under foam-white swells?

Old Griefs Demand Laments Played on Paleolithic Instruments
Clutter 37
Written 6 October, 2016

———————— • ————————

Even on these most placid of autumn days, there are people
Receiving their diagnosis, and would-be mothers who have
Miscarried. There are addicts, who were clean, gone back to using.
The shining infinity of a cloudless sky is the sea
That they are lost in. Yet even in mid-ocean, there are signs:
Lightning flashing a hundred feet under water, Z-
Lines, fluorescing and pointing to some landfall, eyes following
In mirrors the strangers, who, in spite of their sorrow, have
Lived through fragmentation, their hearts cold heaps of crushed-glass
gravel.

No monuments for mourners of the drowned, and for the poem
Unwritten, no weeping readers, only the featureless sky,
And the visageless sea mixing their distant speculums.

When the psychic monolith is crushed, two truths assert themselves:
All things are fluid, all are permeable. The ground-glass shards
Might just as well be raindrops, and the dry infinitude
Of sky might just as well be endlessly heaving ocean.
If you sleep in your pillar of salt, immune to tears, your eyes
Will be fixed on the last of senility, the comatose person,
The tendrils of an abortion, the artificial pumped-up mood.
Only the rainstick siftings of tubed-trapped gravel, and a carved-
Through vulture-bone flute can scratch out tunes to make pain bearable.

Confluence

Clutter 27

Written 7 October, 2016

———————— • ————————

Eyewitness reports from Westerners as late as the nineteen
Thirties prove that when the sage left his ashram, the stream by
His path teemed with following fishes. The birds clouded over
His head in avian prayer. The sage simply claimed that the
Self is one, its affinity mating with the affianced.
I merely note that when waking from sleep that that which the
Vision craves becomes more solid, the watery furor
Of the images more chained to habit. In defiance of Time,
Dream speech repeats itself, as if to fix what it means to mean.

What does it mean to mean — to have a meaningful life, to
Speak with effect, to see what there is to see? The nuance
That connects disparate things eludes a singular truth.

When my mother died, the Mother Coagulation burst free
In brilliant scatterings of stars, all crinkling through the air
That formed my seeing. And when my father died, the repetitive
Phrases of his Alzheimerish speech slipped through the silence,
Confining my tongue to stony repetitions. Death's distance
Had come too near. My sight was streaming and my speech was silence.
There is no central I who sees or hears, only collectives
Moving in unison, fish in the water, birds in the air,
And the sage who is absent, converging divergent streams.

Evanescent Iridescence
Clutter 17
Written 8 October, 2016

We don't clean much, and spiders exploit the niches of our
Neglect with deadly gossamer shimmerings, connecting
Incongruent points to one another. The fibers in
The brain hold, in electrified solution, disparate things:
Elephants, snow, dreams, lovers, angels, the plays of Shakespeare,
The veins in leaves, the faces of refugees, raven wings —
The weirdly unpredictable routinely arising in
The bubble of the normal, the rainbow-serpents writhing
On the depth-defying surfaces of momentary blurs.

This symptom — "The rebellion of the common" — is as common
As spiders weaving in unswept corners. O how we fear
It! Though the bubble thrills us, its bursting is far too sudden.

On the walk before our door, a sycamore tree has begun to
Scatter its leaves, and we track this crumpled randomness into
The house, where eight-eyed spiders are waiting, waiting, waiting
For those slow flies the autumn season brings. As I get older,
I contemplate connections that shimmer like gossamer
Silk as soon as seen, but burst as quickly as a bubble's sphere.
My body, like the thoughts inside my brain, is teaming, teaming,
Teaming with weirdnesses as common as the dirt. What seems true
Seems equally untrue. The webs buzz, and spiders find their food.

Entoptic Phenomena
Clutter 07
Written 9 October, 2016

Sometimes you have to fight for it. It's Sunday — warm. Lassitude
Sticks to you. The eyelids droop, and for an instant before
You jerk yourself awake, you see into a boundless space,
Where blue stars whirl and red spirals swirl, and your whole sense of what
It means to be goes suddenly primal. The cultural screen
Is erased, and those strange figures seen in petroglyphs — unsought—
Come face to no-face: fish-like hybrids, spirit ancestor shapes —
Amphibious, hermaphroditic, the wondrous you before
Your I was born, drawing you down and through infinitude.

In the sanatorium, parental love tried to make
You "normal." But nothing you saw of what they told you to see
Was quite complete. You slept and found a deeper kind of awake.

Sometimes you have to fight against it. The normal seems just so
Soothing. Mother and father both nod their approval, though both
Are dead. They flash their astral concern through jittery eyes
That see how their aging child succumbs to bliss. O! Autumn is
The season of the west, when the atoms of the body
Take their leave, and scatter like homing-bees to where the sun is
Sinking, and where these brief dreams thrive. Is this the larval hive
Of the original honey of creation — odd to
The nth degree, but oddly loving too, like parental souls?

Mining Potash
Clutter 96
Written 10 October, 2016

———————— • ————————

Autumn at this latitude butters the body with slanting
Light on one side and squeezes out ultramarines on the
Other. Every color is enriched, and gray seems not to
Exist. I used to wear gray suits and call on banks. Whole forests
Fell before me as I moved. I could afford to cover my
Pain with fashion, the victim of prosperity. Now the crest
Of Time, which rose before me, falls, and I am destitute.
One collects gray as one ages, and the outward patina, the
Shine of the banker's trust, reveals a final tarnishing.

I return to the forest to sit on a stump — and ponder.
The ultramarines abscond into indigoes. These sigh
As they cloak themselves with night, and smother every color.

From a remnant of woods, red smears gleam forth. If these are the eyes
Of predators, why do they wait? My tears have dropped infants all
Over the stubble ground — food for these nightmare beasts, free for
The taking. And yet the hovering eyes still keep their distance,
Like memories that refuse cathartic purging. But why
Do I speculate? When dawn at last returns, all will be flensed,
And red. I will see my divorce and the loss of my daughter,
As the passage of winter after winter shows the total
Losses of Autumn's scarlet flames as zeroes in dull gray eyes.

Baptism Redux
Clutter 86
Written 11 October, 2016

———— • ————

Feeling lonely, yesterday I labored up a steep fire road
That led to the spillway of a lonely lake. I veered to
A side cut in the steep, where, among fir and redwood, on
The wet side of the ridge, I climbed over and ducked under
Fallen timber, going deeper, bruised and scratched, into solemn,
Inhuman silence. By now we understand the blunder
Of believing in narrative. There is no once-upon-
A-time utterance with talking animals that will lead to
A sleeping princess. This is the wild where metaphor unfolds.

I reach a cleft, where, during the rainy season, a water
Drill bores blunt current to the valley floor. Go back? Go on?
Go on. Go down — the creekbed the only place to clamor.

A rougher road here, over boulders, under snag heaps, skirting
Or leaping cold, black remnants of pools, the mechanical
Habits of the body disrupted, the machine gone sprong
As the broken mechanism reverts to its chemical
Slosh, that bag of corpuscular images, whipped to a foam,
And my mere human loneliness, my old inhuman soul,
Recalls a once-upon-no-time, the muscle of some strong,
Unstoried self, sliming the rock I slip on, and SPLOOSH! a pool
Immerses me in that cold dark, where my first love is waiting.

Stirring Pronouncements
Clutter 76
Written 12 October, 2016

———————— • ————————

Though it's hardly rained here for months and months, last night I
dreamed
Of a watery transparence from which hazy red bursts
Of light arose, and when I awakened, I remembered that
Mud puddles delighted me as a boy. I liked most when they
Had settled and I could drop in pebbles, and see cloudy
Swirlings exploding from their fundament of muck. Boys play
Delightedly in the chaos of beauty that inflicts
The settled with random possibilities, and these strange firsts
Collect in the psyche's muck, awaiting the pebble dream.

Last night I saw the water's conversations, silently
Making their case for incomprehensibility,
For a mysteriousness that would expand all mystery.

As we climb laboriously out of childhood, we ascend
In bodies that become increasingly cloud-like, the settled
Mud of aging and of cultural conditioning disturbed
By the loss of a tooth, a bone-break, or some chemical
Imbalance that releases a dream, years later, when sensory
Delight has dulled. This shakes us out of the abominable
Torpor that elects the settled over the beautiful. Words
Drop into the psyche that are inexplicable.
They defy allegory, and they break Time's mirrored skin.

The Future of the Body is One of Volumeless Prostitution

Clutter 66

Written 13 October 2016

———————— • ————————

Adhering to a great landscape painter's dictum that the sky
"Governs everything," and is "the chief organ of sentiment,"
I note how today a high, white haze serves as a veiling
Backdrop to lower altitude clumps of blue-gray pearls. Place
Anything in a distant visual field, and it becomes
Part of the optic unconscious, like the shadows of tame
Trees on the grounds of a mental hospital, their tattering,
Soft stirrings shading the inmates there, their psychic dishevelments
The beautiful, mutable clumps of reason gone awry.

The shadows are fallen angels, Lucifer's blue-gray pearl-
Clumps dropping to earth with soft thumps, as though to say "Come,
from
These calm bombs we mold our sweet balms for the unreasonable."

Anatomists can now make microscopic horizontal
Slices of a corpse, affix them with high-resolution
Photography, and thus convert the dead to immortal, living
Data, informatics that may be manipulated in
A visual field without sentiment. This new Adam
Has no sky-god father, and no red clay body, and without sin
Or virtue, he exists as a commodified light, shining
His wisdom to whomever can pay the price — reproduction
Achieved without friction, a stable self in a skyless world.

The Deceased
Polyhymnia's Slovenly Widower
For my uncle, George Les Doughty

Clutter 56
Written 14 October 2016

—————— • ——————

After months of drought, last night the rain began talking in
Its sleep, and denying the wicked providence of life
Insurance salesmen. Let's talk about the difficulty
Of creating things with the ubiquity of rain drops in
A rainstorm and the depth of the ocean. Let's talk about the
Photojournalist who takes pictures of an old man in
A dilapidated trailer, drinking himself to death, pee
Stains being his last, truest mode of expression. Let's say why
The heart leaks out Time in bleak dribbles, which smell of urine.

The camera sees the stains, and the reader reads the words, rain
Running incomprehensibly through layers of sleep, while the
Poet's wicked prophecies drown the heart before they find a drain.

We cannot rely on the camera of the eye. It will —
At arm's length — make everything look interesting, but shallow.
You will not smell providence in the flat heaven of its
Projections. You will have to visit where tears — like rain
Drops — fall. The uncle you never liked will be lying in the
Broken down recliner that he sleeps in. He will be in pain,
And he will be drunk. He will call you a son-of-a-bitch
When you try to help him. The stench of his decay will follow
You. This smell will be your muse, your heart's drunk guardian angel.

Lament

For Dee Clutts, one who kept her word

Clutter 46

Written 15 October 2016

——————— • ———————

Great, whirling storms thousands of miles apart slug the continent
On both its east and west coasts — rabbit punches to the kidneys
As political thugs punish their detractors
With trumped-up paranoias. Tomorrow, an old, close friend
With cancer will take advantage of her lawful right to die.
"The voices of torrents," or so asks the poor, bewildered
Seeker, "are from one great tongue — is that not so?" And the Master
Answers: "It is so. But that it is so is a great pity."
How much scripture must the wind speak before we are content?

These arrhythmias destroy long-standing forms, but the Master —
Not a poet, for no poet may master life's storms — as friends die —
In these weird twists of psychedelic pain — accepts the bizarre.

The bizarre — that twisting stereophonic roar that proclaims,
With neon violence, The Wonder of the New in a world
That can never tolerate the old, never find peace in mere
Stability, mere contentment. This ever-raving monster,
Which is the psyche, prefers his poems raw, prefers to die
To each moment by unlawful means. He rejects the Master's
Never-raging calm because — because to die by cancer
Is too piteous, and the trumped-up thugs are too immoral,
And the storms on the tongue are just too exuberant to tame.

Escape Velocity
Another for Dee Clutts
Clutter 36
Written 16 October 2016

——————— • ———————

What do you see when you close your eyes? And for how long do you
See it? I see a primitive city on a desert plain,
As if from an angel-eye view, from a great height, but zooming
Closer, only to disappear before I reach it. One
Thinks of Biblical films, clichés of a veiled woman, sneaking
Furtively down alleyways, donkeys braying, as armed Roman
Troops, in stern phalanxes, hunt down this cancerous one, gleaming
Armor blinking in and out of shadows as the clicking frames
Dictate, the projector's beam a-swirl with smoky curls of blue.

One could conduct this experiment a thousand times, and each
Scene would be unique, each strangely intimate, each flicking
Away as one dream or another, each bright with mystery.

But it is all kitsch, all the overlay of culturally
Concocted images designed to make us see only the cliché,
And to think of ourselves as consumers. My friend — scheduled
To die today — is going to tumble through a longer blink. It
May be that the kitschy scenes that she first sees will start changing —
And breaking up into angelic geometries where spirit
Shows the ancient mitochondrial cities of the cells,
As though she were withdrawing at break-neck speed, moving away
From the Biblical body into unframed eternity.

How We Have Lost Sight of These Heavenly Lights, which Seem to Move in Relation to Ourselves, But Not in Relation to One Another

Clutter 26

Written 17 October 2016

———————— • ————————

Dreams are remembered when we first awaken. But as the day
Expands, the influence of those vivid images wanes.
Yesterday's rain and wind, stripping the autumn trees, reveals
An afternoon of high, white cumulus clouds, which thin to these
Thready silken vapors, golding high in evening's fading light.
Thus, there is this slight residue, like some last wisps of dream
Emotion, by which an image might be reified, some spell
Of the body-schematic, large as a world, which fills with strange
Machines — industrial product replacing the awe-struck brain.

Science has yet to investigate the asymmetrical
Links between weather and our dreams. Our economic plight
Makes it too hard to read these messages from the blood-borne self.

The dome of the skull inside no longer shows sky images,
But a display of advertising kitsch, more fixed than that
Wrong notion of fixed stars. The displays change, but their purpose
Remains the same: reduce the human to a set of numbers,
And make all flesh commodity. The sun has plunged its light
Below the horizon, and the sky, now cleansed of clouds, prepares
For coming night, prepares for a sleep that makes all profit loss.
The brain of the buyer becomes the skull of the dreamer, that
Paleolithic throwback, amazed by the stars' fixed flashes.

Disconnected
Clutter 16
Written 18 October 2016

———————— • ————————

Recordings of all scenes may now be instantly reduced to
A screen that may be held at no further than the arm's length
By which an infant scrutinizes his mother's face: people
Starving in desert landscapes, the great wheels of galaxies
Spinning through distant space, the microscopic mouths that gulp
The air on the underside of leaves, or creatures in deep sea
Darks, spinning their stars in anaerobic zones — what was concealed
By distance, scale, or time, brought close, so that the eyes may drink,
And the mind may sponge sight's indecipherable runes.

But what of the mother's face — the now irrelevant connection?
For the child who self-medicates with pixels, flesh is but pulp
Awaiting the predestined video transmutation.

When the olfactory bulb of the ancient self atrophies
Into tiny, illegible blips, those odor-lights, which told
Of heres and nows, shrink to vestigial organs. The self
Becomes the one cycloptic I. When my mother died, they
Unplugged the respirator and a screen at arm's length pulsed
Wave-forms whose lines ran flat. Her face disappeared from the frame,
And its wave-form features no longer spelled out "Mother," but gelled
Into fears aroused by her spoiled scent. The data-stream turned cold —
Unlit — annulled. By the bed, her son, unborn, sees blank, black grief.

Why We Fill Our Domestic Museums with the Photographs of Family
Clutter 06
Written 19 October 2016

———————— • ————————

A mantle of early snow robes the crests of the mountains,
And, from this house on the opposite ridge, the last of the day's
Light leaves what looks to be a sleeping ghost beneath the first bright
Stars. The house is not your house, and the pictures in the frames
Are — unlike the mountain ghost who will change in the moonlight —
More frozen than snow. These faces were loved by a man who came
Into an icy fixity, when his flesh suffered erasure by
Cancer's mutinous blight.   His life's house — wasted in a last fade
Into starless night — holds only these photographs of past skin.

O seeker after absolutes, you must study these
Ghosts in photography's frozen gaze, and when mutinous Time scythes
Down the faces you love, you must pierce the skin of these thin sheets
…

Pierce through the imageless night, to where — not pain — but pain's demise
Has gathered itself into a lustrous pool. At the deathbed
Of a loved one, you can see the bright eternity of life
Flee suddenly from absent eyes. The last light of day is drained
From the mountainous ghost, and what is lost flows down. If you cry,
You break the spell, and the pool will not dispel your un-housed pain.
But if you are still, as still as a pulseless heart, a sign
Will arise from the depths of lustrousness, and the dead
Will be felt, as they once were — as near as the mountain is high.

Old News from Echo
Clutter 95
Written 20 October 2016

———————— • ————————

After a night of excruciating sleeplessness, you fall
At dawn into a paralytic coma, which is referred to
Explicitly in your dream as "C-consciousness." On a white
Artificial surface are mulberry-colored letters, each
Sprinkled with a pinch of soil. The evergreen steeps before
You, when you wake, flame up in golds and reds, deciduous trees
Saying with here and thereness, and along the snake lines
Of the creeks, "This is autumn, the last room in The House of Light to
Spell out glory. Tomorrow winter's veil of darkness falls."

Did you know that all of the bright-eyed pupils of the season's
ABC's are old? Did you know that these kindergartners
Of Nature spirits learn most from the cycles of moon and sun?

Already there are snow skiffs on the peaks, already the quail
Grow desperate, and break cover to rummage leaf-litter
For final seeds. The skin bruises easily, and cold marks
Of mulberry shadow spread under worried pines. Already
The finest ashen soil remains on the eyelids after
Sleep's comatose speeches. And yet the aging pupil reads
No final sentences in these passages — because the stark
Alphabets flesh out their skeletons with primal Mother-
Tongue — and because the Mother hums: "My beauty can never fail."

The Scent and Sight of Pines
Distill Elixirs of Reminiscence
Clutter 85
Written 21October 2016

——————— • ———————

The valley is filled with sun-gilt mist, whose fatherly touch
Crips crystalline frost. The pines disappear at their roots, while
Their tips of pyramid-shapes arise as pearly silhouettes.
We know that for a while the only distance we will see
Is up, up into that color known in such mountains for these
Mixes of azure-cerulean-cobalt intensities,
Up into that famous lapis lazuli the poet
Praised as orient solitude. With unseen tricks, sunlight will
Reify the pines as the ghost of one who loved us.

These mountains are older than those who live in them. And this
Morning, their rich mutations provide the nebulosities
Wherein our ghostly suppositions may roam through palaces.

Therefore, let us suppose that the first father, who sings of our
Physical bodies, exists inside of us — so strong when we
Were young, but as we age, he ages, his voice becoming a
Whispering imprecation for us to say or to do that
Which would save him. And let us also suppose that our grief
And our happiness have mixed so in his poetry that
It is impossible to tell a present feeling from a
Memory. As the sun ascends, the facts in the valley
Indisputably form solid words from his insolid air.

Mystery School
Clutter 75
Written 22 October 2016

———————— • ————————

Every day about this time, but every day a few minutes
Earlier, the house burns quietly down. Very thin, white,
Orchid-like vapors petal the roof, awaiting orders
From the day-star in the west: "What should we do? What brilliance
Should we express before your absence steals all color from us,
And absence becomes the norm as night descends?" Continuance
Or repetition, these are the mind's addictions, the colors'
Arbiters — "What should I do," it asks. Remember. Hold tight.
Record. But the sun and the clouds refuse. Change is their bliss.

The petaled, but fading roof of the burning house makes wild
Encryptions, which attempt to instruct the bones with the rebus
Of impermanence — the glyphs of bliss. But that is not possible …

Not possible because the aftermath of brilliance will
Not be wisdom, however accurate our recall, but Death —
Our memories sweetened by nostalgia, as orchids might
Sweeten sorrow at a funeral. This is the morbid
Beginning of true genius — this revelation that genius
Loves only change, and change is only an infant in a crib,
Crying to be set free from helplessness. The sun's last light
Cannot read what is missing: the infant's vaporous breath,
The first gasp for the last rest where bliss might still be possible.

Lake Tahoe Shining on the Astral Plane

Clutter 65

Written 23 October 2016

———— • ————

Now, place your hands together, palm to palm, in an attitude
Of prayer. Now, as one body, lean them left and right. Then
Wriggle them. Think of a snake that is hatching from an egg. This
Gesture illustrates how sight and place merge into speechlessness,
How snow-capped mountains round a diamond lake can obviate
The need for prayer. The lake is a crystal bowl whose glass
Draws sky's blue zenith down through its wondrous depths. Here, speechless
Water sprites and wriggling fish converse. How cryptically Zen
Their poems. With their lithe talk, they cut the glass, yet leave no
wounds.

You might see anything here and not be lonely. Still, this scene,
As distilled by the eyes, is not an essence. Sadly, sight's lake
Of sensate blinks is fake, the eggshell of a dazzling dream.

The hands that you placed together will split apart, as the lake
Inevitably fades from memory. Nothing the senses
Fling into Time's rapids may extirpate the body's need for
Calm. A boat, fixed on the image of a boat, is glued to the mind
Like a man asleep at the oars. His voyage, without a wake,
Leaves no breath's trace. The hull of the boat is red, a crimson light,
Contrasting sharply with the man's blue sleep. The quiet oars
Are oaken yellow. The snow-capped mountains, the fathomless
Diamond depths, enact their essence solely through quietude's praise.

Shrapnel

Clutter 55

Written 24 October 2016

———————— • ————————

Changing weather triggers spiritual discoveries.
Yesterday's clear skies spawned high winds, which today bring clouds
and rain.
Forget the unclean flesh of Evangelical adherents,
And a science which eschews the taint of self, we would
Have magic, we would have words that make a link between dreams
And raindrops, we would demand specificity, and we would
Change the illustrious illusions into concomitant
Illusions, illusions that can erase our personal pain.
We would have medicine mixed from the sight of wind-harped trees.

Last night I dreamed of soldiers from a war started three-quarters
Of a century ago. The link? An anniversary
Date. The soldiers wore netted helmets and fought a jungle war.

The netting was woven with leaves, as if the very trees
Were poised to kill. The goal of the magician and the poet
Is the same: psychic transcendence, the body escaping
The conveyor belt of Time by a bodiless dive into
Time's crystal facets — all moments in one glittering sheen,
Where the magician-poet may see all. The magician is who
We are when words and images transport us, when nothing
About the ordinary weather, the ordinary rain, reflects
The ordinary, when angels fly like diamonds through the trees.

The Heir Breathes the
Air in A Forest of Evergreens
Clutter 45
Written 25 October 2016

———————— • ————————

It is said that he secures his domain by the direction
He turns his head when laid to rest. I close my eyes, and the sky —
Quietly overcast, like a coat of paint — suddenly strips the roof
Away, and he who was, but is not, pushes his sky-face
Close to mine, saying "Son." Through an act of relaxed focus,
We may see the cremated father — through Death's translucent flames
—

As this intruding Autumn sky. And we may account him proof
Against mortality, impregnable when we cried
As little children, and his calm voice comforted, saying "Son."

It is said that he secures his domain through the potency
Of his word, a word that only comes when sorrow blinds us,
And we see nothing but this gray film where heaven's light should be.

It is said that the sky secures its light in four directions,
Upheld by the strength of a sacred tree. My father was most
My father in the woods, where he moved like a walking tree,
A singular solidity as giving as a forest.
His green, even in winter, is the air the pine scent gifts us.
We cannot live without this forest. It is happiness
In the midst of agony's clear flames. It is said that he
Secures his life in the fires of absence, and when we are lost,
He is our rooted ridgepole. It is said I am his son.

His Word

Clutter 35

Written 26 October 2016

———————— • ————————

On nights like this, I relive the last years of my father's life,
And remember how the darkness thickened around his mind,
And made his eyes grow bright. Yesterday, the rain hunkered down
For what looked to be a long, dreary siege. But today, the sun
Returned, along with that special perfume, as clean as the ichor
Which wafts from rain-soaked trees. This seemed an ultimatum,
Which said: "Remember, and console yourself. Take a long trek round
A lonely lake." I could just picture him fishing there, the sky's
Deep blue and the lake's bluer blue, lending their lord their lights.

The colors glowed with chromium serenity, as the evening's
Breath infused both sky and lake with its final, finest splendors.
Then, alone there, in my gathering hurt, I heard harsh squawkings.

Above me, flew murders of crows, crisscrossing their ebony
Shapes in contentious flocks, each competing bird, seeking a roost
In the sun-tipped firs, redwoods, and oaks that besieged the lake.
How each harsh word from their anxious throats deepened my wound.
Now everything glowed, and was still. It was as if I had found that core
Of emptiness round which my orphaned planet spun its sorrow.
The birds are quiet now, and the night's eyes shine. In my grief's wake,
Not a single cricket chirps. A colossal darkness rules.
Yet, the lord of this thickening darkness keeps whispering "Peace."

Choked Up
Clutter 25
Written 27 October 2016

———— • ————

As the stakes grow higher, one's reluctance to speak becomes more
Agonizing. "In the beginning was …" Yes, we all know that
"The Word" has consequences.   In the end, my good father
Found speech increasingly difficult, and yet, what a deluge
Of emotion poured from him: whispers, openings and closings
Of the eyes and mouth, wordless vocalizations with huge,
Yet nebulous implications, his composite gestures,
Like today's storm — a whole sky weeping, without our seeing that
One drop of rain or hearing that one word, which would make things
clear.

I do not want to give the impression that these words are
About an old man engulfed by helplessness, when the one thing
That needs to be said transcends even the life of a father.

A single raindrop might roll down the whole interminable
Length of the horizon, like a pearl sliding along the keen
Edge of an interminable pane of glass,
Yet its voyage might say nothing about drowning. To be
Poised here, just on the vertiginous edge, to be rolling
And rolling down that divide, which cuts our silence from our speech —
It is this dilemma, which makes us think of our father's last,
Awful failures. In a moment, something great may intervene
Between lost love and uncertain breath — and here is where speech
stalls.

Undertow

Clutter 15

Written 28 October 2016

———————— • ————————

Even with the bravest of intentions, and even when
Starting from a shore where the ocean's waters are most calm,
Most mixed with brown, uterine nutrients, most buoyant with blood's
Genetic salt, it is a fearful thing to venture too far
Out, and even if the dream is not so fearful as to wake
Us, we remember it still, late in the afternoon. It jars
Us with the terror of depth, and hints that this rain might flood
Into the house, and make a peaceful day disaster. The realm
Of the ABC's in childhood spell XYZ's in the end.

If we recall our mother's perturbed stare peering through owl-eyed
Glasses or the flash of our father's gold tooth when we made
Him laugh, these memories are the alphabets of our lives …

And these letters will be the elementals of our children's
Children's lives, a baby watching his mother's eyes for signs,
A toddler clumping around in his father's shoes, a call
In the night when they tell you your mother is dying, the voice
Of a stranger, which says: "Your father has passed." The rain
Of an ordinary autumn day has presented this choice:
Risk swimming farther out, or tread the shallows. A dream recalled
In the day's calm drift catches us in the current of a sigh,
And pulls us down, down where the meanings of our small words
expand.

Berceuse In a Minor Key
Clutter 05
Written 29 October 2016

———— • ————

A day of solitude. Rain. Green atmospheres, collecting,
Dispersing. Some autumn colors jumping out of neutrals,
As colors jump from an Old Master's palette, rubbed to silver
Luminosity by decades of acute observation.
Learning a song by Fauré, which compares the quiet rocking
Of great ships in a darkening harbor to the calm motion
Of a cradle. Repetition of the French words, to my ear,
Almost inaudibly fading on some of the sad, final
Syllables — *silen-ce* — the sound dropping like last drops dripping.

In the midst of such silences, one is hardly aware
Of the reckless presence of the nearby sea, of the heaving
Margins of risk in the annals of mortal disorder.

In those last syllables, in a foreign tongue, almost beyond
The reach of hearing, are voices at sea in the green mists
Of the day, voices composed entirely of those lisping wisps
Of sound that fall at the end of choirs singing esses,
The lullabies' perhaps of mothers, grandmothers, singing,
Through mortal veils, of immortality, our wishes
For comfort in our solitude granted, but granted by this
Melancholy, this *Tristesse*, that almost makes us wish
To join them — out there — where autumn colors flash in the beyond.

Snide-of-Mouth Obituary
Clutter 94
Written 30 October 2016

—————— • ——————

Rain here is seasonal, and the lips of the earth are always
Parched and cracked before the first fall storms, and yet gratitude
Is short lived, so that after a few days, we long for the sun's
Return, and some relief from the dreary funereal
Mood that comes with rain. Today, I must attend the funeral
Of a friend, "a life celebration" is what they want to call
It, preferring bland poetry to blunt prose. As if the blunt
Blow-to-the-head emotion of death were some affront to
The deceased, and the mourners needed sunshine, and not rain.

The birds seem to know when the rain will take a break, they make
Black streaks across the matt gray skies, and our watery gaze trails
After those flashing lives, watching for some lightning in their wake.

But there is nothing — only the matt gray skies, only the rain
Repeating its un-poetic drips, only the memory
Of flight, and the bliss of the parched earth growing drunk on our
Unreasonable sorrow. The rain here is seasonal,
And needed. And if the skies are overcast with silence, still
The hiss of water running underground through thirsty tunnels,
Where the hardest seeds lie buried, makes sinuous whispers
Beneath our dreary dirges, a subtle, serpentine poetry
For the dead, whose wicked irony relieves prosaic pain.

Halloween
Clutter 84
Written 31 October 2016

———————— • ————————

Sleepless, the night man stumbles drunkenly through an ever
Deepening darkness, watching the streetlamp light hysterical
Trees, the autumn motley of a Chinese privet and a
Sycamore cackling above the house, jocose yellow, jocular
Red, refusing to adhere to the function of the genre.
But … but … what is the function of the genre? "The mad career
Of the night man? he who splits the darkness of dark Death with a
Derisive fervor? the poet of 3 a.m. who wails
To no other wakeful one in the throes of his stormy fever?"

And you, you — the people of daylight, and daylight's colors,
Who, while you sleep, may be relieved to know that your night fears
Are being devoured by the night man's peculiar hungers.

Once the storm has passed, the night man, calm now, may return to
His ordinary self, an ordinary insomniac
In poet-free suburbia, no witness to Death's clowning,
But a clown. The shadows of the trees fill up the house. They
Shatter the floor and walls and ceilings with mosaic laughter's
Thousands of jagged, black gleams. And what do you think he will say,
This ordinary man, in his 3 a.m. carousing
After sleep? And how will you function now, in this place of lack,
When the ordinary day is all that you have to cling to?

Suspended

Clutter 74

Written 1 November 2016

—————— • ——————

My brother-in-law, just three weeks from retirement, was in
Good health, had money in the bank, but he brought a rope to work
And hanged himself. He loved my dad. He took a picture of my
Father, fishing, and through some magical industrial
Process that photo was annealed to this coffee mug, which I
Now hold in my hand. My brother-in-law's trials where not all
Mental. He ventured into a metaphysical sty
Where petty human beings wallowed, and he was drowned. A quirk
Of historical fate — an industrial process — killed him.

But my father was not much given to metaphysical tortures.
He was wily. The Depression, the War, no fate in life
Could kill him. But Time did, Time, which granulates every picture.

In the picture, Dad sits, clothed all in faded denim,
Near a boulder, in tall grass, his wise hands relaxed on the rod,
His handsome profile fixed on the water's surface, the only
Metaphysical thing about him being his skill in reading
Underwater currents from quirky ripples. For him, Time,
Which in this picture can do no murders, has no meaning.
For him, all history twists in the wind, hung quietly
From clouds that do not move. For him, no metaphysical God
Exists — except for these fish that shine where his spirit sees them.

Corpo Vergognoso
Clutter 64
Written 2 November 2016

———— • ————

One of the more excruciating punishments of sleep
Deprivation is the sudden collapse of surface, the step
That gives way to the sinkhole of a dream: Old Self, naked,
Trying again to seduce Young Self's first great love. She sits
On the bed beside him, respectful, yet timid, her eyes full
To the brim with tremulous tears. Shame. Hasty retreat. The wit
To quickly change lust's overtures to fatherly concern. Red
Face gone white, gone ashen, then awakening in a sweat,
Sunlight already flashing round the shadows of shaking leaves.

The poet's guide informs the poet — still drugged with sleep — that he
May not escape the she-wolf's fangs, until he traverses Hell's
Sad corridors, until he faces life at its extreme.

The sinkhole is the Well of Sacrifice. Prepare the virgin.
Garland her with the jungle's lustiest blooms. Pound on the drumheads
With belligerent vigor. Shriek out a chant void of the shapes
Of words. Fall through eons of fashion to the primitive nude,
Then throw the sacrifice into the well. Your shadow crawls
On the wall with the primitive trees, destroyed by the lewd
Intrusions of alien powers. You are punished. Shame rapes
You with Time's prod, your Old self, dying, your Young Self, dead,
While the man alone on the bed embraces privation.

The Vicar of Bones

Clutter 54

Written 3 November 2016

———————— • ————————

This coastal region seldom sees snow, but as a boy, I
Rose before dawn every morning to deliver newspapers.
It was cold. It was dark. There was snow. You get sleepy when
You get too cold, and the snow becomes deeper, more inviting,
And children die in this white blanket, their bodies left blue
And frozen, but their last dreams perhaps being a comforting
Drifting through beauty — passed parental warnings, where they can
Be safe from scolding, or the numbing of noses or ears,
Where they can be innocent always, and have no fear of ice.

Odd, but all my life, when the great parental stressors have worn
Me down, I have had dreams of snow, sparkling under the moon's
Iridescent gaze, and blanketing me in billowing warmth.

And these dreams delivered me gently to old orchards, where I
Might lie in billows of new grass, and gaze up through the branches
Of apple trees miraculously clumped with white spring blossoms,
And making lullabies with breeze-strummed leaves, and choirs of
humming
Bees, and warbling robins. The snow is comforting, deep, and who
I was, who feared those warnings, is now no one. I am a being
Of beauty, a being of cold, an orphan gripped in frozen
Ecstasies. Motherless, fatherless, immune to damages,
I am the primal diamond in the chapel of Death's blue ice.

On the Wintry Origins
of Poetic Inspiration
Clutter 44
Written 4 November 2016

—————————— • ——————————

One of the more baneful yet beautiful traversals one
Must make when one needs the solitude which culminates in
Verse is that of exile from family and friends. Even this
Morning — crisp with sun-soaked autumn — becomes a mountainous
Isolation, a primitive lean-to bound round by snowdrifts.
Who lives here, what bearded codger, what old cantankerous
Predator of strange visions? Is it someone you know, whisked
Into metaphoric shape by the winter winds, some friend
You've forgotten to flatter with your passing attention?

Or is it someone you might dream about, just before autumn's
Sun-soaked dawn: You are in the lair of a black bear, a monstrous,
Intimate beast, who crushes you with pungent intimations.

Animal bulk, inhuman lover, the muse of solid
Mammalian connection, the blood of the mountain's autumnal
Reds crushed under hunks of midnight snow — these are your magical
Companions now, the weight that squeezes your body to squeeze
Out words. You do the simple things. Melt ice for water. Dry moss
For kindling. Stack logs to build a fire. Your one small window bleeds
The red reflections, and from a distance, this weird beacon calls
To one lone trekker, trudging through the cold. The fanged wind howls
And bites his flesh, but sun-soaked splendor flows into his blood.

Bugged

Clutter 34

Written 5 November 2016

————————— • —————————

The organized succeed. But what child has not found the cone
Of a large insect mound, and stuck a stick in it from simple
Curiosity. This first pure need for chaos that is,
And must be, the domain of every child, finds such pleasure
When the workers pour out in programmed panic, unnerved by
The sudden and inexplicable intrusion. They fan out for
The cause, and the child's eyes grow wide, as the severed strands of
nerves
Desperately seek to repair the old construction, the awful
Stick a monument to the horror of the big unknown.

The organized succeed. The collective quickly covers
The gaping wound. The mound is fixed, but the stick stays. It defies
All efforts of the mass to obliterate its lone terror.

The ants or termites have scoured every inch of their domain,
Mapped every pebble, every leaf, every straw, each crumb of soil.
They have arranged the interwoven mess into conflicting
Categories: food or its lack, us or them. Success, they know,
Requires organizing principles, something along the lines
Of a fantasy, which says yes to mindless survival, no
To the wonder of chaos. It is their way of coping.
But it is, in the end, a communal insect way, which the child
Loathes. Although to do so will fill him with an adult's pain.

The Confession of a Champion Bird Mimic

Clutter 24

Written 6 November 2016

This suburban enclave is inured to any general
Catastrophe, the citizens in a permanent drowse
Of anxiety, lulled into petty frets by the supreme
Luxury of too much convenience. Not so the crows. Though
Skilled in magic, I am not a man masked as a crow. I
Am the sun-eating night, the inconvenience of the throes
Of death, the private catastrophe of cancer, the choked plea
Of the betrayed wife, the autistic child locked in the house.
I am the poet of melancholy bliss, the harsh crow call.

Ornithologists tell us that too great a concentration
Of crows will diminish the songbird populations. I
Prefer one live crow to flocks of taxidermied wrens.

Under the ornamental trees, *Au pairs* push baby strollers,
Well-paid dog-walkers walk their employers' dogs, bored kids loll
Back and forth to school, their eyes fixed on their *iPhones*. For them,
Autumn is no harbinger of winter. In a collective
Brain-glitch, they repeat-repeat this suburban exercise.
Not so the crows. When the trees turn red, they shout their native
Chants round the spindly crests of shedding limbs, and rend
The chilling air with creaking pinions. They feel the general
Catastrophe. I am the voice, which sings their jagged aires.

Shadow Birds at Dusk Descending Through Vapory Streaks of Stratocumulus
Clutter 14
Written 7 November 2016

—————— • ——————

Back when I was still a boy at that terrible time when
The handsome young president was shot, one of my earliest
Art teachers taught me a vital life lesson. He was Dutch-
Indonesian with only one eye because the other
Was knocked out by a sadistic guard in a prisoner
Of war camp. He eyed my meticulous drawings with tears
Of compassion, then said, with his odd accent: "You do too much.
Must make mistakes, ten-thousand mistakes," which was the craziest
Thing I ever heard. One slip was bad, let alone ten-thousand.

I had always been taught that blue was a cool color, but he
Painted giant birds with incendiary blues, a color
That jumped at the eye like blood's red, like war's cruelty.

Tonight, when I looked at the sunset, I thought of his hot blues,
And also of the red that jumped from his face at a truncheon's
Blow, and I thought too of the coagulation of mistakes
That have colored my life: divorces, debts, my ten-thousand
Rituals of devotion to the jumbled wounded letters
I try to imprison in vital poems, my one-eyed blend
Of clashing blues and reds — my self-assassinating fate.
The sun dove quickly beneath the disheveled horizon,
And the land became a blob of ink, crowned by feathery hues.

Black and White Photographs Shot Through an Infrared Filter
Clutter 04
Written 8 November 2016

————— • —————

I hope you are not one of those aloof critics who coldly
Vilify this photographer, saying "He walks through lovely
"Forests and on the shores of gorgeous lakes and oceans, and all
"He sees are stumps, deformities — these insect-riddled, wave-
"Battered, wind-torn, moon-blanched, or sun-bleached monstrosities,
which make
"Mockeries of our beautiful, beautiful world." The enclaves
Of the hyper-privileged are full of such critics. "Remove all
"Evidence to the contrary," you say, the contrary
Being this art of death and abuse — these relics of agony.

Animal — and especially human corpses — are so
Repulsive, but there is something about these deaths, which forsakes
Death's horrors to embrace the realm of the beautiful unknown.

Ah, the beautiful, beautiful unknown, a habitat free
Of all you villainous critics, a forest of predators
And prey, a lake or a seashore where cruel climactic
Forces cough up the relics of violence, and lend them this
Luminous, alluring aura. I have studied this face
In the frame of the mirror. I have made it my business
To see this stump of the past as the death of youth's bland critics.
I have looked with the bluntness of a photograph at the scars
Blind Time has hacked, and I see bland bark buffed to a silver sheen.

To An Evangelical Sadomasochist

Clutter 93

Written 9 November 2016

————————— • —————————

After the election, after the unthinkable had
Happened, when I saw behind the hurt face of a cousin
Whose father was a drunkard and a bully, I knew there
Was an actual nostalgia for the vulgarian
Return of viciousness. I knew that millions of abused,
Unwanted children had found a sweet intimacy in
The puffery of a con man, and that her bleached-blond hair,
And her scared green eyes, were only cloaking a barbarian
Need for vengeance, for someone else to be punished as "bad."

I know history. I know that ordinary God-bless-you
Neighbors will ship you off to concentration camps, the screw
In their heads screwed right into your gut, because you are their Jew.

I will not sleep again. How can I? I step out in the night,
And stand beneath the fan of my neighbor's magnificent
Sycamore. It is deep autumn, and the leaves fall, replaced by
The distant, indifferent constellations. It would be nice
To believe that the stars could provide a prophesy, a truth
That would somehow redeem our idiocy. It would be nice
To believe that our neighbors really were neighborly, and that the cries
Of their unloved childhoods will not become the punishments
That break us — but I see a cherub's hands tear wings off flies.

Feeding Hamlet's Capons
Clutter 83
Written 10 November 2016

————————— • —————————

At first light, the sky gleamed in solarized bands of a rich blue
The color of a jay's feathers, alternating with the high-
Toned pitch of an oriole-orange. Above that, and flowing
Up and back towards the west, was an overcast of liquid pearl,
Which finally arced down to dull green pewter. By these dramas,
Mr. Typicus remained unmoved. "Red sky, morning, some drivel
About sailor's warnings," but nothing at all resembling
The eye-food whose ingestion stuns the poet, who wants to cry
Aloud, and change the world with this hallucinogenic goo.

But nothing like that is going to happen, because Mr.
Typicus is immune to sunrise, and he prefers his dramas
To be colorless, and imbued with a chance to get lucre.

Whenever I think of Mr. Typicus, I begin to
Disparage that ineffectual idler who lives on
The over-precious eye-glaze of momentary skies,
And I wonder how poetry could ever have lured me
To this porcelain dish whose food is only shine. It is as
If I were the alien in a world of wooden me's,
The big-eyed extraterrestrial gazer who vilifies
Mr. Typicus' material success, and lives alone
On an air-planet, where nothing lasts, or buys a scrap of food.

To Those Evangelicals Who Cannot Distinguish Opinion From Fact Or Emotional Affect From a Moral Position

Clutter 73

Written 11 November 2016

———————— • ————————

It is late autumn, a time when Death grows exuberant
With blazing, ever-falling leaves. Where I live, on the coast,
The air is a summery balm, but you, you live where the grip
Of winter already fills the air with frozen anvils.
They fall and ring against your biased skulls. I must say, I
Like that distant sound — the ringing filling my ears with genteel
Tones, as of archaic words disgorged by stupid, frozen lips.
I must say that some of your hatred has gripped my heart — a most
Agreeable ice, a hardness like iron that is heaven sent.

Irony is the weapon of the helpless. It keeps my
Poems warm, even when arctic numbness usurps the skies.
It buffers me against your madness, and your victims' cries.

It is late autumn, and Death has bared his crimson teeth with old
Pronouncements. The voters have cast their lots, which came up blank.
The red cloak of the savior has been ripped, and mercy hangs —
Bleeding — from the naked trees. Where I live, I sit — alone,
But alive, and warmed by my agony. I must say, I
Envy your naiveté, your naked acceptance of snow,
Your love of the prose of flat-earth ignorance, and how you thank
The god who bludgeons you. As I happily join the ranks
Of the excluded, I must say that my warmth defies your cold.

Made In His Image
Clutter 63
Written 12 November 2016

———————— • ————————

How delicious it is to sit in the warmth of this sweet
November morning, and feel how the wrath of winter has been
Thwarted. The lawn is still green and dewy, although the locust
Trees have turned yellow, retreating into their seasonal
Dormancy. Because the climate has warmed a few degrees,
A certain beetle may eat our northern forests. The trees all
Stand in brown obedience, dead, in situ, awaiting those bursts
Of flame that will blacken them. We know this is caused by gays in
Florida, whose sin has made our merciful God kill trees.

There is no lunacy that we will not believe, no fact that
Will change our beliefs. Our God protects us from conspiracies
Aimed at upsetting our certainty, and causing us to fret.

How delicious it is to sit in the warmth of the sun,
Knowing we have our guns, and may murder God's enemies
With impunity. How pleasant to stroll through these groves of trees,
Whose blackened Biblical letters, deformed in the mountains,
Can never grow another inch. How fine it is to be
Just as we are, serene in this foretold Abomination
Of Desolation, assured that this deliciously warm breeze
Will loft us, enraptured, to Heaven. And there we will meet
Our God, a Great Black Beetle, devouring this world of vile dung.

Grief that the Autumn Has Skinned the Trees, First Back to Red Viscera, Then Back to Charred Bone

Clutter 53

Written 13 November 2016

—————————— • ——————————

My thoughts buzz with the desolation of bees released above
A desolation of boundaryless waters. Sunday's peace
Calms the exterior of every leaf and satiates
My skin, and yet inside, in the organless interiors
Of the leaves, and in my own organs — my heart, my guts, my brain —
I feel the treachery of water, its depths, the glitter
Of its starry surfaces, the ambivalence of its spate
Of mysteries and deceptions, and this inundates me
With fear for the future, with a terror of what I should love.

For a long time, I have tried to make music from this churning
Effluent in the retort of my body, from my pains,
From my ecstasies, or simply from my choking need to sing.

But now it is November, and even the warm weather bears
A warning. Among the millions of my fellow citizens,
I have witnessed cruelty and hypocrisy on an
Oceanic scale. In the hidden depths of their turbid creed,
Violence seethes. When I saw their idolatry fueled by hate,
It was then I made my ineffectual cry: "O Save the bees!"
For the pollinators of our grounded life are being drowned en
Masse in ignorance. In November the trees are flensed,
Though the weather is warm. And the bees can find no nectar.

Struck Dumb

Clutter 43

Written 14 November 2016

———————— • ————————

Last night's full moon was a rarity, which was supposed to be
Auspicious, as well as beautiful. We'll see. Personally
I look at today's blue sky as a mask disguising an
Evil premonition. Listen: in heaven, a place formerly
Known as the future, the yet to be born citizens will —
If we are to continue to survive as a species —
Wonder what we meant by words like *Guelfi*, Tailist, or sin.
And they will wonder how hate in the name of what is holy
Became the mark for an ignorance that passed for piety.

For the people of the future, the night will appear as it
Is: a black bowl, where the great, white pearl of the moon has settled.
To them, even violence will seem the beauty of spirit.

In Hell, a place formerly known as the past, the zealous
Protectors of the Holy Word were expert torturers
And slaughterers. In the dull gloom of the abattoir, they
Read their scriptures. I read my holy writ as earthly heaven,
The night with her lustrous pearl, the day with his deep, rich well
Of liquid lapis. This pair care nothing of false religion
Or vile politics, or masks of ignorance. They have their say
Without corrupting speech or losing their potency in Time's blurred
Definitions. They have their say as light's auspiciousness.

Fossil Phosphenes
Clutter 33
Written 15 November 2016

———— • ————

Anyone might have seen them, walking from a light space to
A dark one, or vice versa, the normal illusion
Shattered — skies, lovers, lies — all devolving to these plasma
Bursts. They are the blind-eye-swirls of all we have seen condensed to
Their orange and blue petrifactions, all their original
Organic sights replaced, cell by cell, all the way down to
The micro-level. They are the relics of dead silica-
Feelings, which have been mineralized by regret, and have come
To form these stony artifacts from decades of blood-birthed truth.

These preservations of sexual ravings, religious
Manias, viral greeds, family dramas, their details
Jumbled in temporal stasis, are glimpsed again in stillness ...

And, like all such glassy extinctions, polished to completion
By grinding Time. They are beautiful in death. Anyone might
Have seen them, walking from a dark space to a light one, or
Vice versa, oddly cleansed of the mud of their turbulence,
And eternally present in these sudden sun-bursts, all
Of their misplaced catastrophes in place, all of their chance
Disasters crystalized. Anyone might have seen this bright ore,
This agate of their misspent lives, redeemed, what was despised
Now seen as this enthralling, this permanent gem of heaven.

On the Proverbial Slow Boat
Clutter 23
Written 16 November 2016

———————— • ————————

Late autumn, and even at noon, the sun has slid so far
South that the shadows always have a twilight slant, sweeping
Around day's circuit, eventually pouring forth night
Around the last refuge of light, and finally leaving dark
Hollows where poets dream. Last night, I discovered a hollow
Beneath my pillow where a stairwell descended through the dark,
And emerged, just as the myths foretell, in China. Here I
See Li Po, alone and drunk, beneath a moon that is waning.
The night shakes the cherry branches, and showers him with flowers.

Now I sit at noon, idle, but sober, where a brisk breeze
Loosens leaves, gold and red, to bury me. Li Po, I know,
Is both unread and dead, his blossoms mating with my dry leaves.

Autumn, spring, sobriety, drunkenness, I live in evil
Times, where evil people denounce idleness and promote,
With arrogant piety, violence over stillness. In
His Dragon Carvings of a Literary Mind, the sage
Has said: "What lies in the heart is *wish*. Thus it must follow,
"When calm exudes its words, poetry is *wish*. No place for rage
Or judgment in this fragrance. Denounce denunciation.
That is the way." The air is bright and crisp. A burnt smell boats
Its grief across deep blue. I ship to China in this vessel.

In the Ruins of the Never-to-Be Abandoned City, A Few Feral Trees Shed Golden Autumn Leaves
Clutter 13
Written 17 November 2016

——————— • ———————

Instructions are invariably cryptic, poetic,
And individualized for each eccentric. How does one
Move from the one self, embedded in the many, to the sky
Self, witnessing the throng? The enemy is hurry, never
Time, the urge to do in the metropole of doing, the switch
In the head turned on, in the heart, turned off. Watch how the *Flâneur*
In the city's hurly burly, his tortoise on a leash, strolls by,
Amused by the bustling frenetics. He reads the destruction
As jokes, as celestial enthrallments for the social critic.

In shabby genteel, he fashions his own Buddha. A poet
Purged of Baudelairian spleen, his malodorous itch
Scratched, his empty sky-gaze, roaming the sweet realms of spirit.

Instructions are invariably cryptic. How does one
Activate that switch, obtain that tortoise, take that poetic stroll
Through the madhouse city to rest in the gutter,
Another husk of trash, but trash that is utterly at peace?
How does one drift like smoke through the smoke-filled skies, as if one's wish
Were granted by laughing heaven, and the chaos of alleys,
Deranged by such caffeined hurry, were *le boulevard* of stars?
How does one purge one's individual spleen and find that gold?
There are autumn leaves that have fallen at one's feet. Be one.

Coronation

Clutter 03

Written 18 November 2016

———————— • ————————

I suppose you were sleeping when I told you that the whole
Of the city is a ruined dream, is fragments of dreams
That are dreaming. I suppose you have forgotten that you
Are the son of a king, a child who hides in the woods, out or
In there, beyond the shadow of the palace walls, where the oak
Tree grows. You have climbed inside the hollow of the tree, a bear
In your imagination, thinking the kingdom lost. When you
Wake, it is spring, your stores of fat are gone, your body the lean
Ruin of that reality that said: "You are not royal."

You hide the bear inside you, hibernating, and proceed
To explore the city. It was once a great city, but so
Many things have changed, have decayed, in these once noble streets.

It is as if mechanical devices wreaked havoc on
Their own, pounding the peace to death with their hysterics. Here none
Can sleep, although none are awake. But at the center
Of these ruins is a lake, and in its tears, an island knoll,
And on this knoll, a blasted, gnarled oak, and in the oak
A crater, where all past autumn leaves of all past heartaches mold,
And underneath this mold, so deeply buried in disaster,
There lies the tiniest, but the very heaviest of stones,
And crushed beneath this stone, you find your crown. Now — put it
on.

The Violent Return of Resentment
Clutter 92
Written 19 November 2016

———————— • ————————

An arctic fury has pushed down the coast and lashed this forest
With missiles of sharp rain and shaking winds — the last warm days
Of autumn, strangled by a cold, jealous lover. Here, looking
Into the heart's ravine, we see how the golden and russet
Relics of the summer are swept down the slopes in a muddy
Turbulence, and tumbled through the torrent of a stream. What collects
Scattered memories in that chaos of movement is something
Richer than warmth, harsher than scenery, and it proclaims
A pulsing lust that jumps like youthful sex through that deep cleft.

Let us call this the moment of intermingling sympathies,
And let us extend this magic into the watery
Tragedies that roil and raven and muddy the reckless stream.

Perhaps it was possible a week ago to have hiked
The footpath clutching the rim of the steep, and to have calmly
Watched the mirroring creek, tumbling its kaleidoscope with sky
And leaves, and even streaks of bird. Those pleasant voluntary
Reminiscences of sex, are gone, drowned with the love, which dreams,
In perpetuity, of summers without end. The V
At the base of the steep has been forgotten, yet the sky,
Which now rains fury, is strangely at peace, but this is a peace
That does not appease the arctic, nor silence our icy cries.

Temporary Temporal Clearing
Clutter 82
Written 20 November 2016

———————— • ————————

There are tiers and tiers and tiers of spiraled stairway that mount
The rainy sky, and from the topmost balustrade, November,
A weeping giant, leans — the self we could have been. The rain
Is dreary, like a child's grieving for the loss of a pet or
The loss of a favorite toy. The boy is watching rain-
Drops streak the window, all of those slithering paths of silver
Branchings, collapsing the future's possibilities — his pains
All merging in one glistening wet. An old man remembers
His past aspirations, and the boy inside him gasps out loud.

The fantasy of being bigger, smarter, has fossilized
To giant human skulls, all trepanned, and found in one mass grave,
Along with the bones of mice. This grave sleeps in the crying eye.

And the boy at the window, the old man in the glass, the two
Both streaked with the dreams that were never to be: November's
Species of late autumnal storm, awaiting what December's
Cold will bring — these are the ones growing older, but never
Maturing. They are the reasons the giant weeps out his pain
In tears and tears and tears of stormy losses. The brain pours
Forth its longings, and for a moment, they streak the glass with weird
Distortions of both past and future — an instant of glitter,
A day of greys, a spot, high up, of momentary blue.

Notes on the Risks of the Ectotherm's Primal Joy in the Throes of Minute Discoveries
Clutter 72
Written 21 November 2016

———————— • ————————

After days of violent, drenching rains, the storm rolled east,
Leaving a morning of blue upper atmospheres, ringed by
Horizons of white mists. Those mists, this afternoon, have bunched
Into armadas of white ships, plying heavenly seas
Free of anxiety. But we are anxious. Because the hulls
Of those low hanging vessels spread shadows, the piracy
Of uncertainty, unpredictably, with a sudden crunch,
Making us food for Chance. Even on bright days, anything might
Happen, Time being hungry, and our little plans his feast.

Our eyes tell us nothing. We must rely on chemo-sensors,
Reptilian tongue flicks alert to dangers that the gulled
Human brain, distracted by culture's trinketry, ignores.

It may be that the astute practitioner of emotions
Still has access to the reflexes of an ant-eating
Lizard. He tastes something in the air, something in the masses
Of myrmidon distractions on the ground, and with open
Jaws, he snaps his head around, ready to eat these words — the full
Significance of which are only digestible when one
Is not stunned by the predator-culture. His tongue caresses
The air for a subtler bliss, something genuine, hovering,
Something beyond those ant-facts, which bred his lizard emotions.

How the Sun-Shot Effusions of Iridescent Droplets Hides the Shooter on the Grassy Knoll

Clutter 62

Written 22 November 2016

————— • —————

Mystique is a great thing to have, you deny that, and you
Eject yourself out of existence. Let me elaborate.
The sky today is an uncertain conglomeration
Of vaguenesses — soft blues, pinks, lavenders, the sun imparting
Goldish cool diffusions, so that the eye, uncertain always
About what it is seeing, must enter that made-up thing:
The heaven of imagination, the poet's palace in
The mists of day, the mystique's wonders where elaborate
Ornamentations stand nebulously in place of solid truth.

"Today," you say, "my body is not here, and this mist," you say,
"Of flesh, was never real." And I say, "Whatever you say,
Is air, the vaporous hair of angels wound round the day."

Who then embraces the richer of two illusions? You,
With your body whose solidness will soon feed crows, or No One,
This crow of multicolored smokes, whose chief delight is to make
The solid insolid? Note: Your crows are black, the composite
Of daytime's brights, the rifle barrel that the sniper aims,
Which — crack! — from ambush, assassinates your thought, and makes
its
Emptiness apparent. So, I repeat, "Mystique is a great
Thing to have, a sad thing to lose, a nebulousness that comes
In vague dreams as a poet who sings this untruth as his truth.

What All Those Flashing Lights and Loud Noises are Saving Us from Knowing

Clutter 52

Written 23 November 2016

———————— • ————————

Affixing midsummer solstice as the rim of a crater,
We see we have been on a winding downward path, a journey
Growing darker and colder as we descend, the brilliance
Of autumn, as bright as the brilliance of spring, but a precursor,
Not to life, but rather to ... Stop. Wait. It is far too risky
To finish such a thought, and we have invented a hoard
Of devices to reliably spare us. We look askance,
Having noisy contrivances to blow away dead leaves,
And intricate diversions to entertain us — clever ...

Or so we think. But the descent is also in our bodies,
In cells that convert spring's light into tumors. There are heaps
Of autumn reds mulching odd concoctions where we cannot see ...

But we can hear. They make the sounds of those machines,
Blowing dead leaves to another dimension, the dimension
Where unaccepted pain is magnified. The dead remembrances
Of spring, in livid blazings, have not been blown away, they
Were swept into the crater, down where all that we denied screams
In the dark, and the thought that we dared not finish now brays
Out pain with mechanical constancy. The silences
That might have brought us comfort are ground down by an autumn,
Angry that her one great lesson was dumbed down by smart machines.

The Old King's Premonition
Clutter 42
Written 24November 2016

———————— • ————————

Last night the cold polished the estuary creek to
A glassy anthracite with sculpted basalt water fowl
Carved in its still tableau, the heaving muscles of the tide
Working without a ripple. The moon left the night unburnished,
Yet rose early this morning to be chased across a bright blue
Sky by a sun that hurries to set too early. The great hush
Of awe that should accompany this drama is absent. Why?
Because the glass that our children obsess about has pixels,
Gumdrop bits of light that render these primal dramas moot.

Last night I dreamt that I was jailed underground and was forced
To shower in a mildewed tile room, filled with soggy rags. Who
Or what compels me, I cannot tell. But I am depressed.

It seems I shall never see the sky again. After — awake —
The calf of my left leg cramping, I rose and hobbled through
The baffles of a cold house, filled with desires that could not be
Satisfied by candy behind a glass. I went outside.
Frost crinkled in crinkling starlight, as a 4 a.m. half-moon
Just crested the eastern horizon. A hushed awe froze the sky,
Froze me, and I stared like that first human who wondered what these
Nocturnal miracles were saying. I did not want to
Sleep, yet, I felt sleepy, and I knew that sleep would be my fate.

What If the Bigger Life We Are Seeking Is Not Fame and Fortune, But Weather and Words?
Clutter 32

Written 25 November 2016

———————— • ————————

The blue of yesterday's high, bright sky invited a warm
Intimacy, but today an arrogant old man cold
Shoulders us with his celestial snub. This is why we deny
That the weather is an entity, a fickle friend or foe
According to moods sculpted on a grander scale than any
Of our own, and why we remain atheists in that most
True sense, and strangers to the air we breathe. But sometimes
We feel twinges of a believing self, a primordial,
Vaster being, who allows the sky to take more human form.

Do our days collect as one Monad, having many moods, or
Are we pagan polytheists, our gut peopled with any
Number of deities — and where should we seek an answer?

Suppose you had a dream, your body profiled in a walking
Pose, but trapped in a wooden, black frame. You are not moving
Towards the edge that you cannot transcend. You are stuck in your
House, in your bed, in your oscillation between a sleep self
And a waking one. The sky inside, and the one that bleeds
From above, too publicly — is this the primordial
Deity, both one and many, presenting you a picture
Of a truth that your paralyzed, little, unbelieving
Self cannot accept, unless your waking embraces dreaming?

Equine Ennui
Clutter 22
Written 26 November 2016

———————— • ————————

Quiet afternoon, grey skies, intermittent rain, the mind
Its own musical progress — *andante* — with *pizzicati*.
One of the more famous romantic composer's obscurer
Sonatas, the piano dropping black pearls in blood pools,
As the cabman's horse droops his head, awaiting the return
Of the young gentleman from his assignation, a fool
Again for crinolines, the lady beautiful, but a bit more
Practiced in flirtatious cruelty, a bit more flighty,
Than his heart can stand. The horse wears blinders, but is not blind.

Listen. Simple horse sense will tell you that rain is wet, the day
Too cold for waiting, that even should the violin burn
In excesses of grace notes — *fuoco* — the day stays grey.

Listen. To feel, to really feel the effluents of these or
Any words, you must traverse miles of sonic penury,
Plodding along the streets in dreary weather, the raindrops
Blurring your vision under the blinders, the streets a jumble
Of meaningless sounds and motions, with only the curse
Of the cabman's whip and voice to drive you on — animal
That you are, and have always been. You fix on the clop
Of your own unmusical progress, and stop on a street
Where a house, like all the others, leaks music through its locked door.

Burying Sapphires
Clutter 12
Written 27 November 2016

———— • ————

On days like today, when the clarity has about it
A gem-bright permanence, as yesterday's raindrops drop-drip from
Leaves and eves, and all seems falling brilliantly back to earth, I
Lift my spirit-visage to the heights of heaven, while knowing
I too am descending. The histrionics of advancing
Age derive from this division, my sky-part aspiring
To jewels, while my earth-part — granulating — drip-drops sighs.
Two angels call me now, one vapor, one dirt, and both say: "Come."
What am I to do, or say, dissected by this sharp split?

It is taboo to speak about these two, one sliding in
Runnels, draining my dissolution down to roots, one lifting,
Like breath, an essence of essences, to mate with that blue gem.

It is taboo to be one with these two. The split says, "You
Must choose." I know I have always chosen the sky, always
The vaporized sparklings of nebulous news. I know I
Have always slighted earth. Yet now that I feel my solid
Underpinnings breaking apart, their tiny bone-grains flowing
Down and down into a comforting darkness, that which is solid
Calls me back to dirt. The angel of poetry's lies
Grows hard in space. The last trump of the best news cannot play,
But sticks in air as final silence — a clear, false note of blue.

Sanctuary
For Patricia Keel
Clutter 02
Written 28 November 2016

—————— • ——————

On the island of Malta, archeologists — those lovers
Of past passions — have discovered a shrine for the goddess,
A rock city of the dead, carved with stone mallets and picks
Of horn. Over the course of millennia, the limestone,
Smoothed with small flint blades, replicated, so deep below the earth,
The ochre-hemorrhaged inside of an egg. The surface limestone
Is alive with spirals, honeycombs, dots, circles, those tricks
The brain makes on our closed eyelids, as the waking consciousness
Starts to dream. The goddess lies at this Hypogeum's center.

She was born fat as an egg — and sleeping, and she has been
Sleeping for more than six-thousand years. Suspended, like our breath,
And colored red, like birth, she calms the dead and welcomes them.

The sea cradles the island, as well-worn slippers cradle
Cherished feet, the feet that have crossed the brightest-chop of waves,
So that our spouse of many lives and years can whisper, lip
To ear, her secret message. Her words for this — "I love you" —
Are fraught with passion, the passion of her never-aging earth.
She cradles in her arms our deathless wishes. "I love you."
That is what I think when I see these well-worn slippers that sit
On the well-worn carpet by the slept-in bed. What could I say
That is better than these words, to tell you how I fell, and feel.

I Drive Evil From the Body, and Free Spirits Trapped In Demagoguery's Snares
Clutter 91
Written 29 November 2016

After the election, it became all too clear that there
Were millions and millions of citizens who were growing
Obscene tumors in their small hearts. These cancers, more properly
Called "teratomas," can grow hair, teeth, bone, misshapen torsos,
Or skulls with red, blind eyes and brainless tongues that only bleed.
Bluntly put, they replicate the bullying, drunk fathers, who
Rape children. To crave fear, that is the symptom of their disease,
Which has no treatment, but murder. They welcome the coming
Catastrophes as the prodigal was welcomed by his father.

Sad ones, do you know who I am? I am one of your children,
One of the Principal Ones. I am Mother Touch, she
Who may read the Book, which contains the language of the chosen.

My words speak sky-music. They fall from above. The songs they hum
Rise up from earth. They shine on water. They blaze in flame. They
Are little luminous puffs of medicine. They come to my
Sacred tablets, and with fond care, I nurse them. This is the Book.
It is not your Biblical black. It is what happens to me
When I am chosen, when I choose the Principal Ones. I look,
And I see the executioner. You hear, and you praise lies.
Sad ones, how is that your hearts have grown so sick? Your pulse brays
Ignorance, and takes a bully's boastings as Christ's sweet balm.

Surprised Tears Fall When You Learn That The Coroner Listed The Cause of Your Father's Death As "Accidental?"
Clutter 81
Written 30 November 2016

———————— • ————————

Attention: you are now entering that consciousness zone
Where sexual tension is maintained throughout a nocturnal space
By the chromium repetition of a baroque theme.
This music stimulates beautifully and complexly,
But its coda comes without resolution or release.
The drizzle of raindrops on the roof, a coronation scene
With millions of infants tapping xylophones — now you believe
It: Emotion is a chemical arousal with no trace
Of identity, a dream of aqua sounds, not flesh and bone.

There are lulls in the fighting, but never in the rain,
Lulls, when the comic dictator revamps his war strategies,
But his bloated egotism no longer causes you pain.

You have fallen so many times. You have grown old falling.
But the chromium music stays bright, though your hearing fails. For
You, the mechanical tones are choirs of voices, the people
You knew, the person you once were, collecting these ecstasies
And griefs, as if they existed once in a history
That built itself with names. For you, the precipice is a scene
Of falling — the father of your body, growing senile,
And trying to get out of bed, but always falling. For you, for
You, he sings. He is singing with teardrops. Are you listening?

A Tiny Raisin Craps a Giant Grape
Clutter 71
Written 1 December 2016

———————— • ————————

Is this the 3 a.m. insomniac's discovery
Of the grotesque? Eras, seasons, peoples, at some point, all
Combine senile, decaying, deformed images with the
Gigantism of free-floating angst. The frost on the roof
Eats the reason's illusion of a classical completeness,
And the mind swells with ridiculous terrors, the crone muse
As laughing goddess, pregnant, but senile, the last hope, the
First fear, the climate of one's last years become combustible
As autumn's reds drop down to winter, and winter's poetry.

"Now," was the word, but now the word is "later," perhaps too late,
Although the goddess laughs as though she mocks her crone's barrenness
With the impossible birth of an impossibly living clay.

The insomniac is reminded — with this raw power
Of uterine contractions — that transcendence is not the sole
Province of the holes in the head, but also comes through those
Obscene cavities below the omphalos — screwing, pissing,
Shitting, giving birth, as the body accepts its collapse
Into wintry bones. An ancient, grotesque kind of carping
Sings of death — but not the death we feared, not that clichéd, lone
Skeleton, robed in masculine black, but this, this comic old
Renewer, this figure bent double with chronic laughter.

A Redonian Antidote
to Violent Conflict
Clutter 61
Written 2 December 2016

———————— • ————————

Would you believe me if I told you that one of the most
Beautiful souls on the planet time travels by sky watching?
(Beware! I prey on the gullible.) You might see the deformed
Bloat of his body as a no account idler, but he sails,
Vaporous wisp to wisp, across an immaculate blue in
A boat of polished abalone shell, its great sail
A sheet of beaten gold. The Virgin, head bowed, calms his heart's
storms,
So that near her, at the tiller, he may steer by the heading
Of desire's star, on a plane of glass unframed by any coast.

In a time of peace, in a decades-old war, this boy lives on
His father's estate, and need never choose an occupation
From the necessity of earning loot or the need to fawn.

He attends the old, stone country church, its medieval
Stained glass panes washing soft vagaries of light across the small
Hands praying before him. An exquisite music echoes
Through the rustic nave. Fantasies of the most vivid angels
Play round his steepled hands. He decides, through revelation,
That his religion will be the art of imagination, that pastel
Will be his medium, his goal, chromatic innuendo,
His object, mystical beauty. He decides that the boat's sail
Will be filled with golden breezes woven from life's dark evils.

Bright Permanence in Turbid Flux
Clutter 51
Written 3 December 2016

———— • ————

Binge watchers of the calamities of others, we have all
Seen those hooded prisoners, often journalists, in the
Custody of true-believers, those unfortunates, breathing
In the smell of vomit and sweat, while we watch their torture or
Beheading. But who among us feels their true condition?
The suburban poet, hooded by middle-class comfort, bored
By the terrors of media inanities, keeps probing
Into the stench of this predicament. Why is it, if the
Poem means death or life, that to others it seems so banal?

Binge talkers, repeat and repeat, with hard breathing, something
Which flows beneath those perfumes trapped by the hood, something
akin
To freedom, something akin to rivers, alive and sparkling.

These flashings from the stream of green spirit take the shapes of sounds
In the ennui of mundane speech, the shapes that form stories
From snippets of journalism, the myths of death that blossom
Into spring. Like the sun retuned to the darkest winter day,
They announce to the terrified captive his true condition.
The hood stays put, but the poet hears, beneath those profane
Binges of middle-class boredom, that gasping for freedom
In the prisoner's lungs. And from these rich, treacherous eddies
In spirit's river, his glamorous voice turns wounds to sounds.

Elementary Zoology
Clutter 41
Written 4 December 2016

————————— • —————————

Take a toddler to the zoo, and you will discover that
The animal over there, caged, however exotic,
Holds scant interest compared to the pigeon, right here, at your
Feet, which is chased with outstretched arms and screams of shrill
delight.
Turn your old eyes around, and see that the uncaged and close
Is much more dazzling than the consensus trance. Inside-sights
Always arouse exuberance. You may be repressed, but your
Raw self, untainted by leaden experience, and heartsick
With habit, may suddenly see, and be stunned by the contrast.

That which appears and disappears — the iridescent gleam
Of the pigeon's throat, or this beast, striped grief-black and orange-gold,
That pounces when your eyes are closed, as though emerged from
dream.

A peek-a-boo blinking of insight and night, in one strike
Of lightning, a child in quartz-pink light, in another, an old
Tiger, his face a blur of shadowy blue vapors, with you —
The common exotic creature, caught between them. Over there,
Not so far away as you want him to be, is a morose
Stranger in a cage. He paces. He grows bitter. While in here,
Is a sudden shudder and clattering of wings. And what will you
Chase with your toddler's outstretched needs? The cold
Relic of formerly savage things, or this bright flash in flight?

Soporific

Clutter 31

Written 5 December 2016

———————— • ————————

'Tis the season ... and the pianist at the white concert grand
At the foot of the escalator of this snootiest
Of department stores plays arpeggios in his sleep.
The shoppers, slathered with this year's fashions, slide up, slide down.
He dreams of the Goldberg variations, Bach's masterpiece, composed
For an insomniac. Asleep, his hound's paws twitch, then bound,
Then zigzag after bounding game — variation seventeen:
The left-hand figuration rises. It thrusts an anarchist's
Bomb into the G clef, which blasts the melodious right-hand.

For Christ's birth, millions and millions of shoppers throw away
Their lives in sleep, their slatherings of fashion's shiny clothes,
Burning away to skeletons as naked as primal shame.

But the music, Bach's music, Bach's brook, flows on and on, spilling
Through crashing chords of a moonless surf, where an artist, bereft,
Walks the deserted strand, troubled in spirit, seeking some sound
To drown him, some sound to drag his old dog's body down, down
Where the primal Mother calms her baby, her voice, composed
And comforting, her song, a balm. The waves rise up, crash down,
Their rage, however violent, mere surface motion. Their harsh sounds,
Distant now, are smoothly soothing. At these profoundest depths,
The lost child, found, now blithely dreams of serpents serpentining.

Said Unsaid

Clutter 21

Written 6 December 2016

——————— • ———————

Coveting the usual masculine delusions, like
Most men, I seek maximum illumination, noon being
The best time for decisiveness, no matter what the wind
Is whispering on the hillsides. The sky is bright, but a few
White clouds splash racing shadows down the mountains, and those
ragged
Ghosts, formed by the wind-sky-forest trinity, introduce,
Even at noon, a lunar uncertainty. A force akin
To gravity, an anti-noon, that does not need the shining
Masculine sun, pulls me beneath a sea of primal night.

A sudden narcoleptic plunge drowns me in the feminine's
Fertile questions — a view down a rugged coast, born from ragged
Skeins of fog and the plunging roar of surf from a blood ocean.

Someone resembling who I used to be stands on the sea cliff,
Watching the storm roll in. The wind parts the grass at his feet,
And reveals, by lunar shine, a figurine of wax. Someone
Has plunged a nail into its chest — an omen, in black, that
Speaks of feminine spells. Where the nail goes in, a drop of red
Emerges, not the blood of menses nor of birth, but of that
Which stains the thoughts with indecision. I blink, and the vision
Drowns in the flood of noon, as the sun returns with its indiscrete
Intrusions. I would say more, but a salt drop seals my lips.

Scavenged

Clutter 11

Written 7 December 2016

——————— • ———————

This late afternoon overcast has a jaundiced hue,
Its yellow always turning gray whenever you try to
Look at it directly.   It has been more then seventeen years
Since I first discovered that each small island of awareness
Is ringed by a luminous void where flesh is purified.
Before that revelation, whatever soul I possessed
Was but one gelatinous blob in a star-spawn mass of tears.
But since then, my bit of ovum, having been fertilized, brewed,
Has been a node where the particular can start to accrue.

Such experiences cannot be planned. One is simply
Burned alive or is drowned in negation. The body dies,
And is hung high up in the arms of the nervous system's tree.

The gray men who write scholarly articles on the subject
Of excarnation tell how some tribes de-flesh the deceased.
They place the corpse high up to feed buzzards. "Sky burial," they
Call it. But what do they know of the eye of the butcher priest,
Who must perform the rite? I tell you it is like this sky,
Overcast, cold, jaundiced — a void, not to be directly
Gazed upon, but allowed, like his red knife, to devoutly flay
Experience, to purify it through buzzard guts, and be
Flensed down to nothing, but these yellowed bones the soul infects.

This Muted Bellowing
Is Not The Last Trump
Clutter 01
Written 8 December 2016

———— • ————

In the spirit's ear, everything is poetry, in its eye,
All is splendor. The backyard's pear tree, ruined by the routine
Of autumn, contrasts its last yellow leaves against the flannel
Grays of a weeping sky, and as one — anyone — your one,
Looks out the storm-mad window, one sees the hospital. Are you
Surprised? In the hospital the president-select stuns
No one with the wealth of his diseases — and though brown missiles
Rain down in ceaseless torrents, they cannot wash this turd clean.
No matter. In the spirit's maze, poetry trumps all lies.

Surprising though how the blatantness of evil appears
As good to those who delight to wallow in Christ's blood. You
Might think that they court crucifixion, and mistake fear for ardor.

And surprising too how the intricacies of autumn
Can still give succor to the Biblically blighted ear,
And to the suppurating, fundamentalist eye. Perhaps
It is this appliqué of the last leaves on the weeping flannel,
The gold on gray, or the L-sounds in "gold" and "flannel" that move
The L in "hospital" to pity, and make the muted gospels
Prate sad truths. Whatever. The spirit meditates, even laughs,
Because a pear is not an apple tree, and the primal fear
Is not the final terror — no matter if the skies rain dung.

The Devolution of the Species
Clutter 9
Written 9 December 2016

———————— • ————————

As the year unwinds in winter, we are often confronted
With the limits of what we can bear — the deaths of loved ones,
Friends, the realization that the body can no longer
Make complete repairs, and the more profound realization
That these truths have always been dreamily hibernating,
Even in those first blushes of youthful love — where no one
Dared to seek them. The Paleolithic cavern — Time's bore-
Hole in God's rockface — or the hollow tree trunk, these bastions
Spell isolation, where the dreaming body can meet the dead.

This is not the amazement of the old discovery
Of the animal self, but the stark amazement clinging
To that human to whose locked heart only spirit has the key.

That the human beast with its unique capacity for
Wickedness and destruction has arisen in the body-
Politic, there can be no doubt. The revelations in
Our dreams prove that. We have reached the limit, the great collapse
Of a warm autumn into a drear winter, where foreboding
Chokes the future in a fretful vision. But are these the last
Breaths of sleep's nightmare, or the first heart-beats of a human,
Awakening to the word "farewell" with an ecstasy
That transcends death, where the bestial-angel clumsily gets born?

The Worst Apology
Clutter 8
Written 10 December 2016

———————— • ————————

What is it about this rain that has persisted through the night,
And which conjures the vision of a procession of horse-drawn
Hearses, each hearse bearing the incorruptible corpse of a
Black-clad nun? The horses are black too, and each sports on its fine
And blinkered head, a black cockade, capped with red, which, with the
high-
Stepping gait of the teams, tremble like autumn leaves on the fine
Black twigs of almost barren trees. The nuns' bodies bear no stain
Of sin. They are ideals, the ideals that arose in the dawn
Of youth's first loves, and which now show this sad, but comforting,
sight.

I cannot say that some entity outside of time has shaped
My histories with women, so that today, in this rain, I
Would write this poem. But it seems so, and seems a cure for shame.

Appalled that I could love you — my wives, my daughter, my mother —
Only in that corrupt way of an idealist, whose
Flesh was always the open mouth of need, whose mind was crystal,
And whose heart was sentimental. It seems this entity has
Extracted these poison chemicals to change the lies
I was always telling to myself into verse. What has
Happened, happened, and if the pains or joys of this persist, all
I can plead in my poor defense is this: I did not choose
To hurt you, but to love you, and to grace dull words with splendor.

A Family of One
Clutter 7
Written 11 December 2016

———————— • ————————

My nephew, who is a grown man now, and the same age as Christ
When crucified, was slow to talk. He teaches music theory
These days, and is an avant garde composer of some repute.
But I remember watching him babbling to a Blue Jay
In a fig tree, and though he was nearly four, his weird squawking
Was no more comprehensible than the jay's. That was his way.
Understand, I could have substituted "son" for "nephew,"
Or "reader," or any relationship term, and my theme,
Although altered, would still be as ineffable as bird cries.

Listen: the leaves of fig trees are large, and their music, when stirred
By the breeze, mimics largeness. In the same way, the jay's squawking
Is not that of a crow. My words for this are not a child's words.

The music of these words does not link sign to signified,
And babble on about fig trees and blue jays, and children
Who are slow to talk. Yet there are linkages here much like
Those of heartbeat to blood flow, or sunlight to leaves, or bird
To boy — linkages mysterious to those who are searching
Only for that shallowest sheen called "meaning" in these words.
Mine are the exclamations of an avant garde that crucify
The reader with relation, as of the squawks of slow children
Or quick birds, which connect the pronoun "you" to the pronoun "I."

X-Mess Celebration
Clutter 6
Written 12 December 2016

———————— • ————————

I found a thirty-three second video of my grandson
Today. He is six-months old, and lying on his blanket.
He seems curiously bemused at the giant stranger
Looking down on him with his metallic-glass-cycloptic eye.
My daughter's stockinged foot enters the frame from the lower right
To comfort and to tickle a reaction. The world slides
Once more towards a precipitous verge — now, because cyber
Hackers have corrupted our elections. Rumor destroys fact
With the alacrity of religion crushing reason.

You could not take my grandson's babbling for prophesy,
But it is a kind of promise that the disastrous flight
Of a world flirting with death might not end in calamity.

My grandson will be four on Christmas Eve, the day before
Fanatical consumers will divert themselves in orgies
Of gluttony, envy, and hypocritical belief.
He will shout with joy or weep with disappointment just as
The programming mandates him to do, and whether a lie
Or the truth infects the virtual news, both will be as
Irrelevant to him as poetry is to cyber thieves.
Jesus will weep, but that program is a rerun, and we
Will flail through actual chaos, fearing what may come after.

Twister

Clutter 5

Written 13 December 2016

———————— • ————————

The day woke as low clouds, and crept slowly, with an infant's
Crawling progress, into midmorning hazy sun, only
To collapse this afternoon into duller atmospheres,
Spitting rain. I grew up in the Midwest where weather
Reports took precedence over any other news, because
Farmers and shopkeepers still looked to heaven for their worth
Or dearth, and not to the Dow Jones or the NASDAQ. The future,
If we have one, will wonder at this change. How could hope be
Consigned to entities, full of dollars, but void of sense?

I remember the summers there spawned tornados, entities
As capricious as the Christian God whose arbitrary laws
Were kept with punishments and blessings just as arbitrary.

This morning, I found a photo of myself, holding my
Grandson for the first time. I had flown in from the coast
To visit this Midwest backwater where my daughter now lives.
It is summer, and the sun shines through a make-shift curtain,
Backlighting a happy man and a shocked infant, who kicks his
Bare feet and grabs his toes for comfort. I had just been
To see my ancient father, where I knelt, yes, knelt, to rub his
Wrinkled feet. We never met again. Ah, is this one of those
Cyclonic moments, when joy and grief make the same puzzled cry?

In-digestion
Clutter 4
Written 14 December 2016

———— • ————

Suppose you say to yourself: "Today, I am sad and lonely."
Naturally, you will want to attribute cause to your
Diagnosis. If your gut's python has swallowed a lion,
If the town you live in has decayed, if the bigots at your
Church have ostracized you, or the city, so glamorous
Once, has become a dump, naturally, you want a cure —
Naturally. But there is no cure in nature. The heavens
Are only vapors dropping rain. There is no steel monster
Aloft, dissolving in frigid rage, no grand identity.

Nostalgia: the bliss of looking through old black and white pictures
Of family, who are dead, and recalling only virtuous
People and heartwarming moments, only The Unreal Pure.

Suppose you could be happy without nostalgia, that you
Did not require purity in others, or in your
Apocalyptic gut, and the overbalance of pleasure
That you seek could be obtained through a kind of metrical passage
Of honest speech — honest, of course, with a tainted kind of curse,
That curse which comes when the rage for purity dies, and a rage
For solitude and words begins. Perhaps a blighted pleasure
Might ensue, redeeming, partially, your sadness. Your cure,
Perhaps, is here, inside of you, in poetry's half-truths.

Asteroids

Clutter 3

Written 15 December 2016

———————— • ————————

Slow learner that I am, and less permeable than a stone,
Occasionally, like the packed, cracked earth of rain-starved dirt,
I will, in response to some violent emotional
Deluge, reluctantly accept a drop of stillness. But why
Now? Because we argued? Because your eyes grew hard? Because the I
That sticks fast to the phrase "I love you," and thickens, and dries,
And cries out, like the stones proclaiming Christ, "I am right!" while all
The while my "I" is drowning, granulating, changing its dirt
To mud, and pleading, turbidly, to be loved or be left alone.

Where do the tears go? — bluing and blurring the earth, the tears
I long ago choked back, and refused to shed? They flowed inside,
Bashing away with insistence, saying my word "love" meant "fear."

Outside, another arctic storm is raging, having rampaged down
Thousands of leagues of ocean-pounded shoreline, relentlessly
Crumbling the continent's rock lips, black thunderous water-walls
Taller than city spires, shattering in moonless night, a trillion
Bubbles accepting the nothingness of wind before they die
In great cacophonies of egoless, wondrous destruction.
You and I, I and you, our words, our pledges, our raging squalls,
Are mist in mist, rising above lust's violence to be,
Yet not to be, calm in new heights, and still as space or stone.

A Note to Distant Kin
Clutter 2
Written 16 December 2016

———————— • ————————

Sadly, I cannot even credit myself with the virtue of
Honesty by simply admitting the obvious: I do
Not know what to say. After three days of tree-breaking storms,
High tides, flooding, today the sun shines and conducts its chorale
Of bird chirps, dog barks, the rattle of suburban machines
As though nothing tragic could ever occur. The past swells
Inside my head as the blue swells above it, both now re-born
In a nostalgic mood that has me looking tearily through
Old photos of the dead, as if I could somehow see their love.

But I only see grainy, sepia-toned faces — symbols
Instead of flesh that could mean anything to anybody,
The shape of a skull, a toothless mouth, patched pant-legs — crumpled,
soiled …

Poor people who wandered through life's temporal maze of decades
As outcasts in an interminable forest, where live trees
And broken dreams perverted every path but one: the way through
To a ragged, unfinished end — and I am following them.
Ring out the intricate sponge of my old brain, and you will see
This rotgut distillation, this cheap whisky of a drunken
Memory seeking to make life count for something. No doubt you
Have your own dead to attend to — and your unborn, your bent trees
Chattering in an after-breeze, not knowing what to say.

Fakir

Clutter 1

Written 17 December 2016

——————————— • ———————————

The final apocalyptic dawn has sounded a cannon
Shot, scattering white gulls off the vast trash heap of our dreams,
Settling round the house like frost flakes, each with its glitter
Of revelation, each as bright as this new day, bursting on
The scene — a cold and blue-starred presence. The residue of
The dump's ghost is a gruel of crushed objects and occasions,
A right hand removing a left hand's wedding ring, a child's tear
On a broken toy, a grandmother smiling with white, false teeth,
Spent candles on too many birthday cakes, naive hearts — conned.

I can tell you the specific date when my mother died,
But when did I first realize that these images Time stoved
In my head were not the junk of my brief, personal life?

When did I first smell the hot crush of melted transpersonal-
Trans-human existence? the heat of collective mineral-
Vegetable-animal-temporal feelings, making this
More than intense form of being that cried out to be salvaged
By rag-picker words? No stranger sight, nor more perverted love —
An old man toddling through his daze, immune to killing age,
Bereft of the coffins of bronze baby shoes. If there is bliss
In this gaseous mess, it is the bliss of traversal,
Of having crossed the hours of eons with words that walk on nails.